A Road to the Left:

A Road to the Left:

Life on the Left Side

By J. P. Brunette

Xulon Press
2301 Lucien Way #415
Maitland, FL 32751
407.339.4217
www.xulonpress.com

Paperback ISBN-13: 978-1-66283-512-4
Ebook ISBN-13: 978-1-66283-513-1

Table Of Contents

Introduction

Have you ever thought you were something—the tough guy, suitably qualified for anything life's gonna throw at you, experienced because you've heavily involved yourself in everything possible, the right fit because…well, you just are—only to find out you're not any of those things? You're just you, and the you you've become seems to be the least desirable version anyone would want. Does hopelessness set in? Have you let despair take over? Do the mistakes you've made rule your every move? Have they created the you you've feared would manifest? Has others' disdain and rejection forced your hand and knocked you off your feet? Or like me, has an unexplained disability driven you to your knees?

Now what?

Might I suggest all is not lost? That God is at work. And the road He's about to illuminate will lead to His glory and your freedom if you embrace Him. Flip the switch called Trust and join me on a remarkable journey down the bumpy yet amazing straight and narrow. I'll wait while you take a breather to decide. Don't take a long time to choose, though. You'll miss out on so much if you stay on the road to the left. Maybe the stories in this book will help you decide. Flip the page!

Do not turn to the right or the left; keep your foot from evil. Proverbs 4:27

Dedication

I dedicate this book to my wonderful, beautiful, patient, loving, gentle, emotional, longsuffering wife, Heather. Without her, I'd still be wandering blindly in foolishness. She has modeled the love of Jesus since the day I met her, and, although she'd tell you she's far from together, she certainly has been the glue that has held our family together through these stormy seasons in life.

LORD, Jesus, thank You for blessing me with such a marvelous woman to call my own. She's a beautiful gift, a faithful wife, an excellent mother, and an inspiration to so many. Bless her, LORD, in every way in Jesus's Name.

I, also, dedicate this book to Miss Connie from the credit union. Years ago, when I first sat in your office, you listened to a guy in his middle twenties talk about his crazy life. I must have appeared to you as quite the storyteller because you encouraged me to write a book about all the bizarre events I flew into your office to freely share. Well, here it is. It's certainly not the direction I thought the book would go, but I followed the LORD's leading and your encouragement. Thank you, Miss Connie, for being such a tolerant listener and a beautiful soul.

Chapter 1

REJECTION OR HARSH REALITY?

Everyone has dealt or is dealing with some sort of rejection. For me, it seems to have been a constant daily battle that's never diminished. I've felt rejected in multiple areas of my life from an early age up until now. Be it socially, on the job, relationally. By my family. And especially now since I've undergone a life-changing event.

Wow! What a way to open a book! Depress the reader into slamming the book shut right from the beginning.

It's not all bad, keep reading. Trust me. I gotta share the truth about who I've been to paint the proper picture of where I've come from to where I'm going. Continue if you dare.

I gained the rightful label *troublemaker* from an early age. And sadly, gaining that label doesn't shield one from rejection. *Always in a predicament aren't ya?* Doesn't help. Who likes a troubled youth turned adult? One who drags around his excess baggage and displays it for the world to see. *Can't you be like any normal person and at least act like you have it together?* I should have been more like my sister. Like the kids who developed common sense. That guy over there in the black suit. Anyone else.

My sister, Jessica, was mild mannered and embraced by everyone regardless of where she went. Why? Because she was a goody-goody? She was calm and collected. I gotta give her that. Very understanding and compassionate. *You say mean things to me. I melt you with my smile and now we're best friends.* Hardly anything riled her up, and she loved to smell the proverbial roses every chance she could. In fact, roses were her favorite. Go figure. I on the other hand was feisty (and still am), easily angered and couldn't give a hoot about the finer things in life.

What?! And be a sissy? Get real. A dude's gotta be tough and rough and full of stuff.

But back then seeing Jessica's blossoming sainthood, everyone nodding their approval, truthfully everything caused me to embrace jealousy on every front and serve up a picnic from hell. *She's gonna pay for this! And so is whomever else who dares reject me.* All the while I acted tough I continued to whine: *why won't people accept me for me?* I was blind to the fact of what was really happening. I was being tortured by my own battle cry—*Make 'em all pay because I'm good for something, too! I'm loveable! And relevant. You'll see.*

For Jess, sweet and innocent came naturally. It wasn't an act. You know the mean girl, the fake-acting-nice one? Not my sister. She was so genuine it was sickening. *Screw up, already! Take some pressure off me for crying out loud!* Numerous times a day her perfect behavior would irk me. *Why ya gotta always be accepting of yer reality*? You know, the glass half full kind of crap. Gross! *Just hulk and get it over with. When things don't go your way, throw a hissy fit! And make it a doozy! You're making me look bad.* Nope. Hardly a sign of frustration. She was almost stoic in tough situations. Years down the road I realized she was more of an inward person. She'd store things away. And that girl could store a lot! She'd download a mess to the memory bank, accept the reality, and press on. But when the file folder swelled to max capacity—explosion! *Wait one minute...Jess has a flaw? Remarkable! Ooh, things are heating up!* I promoted her rebellious streak the moment I caught on. *Welcome to life, Sis. It's about time you slip up. Thanks for the needed break. Eyes are finally off me for a moment.*

Fireworks erupted one day when Jess had defied Mom a whopping three times! *She's doing what?! She's hiding in a closet to avoid a spanking?! Epic!* It was the worst behavior I'd ever seen out of my angelic sister. It almost terrified and satisfied at the same time. Mom had hulked and dragged Jess screaming and fighting out of that closet. *Go Mom! Didn't know ya still had it in ya!* Swat and correct Jess without a struggle? No way! As rare as it was, her defiance that day made my past fights with mom look like kittens cuddling. The "who cares" flag was cracking out a wicked tune at full mast with no sign of giving in.

Unlike Jess I endlessly fought back. No wonder I idolized the Tasmanian Devil as a child. I clearly enjoyed a bloody free-for-all. But after Mom cleaned up the aftermath of Hurricane Jessica, all went back to normal. And all eyes refocused on me, again. Jess returned to being gentle and obedient, and left the land of the wicked. *Come on. Really? The crowd's yelling encore!* But the encore never came. And I was lonely in the crowd. The only storm that raged after that was her candor in our relationship.

"Go away, you're annoying."

I heard this phrase like a worn-out Patsy Cline record. I had perfected the art of annoyance; she performed her role flawlessly and so did I. But instead of celebrating her individuality, I tortured her. I'd yank her hair. Smash her doll's faces in when she left them in the car. Attacking her dolls was a perfect gig, especially in winter. When they'd get cold, I'd take both hands and squeeze! The face would concave, and it'd stay that way. When she found them she'd cry! Oh, how she'd cry. I'd especially go after her Cabbage Patch doll, Bridget. She always cradled that thing, wrapped her in a blanket, dressed her up. *Yuck!* Bridget's demise became my ultimate goal. However, even though I tortured the smile off her face most days, all I wanted was her acceptance. Her approval. Her love.

"I just wanta play with you, Jessy" I'd plead.

"No, go away I said. I'm reading. And don't call me Jessy."

She loved books. Mushy, sloppy, sickening love stories. She'd read one right after another, disappearing for days on end. And it would bug the life outta me.

"I'm not annoying, you're annoying!" emphasizing it with my pointy tongue.

"You only wanta read your stupid books. Fine, I'll just play by myself, and I hope you feel bad! *JESSY!*"

Nothing I did mattered to her. She never looked up. I could've stuck my tongue out until it cracked off, and she'd sidestep it. That day I continued shouting sassy slurs until I ran out of nastiness and then slammed her door. I figured that would light a fire behind her beautiful green eyes. Nope!

"HEY!! STOP SLAMMING THE DOORS!!" Dad would yell from his recliner.

Why am I always in trouble? She's the one being mean!

I could never figure out why Jess wouldn't play with me back then. However, seeing how relentless my kids are right now, I can fully understand why I was the lonely rebel. They refuse to read the room no matter how many times I suggest it. Jess' misery with me around: crystal clear. Her girlfriends would come over and I'd taunt them, too. Without warning I'd shake my butt in their faces, dance a little jig, and then would run off. It was guerrilla warfare, man! I'd take note of how many times they'd scream and up the antics accordingly. The torture never ended. Even into adulthood I pestered that poor girl. Sadly, a Grand-Canyon-sized chasm between us continued to form until she passed away. We talked occasionally and enjoyed a lunch date once and a while, but I felt the strong separation. It wasn't until Mom and I tearfully reminisced fond memories after my sister's death that I finally discovered the reason for the rejection I felt from her.

"You love Jay more than me."

There it was. She felt her own form of rejection.

"No, Honey. I love you both equally" Mom declared.

But was Mom's rebuttal enough to fill the gap between us? Sadly, no. She broke down and cried all the more.

"Well, you spend more time with him instead of me."

What?! I had caused her to feel rejected? I wanted her approval, spend time with her, annoy her, play with her. *How could she feel this way without me noticing?* Mom knew the truth.

"No, Honey. It's not like that. Your brother requires a lot more attention because he is so busy."

Busy?! Wow, Mom, you're gentler than me. The conversation would've gone something like this.

"Well, you know, Jess. Your brother's a dink. Somedays I'd like to slug the crap outta him. I'd get to spend more time with you if he wasn't such a puke."

As an adult, I never gave her pain much thought because I was self-absorbed. Felt rejected myself. Mom reminds me every chance she gets of her need to "pass herself in the hallway" correcting me. She deserves a medal for her dedication. I was more than a handful back then, and appropriately I'm reaping tenfold my just reward through my children's tenacity.

Now I'd give my own life in trade for another moment with her. To put a smile on her face. To seek forgiveness and correct my mistakes. I'd hit the rewind button. Smell the roses with her. Buy her more books. Celebrate our differences. Get more popcorn chicken and fries with gravy on top.

You Better Shape Up, Mister!

Remember the mom who never gave up? She called in reinforcements. Through repeated cuffs to the head; wooden spoons, paddles, dowel rods, and the occasional bare-butt open-handed slap; constant coaching, reminders, conversations; I slowly crawled to the plate and made better choices. Sluggishly and defiantly, I might add. But I'm exceedingly grateful that she never gave up. I needed those "beatings" as today's culture would define it. I had parents who stopped at nothing to put me on the right path. I owe them more gratitude than I can ever express. They weren't perfect but no one asked them to be. Could they have done better? Depends on the outlook.

I remember the new path I started walking on was horrible. *Where do I belong?* I couldn't shake the feeling of rejection anywhere I went. *Rebelling was so much easier. At least as a troublemaker I was accepted by other troublemakers.* And from an early age I was never into fashion, so I struggled even harder to fit in. Growing up in the eighties and nineties and rejecting mainstream fashion was pop cultural suicide. If you didn't have Air Jordan's, Nike anything, root for the Chicago Bulls, you were a social outcast. Worse yet my lack of fashion not only stood out, but people pointed it out. I had no chance. My parents were steadfast in their fashion and modesty convictions, and it destroyed any and every chance I had of fitting in. *Go ahead and stick that loser label on my back.*

What happens to unpopular and socially awkward kids like me? They get bullied. For being the exact loser, geek, and nerd he or she longs not to be. My favorite words —rad, totally tubular, psychedelic—would never describe me. So, I quit using them. I stuck out like blood splattered on a white shirt. I was an alien, wearing plaid shirts and pleated pants, walking down the elementary halls. My parents never allowed me to wear shorts or t-shirts at school. That made matters worse. Like most growing kids, my head was disproportionate compared to the rest of my body, causing kids to repeatedly call me "ET." Or "frog face" because my eyes were huge and awkwardly spaced. Also, my feet were gigantic for my age; I was quite the sight. And calling boys gay for no reason at all was popular in the nineties, so kids spread schoolwide that I was a homosexual because of my awkward appearance. You get the picture; I can move on.

My only dream was to fit in. To have my name carved anywhere but the bathroom stalls. And without horrible expressions after it. All this stress caused me to test-fit the good-kid persona for only a moment, but when the groundwork for ridicule is already laid and there's no end in sight, good and bad becomes irrelevant. A kid's gotta fight to keep from being stuffed in a locker or thrown into the dumpster. Luckily, I had a few good friends who liked me, but I began to long for the popular seat. To be the good-looking kid. The jock. Everything seemed hopeless, and I began to cave under the pressure.

It's All Your Fault

With that desire ruling my thoughts and choices, I began blaming my parents for ruining my chances at the good life. *No wonder people hate me. Look at this stupid shirt! I look like a geek. I wish I had parents who loved me. Ones who supported me instead of embarrassing me.* I knew it wasn't their fault, though. Dad worked his tail off to provide for us. He barely had a choice back then. But I resented him because he rarely had time for me.

Why not blame the bullies or the parents who don't teach their children the valuable tools of acceptance? There seems to be quite the lack in parenting these days…the American Dream, don't get me started on that. Children are being left to their own devices, many because of greed.

How about pointing a condescending finger at a broken school district? We all have stories about the rotten, no-good schools in our area.

Careful, Now

I decided to shelf my desire to become a goody-goody after I realized how many people disliked me. *What's the point?* Kids at school hated me, teachers seemed like enemies, people at church spoke up against my behaviors. *Everyone gets a check mark.* The adversary list became well-populated, circled, and highlighted. What was I to do? I couldn't win. What choice did I have? No one would help me. *Why not build a wall to keep people out? Construct the fortress of Jay. I could hide behind it and be myself. Let very few people in, if any. Everyone can publicly crown me the unpopular kid, I don't care! I'll become the king of my castle.* Deceit, lies, viciousness became the new norm; I was determined to fit in even if I had to smash the moral compass. Strangely enough, however, I never wanted to be this new guy. I longed for acceptance not war. But I had reached the pivotal point, the crossroads of who I'd become. Straight ahead or swerve left or right. I had landed on the prime location where I'd start laying the groundwork for the devastating foundation that would take years to destroy. I had created the "tough guy."

Marching Orders

Armed with the new attitude, I started undoing everything that would label me weak. The walls flew up, and I dug the moat and began filling it with disrespect and sarcasm. Every teacher gained a new, mouthy student. Me. And little by little I sabotaged every good-guy area of my life. The tactics I employed were careful and calculated, however. Just enough to frustrate but never enough to alert the folks. Otherwise, it would complicate my covert ops.

In the hallways and out of earshot of any adult, I adopted the mouth of a sailor. My new go-to had become the F word in every sentence. I considered it my glowing ticket to relevance. Picture this: the dorky and unliked kid, me, in a yellow and blue sweatshirt I had sown in Home Economics torturing and cussing at the nerdier kids. Right in front of the cool crowd. I had lost all control. Everyone saw the new kid in action. Well, except my parents and teachers. I had finally emerged as the tough guy and with a rock-solid plan to assert my coolness.

But I was completely torn. I knew it was wrong, and I felt terrible for tormenting the nerdy kids because they were my friends. They were the only ones who somewhat understood me. But were dropping off one by one I might add. *Time to tweak the plan.* I'd be the good kid when it mattered the most, that way I'd ensure retention of a few close allies. But I'd become the Tasmanian Devil when my hard reputation was at stake. *Brilliant!* Yet oh, the inner turmoil. I wasn't this new guy. The work it required took a toll. and I wondered how I'd keep up the charade. *Hey, Pansy. Remember the rippling "who cares" flag flying over your castle? There's no surrender. You might have to lose a little to gain a lot, so keep moving! Collateral damage is a part of war. Conform or be torn apart. Fit in or die trying.* I had to fortify the wall against hate and rejection and squash the desire to be a good kid before it disrupted the progress.

What about making my parents proud? Honor my father and my mother like they said at Sunday School?

Well, the solution I found to the treasonous rantings of my conscience was quite simple. To succeed in my plan, I'd have to become a great little actor. Easy, right? Some of my favorite people in the world were actors. They seemed happy. And if Zack Morris was popular at his school, I could be too. Afterall, we were both blondes with a rad combover! At least one box had a checkmark. Putting myself through self-taught acting classes, I examined the way the cool kids swore and mimicked it in the hallways, and then learned and quoted Bible verses while at church. I wrecked my friends with hate speech in between classes but tried to smooth it over at lunch. I deserved an Oscar, I thought, because for a moment, the bullies left me alone, and I took their place. But the casualties of war piled up as the friend count took a staggering loss.

"What's the matter with you guys? I didn't do that!" I shouted after I was uninvited from the lunch table.

"You told Kim to F-off, Jason, when she asked you to stop teasing her friend. You've really changed, Jason. We aren't like that, so you're not welcome here if that's who yer gonna be."

I couldn't deny a single bit of it. Totally should've owned it, but I chose to be the tough guy instead.

"You guys can go to hell if you think I'm gonna take this abuse from you. I don't need you or anyone at this table! Bunch of losers!"

Everyone within earshot perked their ears. *Score! Relevance cemented! Now I'd be respected because I had told the majority of the cheerleaders right where to go.*

But I gained relevance in no one's eyes. Respect remained elusive and I became even more withdrawn. Lonely. Afraid of losing the battle. And was bullied far worse than before. I ramped up my own efforts but only blew my cover. Multiple trips to the principal's office, phone calls home, I lost major ground and gained heavy battering on the barn door that held up my Wranglers.

I, like any kid, was not equipped for such a vicious battle. I never wanted all the stress; I wanted the war of rejection to end. Still a nerd at heart even today, I love doing any kind of research, but mostly on health and wellness. When I recently read that a child's brain won't fully develop until about age twenty-five, my immature childhood behavior began to make perfect sense. Especially when I read the part about the section of the brain dealing with love and acceptance being one of the slowest developing areas. However, if I use this as an excuse, as scientific as it may be, it would only be adding to my own stupidity. I knew all along what I was doing was wrong. I just didn't care. Additionally, we moved around a lot as a family, so I was no stranger to loss. The first few moves I struggled to cope but after several more I began to grow cold toward losing friends, familiarity, happiness. *I don't need your address to keep in touch. I'll just find a new friend. Who cares!? I'll be cool one day.* But the opposite occurred. The more we moved, the more confused, angrier, and less friendly I became. Causing more of a downward spiral.

Never Give Up On Love

But listen to me for a moment. No matter how many times a child rebels, angrily rants, acts rashly, never stop expressing your love. I remember hating when my parents or grandparents, even people at church, would say to me, "I love you" and "you're all that matters." But honestly, it was the love of family and friends that pulled me through until the dark clouds cleared. Thank you, all of you who dared to stick around, for loving me.

For The Love Of Questions

Let's hold up for a moment and ponder a few questions.

Is anyone truly accepted in today's world?

Who sets the standards of acceptance?

Why is everyone in a frantic fear of rejection?

Let me tell you what I've come to realize the hard way. If a person cannot accept rejection in any way, shape, or form, it'll rule his or her life. As you can see it controlled every aspect of mine. I desperately feared rejection, and as a result it continued to get further outta hand. I agreed to and cultivated that fear before I decided to develop the tough guy foundation. Even though people expressed their love for me, I believed everyone to be a liar. At an early age I had already formed the belief I was overly rejected, and I never understood how to process it.

A haunting memory of my grandpa seems to have locked this fear of rejection in place. Of all people, I wanted acceptance from my grandparents the most. But try as I may, I could never release the felt rejection because I never got closure before he died. The one and only time I remember sitting on his lap, I was showing him a picture I had colored. I was possibly five or six.

"Look, Grandpa! Do you like it?"

Instead of praising me, he began pointing out the many places I had gone out of the lines and said that I could have done a better job.

Hold on, now. Before you blast my grandfather with word curses, understand this: I do not know the context of his coaching. I was too young to remember the whole conversation.

I do remember Grandpa loved to work hard. *Do it right the first time!* But this memory made a huge impact on my thought patterns because I took it as rejection. I remember jumping off his lap utterly defeated. And shortly after that I started going the wrong way. I'm in no way blaming him for his seemingly harsh assessment. I felt rejected, but I now believe he meant it as constructive criticism. There's no child out there who likes to hear of his or her mistakes, especially when crazy proud of his or her accomplishments. Totally understandable. All I wanted was to be accepted and praised for my picture because I had worked so hard.

Ironically, while I was writing this chapter and considering this story as an example, I began to heal from the situation with a new outlook. He was rejecting my work, but he wasn't rejecting me. Grandpa pointed out a harsh reality. I was young and inexperienced and overly sensitive. What he may have wanted me to realize was that if I worked a little harder, then I'd do better. *There's always room for improvement.* If I continue to believe Grandpa was rejecting me, then I'll never get over it, and the memory will forever haunt me. I'm gonna offer Grandpa a little grace here.

How does an adult, much less a child, decipher between a harsh reality and rejection?

Target Practice Is In Session. Beware!

One of my tough guy decisions was to focus my anger at my dad. And why not? He didn't give me everything that I wanted. He seemingly robbed me of the tools to fit in. He made me follow rules. He refused to let me stay up late and eat junk. He made me go to school. I was being held against my will. And since his methods were just like Grandpa's, I couldn't handle his harsh approach. Guess who struggles with gentleness? Uh huh. This guy. Like father like son as the saying goes. But, as I look back, several of my anger bouts with Dad stemmed from our different interests at the time and not his character. Dad loved physical labor, to work on cars, run heavy equipment. What kid likes that?! I wanted to be just like him, but *don't tell me what to do. Gimme your time and attention, Dad, but on my terms. Ok?* Classic kid moves, right? Our personalities clashed from a young age, so I blamed it on his harshness. A competitive and disrespectful spirit arose in me, and I set out to show him how wrong he was. *I'll show you I can do everything you do and more.* When he tried to involve me, I acted disinterested. When he attempted to teach me things, I reacted unfairly. Pouted. Stormed off all mad for myself because I didn't wanna spend my time on what interested him. I couldn't see the dad who loved me and wanted to spend time with me; I saw a dictator. A tyrant. *May I have a replacement model? This one doesn't listen.*

How Ironic

Dad was a car enthusiast and an excellent mechanic. He could fix anything with a motor without a manual. Guess who's spent many years a car enthusiast, an at-home self-proclaimed mechanic, owned a whopping thirty-two cars and counting.

You're A Meanie

Have you ever heard a child say, "You're a meanie-butt"? Does anyone know what this means? That's been a popular phrase in my household for years.

Dad was a meanie-butt for trying to show me how to fix a car. For showing me how to use a planer, an orbital sander, a torque wrench. *Spread peanut butter on one piece of bread and then marshmallow crème on the other.* Nope! I want a different teacher. *This one's trying to do his best. What's up with that?!* Whether I wanted a gentler teacher or not, one who adhered to my schedule and tastes, I was behaving like a typical defiant child. One who was employing disrespectful behaviors God frowns upon.

Because of my drive for separation, I aspired to do things he didn't think befitting of a boy. Let me explain before you jump to conclusions.

I didn't want societal norms dictating my daily activities, but Dad subscribed to the ideal that boys hunt, fish, work hard, and rule the roost. *Nobody tells me what to do. I can do all things! You'll see.* I took up piano lessons because one of my friends could play. I planted flowers and built beds to mimic the ones my pastor had constructed. I became an artist, painting on cardboard and chunks of wood. *You cross-stitch? So do I.* This mentality followed me into the future. *You decorate cakes? I offer wedding and birthday cakes on the side, too.*

Before you laugh at a guy decorating cakes remember I could eat a slice of cake at any moment. *Make fun of me now, Friend!*

If I wanted to learn it, there was nobody who could convince me otherwise. It was exhausting, but I just wanted to make my dad proud. To see that I was worthwhile in his eyes. *Only be kinder when expressing your opinions for crying out loud. The whole world already hates me. Please accept me for who I am.*

Dad accepted the good kid. The one who followed the rules. *Don't be disobedient and you'll be fine.* But I wanted it both ways.

And this caused me to reject him fully. And look for a softer source of instruction. Besides, the more I learned, the more I'd be able to assert to everyone my relevance. Sadly, I never found what I was looking for on the quest for besting my dad. It only pushed me further into the pool of hard feelings. And a severed relationship. The water in that pool is disgusting, friends. I think it's filled with sewage.

Anyone who currently knows me has learned that I'm relentless. I'm just like my dad: pounce on a project wholeheartedly until it's done. Never give up. Never quit. But many also know of another fact. I lack finesse. An increasing number of people suffer from this, so I'm not alone. But look at what it takes to fill this void: you gotta want a softer touch and be willing to use it. The biggest step: you gotta actually do it. Actively work on it. I've known for years I've been recklessly brash. However, I've come to understand that if I'm unwilling to do something about it, then I can't expect others to treat me differently than the way I treat them. I demanded gentleness and acceptance from everyone else, but never once had I offered the same to them. In Dad's case, he was the problem and that was that. Everyone else complicated things. End of discussion.

Standards

Who sets the standards of acceptance? Who's to blame when things get off kilter? I do believe I've been quite honest and transparent here. Will you do the same?

Alarmingly, society finds it easier to blame its shortcomings on others. Why not dwell on someone else's mistakes? All responsibility is magically absolved and lands on another. That's what I believed. I blamed others for the mistakes I made and never internalized my own blunders. I ignored my own slip-ups, especially if someone pointed them out to me, and focused on everyone else's flaws. *You wronged me. Period.*

It takes a strong person to admit and self-correct. No wonder most ignore this crucial step in keeping a balance in life.

But to answer the question I asked earlier about who sets the standards.

God sets the standards. No one else.

He perfectly planned them to work out for our own good. His standards are doable, but not without daily surrender. They only become lofty and unattainable if we choose to complain and look for a better solution. If I choose to deny His standards, then I'm left to handle the outcomes of my life. And that is a scary choice to make. But, if I fix my eyes on His standards, I'll be able to willingly accept harsh realities without taking on the damaging feeling of rejection. And then live in His blessings. I could easily sit back and blame the world for my lack of acceptance, but if I know I'm doing wrong in order to be accepted, I'll lose acceptance with God. And He's the only One I gotta worry about disappointing.

The world's a cruel place and isn't gonna get any better just because I want it to. People will be downright nasty when on a quest for the incorrect kind of acceptance. But I've learned that accepting God's standards allows me to feel worthy in His eyes. Then I can consider others' opinions and harsh criticisms without allowing rejection to destroy my sense of belonging. Constructive or destructive.

I was rejecting God's standards and a relationship with Him. Dad didn't push me into that. Kids at school weren't to blame. Once I began to understand my place, my worth, my competency in the light of the Cross, I began to accept harsh reality not as rejection. Trust me, it begins with the personal choice to surrender to God's standards of acceptance. The world will not accept you for the way you are because the world's standards change with the wind. When I looked to win over the crowd, I became an enemy of God. I wanted large-scale acceptance, but it came with a large-scale price.

I've come to realize…Whatever's today's acceptance will be tomorrow's rejection.

Let There Be Peace

Even with family and friends spending less time comforting and consoling me in my current time of need, I completely understand and respect the harsh reality that life is busy. People today are overwhelmed with their everyday activities that detract them from spending time with each other. And even though this doesn't make it right, we're all guilty of it. But if I think people are rejecting me because they don't take the time like they used to, I'll forget about the harsh reality of it all: they're busy. They've got a lot on their plate. I gotta believe I'm loved until proven otherwise. Because if I don't, I'll perceive reality as rejection and will in turn, reject them. In essence, rejection becomes a mental choice. One with a lofty price tag if made unwisely.

Where should our acceptance come from then? Should we only seek approval from a select few if the world is bent on disapproval?

My answer's quite simple. Only seek acceptance from God. Only He can give us peace about who we are, peace from the hate that rails us day to day, and peace from the fear of being rejected.

Still unconvinced? Picture this: Jesus was perfect, led an exemplary life, and loved everyone beyond their shortcomings. Yet He was despised.

Why would anyone think the world will openly accept him or her? John 15:18 in the NIV speaks of a harsh reality and rejection: "If the world hates you [as a Christian], keep in mind that it hated me first." BUT back it up to John 3:16 NIV and receive some hope: "For God so loved the world that He gave

His one and only Son, that whoever believes in Him shall not perish but have eternal life."

John 3:16 started the first official crack in my tough guy foundation. The power in the Hope of Christ demolishes strongholds. Breaks chains. It has the power to lead the rejected back to where he or she belongs: accepted in God's Love. And with that first crack, room for a building faith appeared. Room to produce a trust in God that would flourish. And blossom through the storms provided I didn't fill the room with selfishness again. I'd hafta remain open to God's design. Be laid bare. Promote exposure.

And so it starts, *Life on the Left Side.*

Chapter 2

I NEED A BREAK!

Have you ever reached the point where you've begged for a break from your reality because life has thrown a Buick at your head, and you've buckled beneath the weight? Instinctively you've ducked for cover, and waved the white flag, hoping to avoid being rammed ruthlessly straight into the ground. You're on your knees, wincing in pain, pleading for a resolve. Sound familiar? I think we've all experienced this at one point or another in our lives.

But have you ever noticed what slips silently under the elusive door to freedom? Buyer's remorse. Seconds into the break, you begin to complain about the breather and wish to have back what had previously destroyed you. Is there any reasonable justification for this? An explanation why nearly every honest human on this planet can relate? What a sick joke!

It usually goes something like this…

"Set me free! Somebody get me the heck outta here!"

"Wait, hold up! I wanna be free but toss in a smidge of bondage, too."

"Pump the brakes. Jk. I didn't mean anything I said. Gimme it all back. I didn't really mean what I said when I shouted, 'I can't take it anymore.' Can I get a do-over?"

That's embarrassing for most, but what's worse than this happening to the average citizen? When it happens to a tough guy. Because tough guys can catch that Buick, deflect it without wincing in pain, and send it into orbit. With one arm.

Who am I trying to kid acting out this role? I'm the bald white guy tipping the scales at a whopping 150 pounds. The one who's accustomed to hearing "muscle shirts are for muscles, Bro." Yet I've been that guy exuding a superhero air. Always got something to prove. Gonna win that argument. *I'll do it!*

Grab the door for the little old lady because it'll make me look like the hero. Carry her groceries to her car cuz it might win me cig money. Yell at the guy who refused to help her, and who would've let the door slam in her face. *Luckily I was there to save her!*

If I heard from anyone daring to defy me, *take a break, Jay.* I'd follow it with *who me? I don't need a break! I'm on call.*

I determined to save the world even if somebody knocked out my teeth and took me out at the knees. Because if I didn't, my rep would be at stake.

Was anyone shining the distress beacon to draw me into action? No. Yet despite this truth, I convinced myself of the realm I thrived in and forcefully achieved daily perceived victories. The walls I had constructed around my castle would protect me against the naysayers. Cutting vocabulary, offensive body language, a foul demeanor; they were my armor. And no one discipled me in my tough guy beliefs. Sure, I allowed society to enculturate me and learned from the bullies from grade school, but I honestly needed a break from myself because I answered a mysterious call when no one was calling.

Softly and Tenderly

Through all this I wrestled a softer side. I longed to be anything but what I had become. I scrambled to cover up the inner turmoil so the good guy would shine.

No one saw that, right? How could I have let this happen in full view?

It was all so confusing. And damaging to my health.

But then, Jesus. He began constructing siegeworks to begin demolishing the tough guy walls. Through my kids.

When I think of siegeworks, I think of movies like Braveheart or anything to do with King Arthur. It's blood and guts and valor and princesses. *Close your eyes, kids! Wait, why are you even watching this?!* But that's not what the LORD used to correct my path. It wasn't lances and war hammers and bludgeoning tools, but a simple bewitching tool called love.

The magic children have is astounding. They're powerful and don't even know it. They dump out undetected spell potions in a slobbery kiss. They scatter pixy dust as they perform a mesmerizing ballet pose. Their squeaky voices hypnotize as they call out, "Watch this, Daddy". Their little warm embraces scream out I love you and hide the flick of a wand.

Where do they get this power?! I need some of that to save the world!

All I remember hearing from my parents were the phrases "some days, kid" and "would you please just find something to do? You're driving me nuts!" Every parent says this. Me included.

The Cheese Grater

Why do we release such comments into the air? Out of pure frustration? Because we're in charge? Because of the unending chaos rearranging the living room? Because of the duck-and-cover-or-get-pegged-in-the-head-with-a-flying-toy-truck reality? Or is it because we crave the ever-so-elusive alone time we once enjoyed before the little monsters debuted on earth. The struggle's real, I get you. If you disagree and live in the false reality that *my child's not like that,* lemme feed your little beast a slice of double chocolate cake washed down by six swigs of Mountain Dew, and then hand you a ticket to the freak show. No joke. Life with children is relentless. Challenging. A cheese grater.

But the way I felt as a youngster when I heard those hurtful comments was rejected, unwanted, worthless. And I see the same pain on those adorable faces when I slip up and angrily spout off. Don't misunderstand. We gotta crush some dreams now and again. White cabinets aren't suitable canvases for up-and-coming marker artists. And peanut butter cannot substitute real butter when making scrambled eggs. But we gotta be careful. We can't downplay when we've senselessly and harshly crushed their hopes and dreams: our frustrations.

What if the desperate cry for a break is because we've let too many occurrences add up? I've learned to pick my battles and forgive the silliness before it becomes a war, and I get dragged across the cheese grater. Again.

Most tough guys would disagree. I did. But experience has taught me that I'm way too harsh. I've always been able to detect the pain welling up in their eyes seconds after I've crossed the same line for the hundredth time, so I've got no excuse. It's no surprise when that kinda hurt, annoyed, and frustrated expression disfigures their smile. It's time for a change.

The Forgiving Nature We All Need

Have you noticed at a tender youthful age that, even though we grind children's worlds into powder, they easily forgive and bypass the rejection to prove their love for us? Time and time again. It's like they get punched in the head like the inflatable clown who hits the floor and rebounds for more. It's only the out-of-control parent who wants love from them, but on his or her terms and usually when things are good. *Ouch! That one clown-punched me in the throat.*

Not now, Johnny. You just peed in the wastepaper basket. Give me a moment to compose myself, son, because I'm sopping up urine and you want a hug! Yer kidding, right?!

Yup. Two out of my three children have wizzed in a trashcan. Kinda lost my cool…

But then sometimes we enjoy the hugs and kisses, even after they're found guilty of normal childish crimes. But there's definitely a limit. My middle daughter's good for this one.

Okay, okay. You just kissed me 78 times. That's enough. Someone wanna grab a mop for all this slobber?

Or what about the times when they hulk the air outta your lungs and you nearly hafta club 'em over the head to break their grip so you can breathe again?

The love is enjoyable, the chaos amusing, the songs memorable, but they sometimes cramp our filled-to-the-brim lifestyle, and that's when I think we explode. We still gotta forgive, though. *Help me, Jesus!*

The Lid's A' Rattlin'

I own the right to bark. So back down. Because justification came when I snapped for the umpteenth time today. If they woulda listened the first time.

Yup. Classic me. Tough guys throw their weight around.

But they're just kids… says anyone with the understanding that children need gentle yet firm guidance.

Okay. If they woulda listened maybe the second time I said it, the glue would've held. Now YOU can deal with it since yer all calm and collected.

I JUST NEED A STINKIN MOMENT, PLEASE!

Why don't children understand the detonation? It's obvious they weren't just spectators at the crime scene, yet they claim innocence with one hand still in the cookie jar. *Should I really hafta repeat myself until my tongue falls off?* Sometimes I'm convinced my kids' heads are composed of solid brick, and I'm flapping my jaws at the dripping mortar. I gotta be a broken record, yet they can instantly get crabby when I tickle too long, or when I poke their flubby bellies every time I walk by. Why don't they grasp the special kind of crazy they're yanking outta me?

The tough guy education I'm teaching is the issue. My poor attitude is the subject of choice.

Sit down, you little brats. Yer gonna listen or I'll take yer birthday away. When I tickle, ya better like it. If I poke ya, crack a smile or I'll give ya two cracks in that rear of yers. Oh, and, ps. Don't behave like Daddy. Just do what I say. Class dismissed."

It's time I adjust my behaviors if I want them to adjust theirs. I demand them to cease ridiculousness. Straighten up or else. But why don't I stop for the proverbial crosswalk lady when her flashing sign nearly blinds me? Not being compassionate by nature, I nearly morph into all kinds of crazy the moment they push the limits, and it's time to stop. Something doesn't add up here. I'm employing the old saying, *do as I say, not as I do,* that once drove me further into rebellion. And in that rebellious-brat stage, hearing the phrase because *I said so,* instantly fueled my fire.

I've come to realize angrily mouthing phrases like these isn't parenting. It's being a dictator. Parenting requires gentle guidance.

And what's the point of this domination? Wouldn't this breed an unhealthy resentment instead of building trust? Are my kids in basic training or in a loving home?

Troops! Fall In

Whenever the drill sergeant in me came out, the ranks momentarily tightened, but then went AWOL again. Children will briefly listen, and it breeds an overall sense of victory in the parent's minds. Until…

I'VE HAD ENOUGH! If you wanna play, you had better listen!

Temper flareups from Dad have never changed my kid's ideas toward fun; they've always endured a vicious butt-chewin' until the magical "go play" is uttered.

Have a blast is what registers with the words *go play*, whether said angrily or not. Go play is what drives the silly train. So, remember a harsh reality, parents gotta watch their kids no matter where they are, so telling them to get outta your face is not only hateful but also pointless. I've learned a single victory is never won by exploding and sending them away. All it does is ramp up the explosives for the next mischievous event. Maybe try a calming exercise? Count to ten. Take deep breaths in through the nose and out through the mouth. *Don't explode!*

Two Things

What I know when I'm frustrated: my kids are in my hair, or what's left of it, and I need to make them disappear temporarily so I can catch my breath. What I need to discover: where has love gone? Do I need to send my kid outta the room or get love to come back into the room? Does God immediately slap us around when we slip up? Or does He offer compassion and tenderness in a hairy moment?

Come on, Jay. Take a deep breath and don't be so rigid. Remember 1 Peter 4:8 NIV when it says, "Above all, love each other deeply, because love covers over a multitude of sin."

My kids used to call my facial hair *the pokeys* when it'd start growing back in after a clean shave. Heather would sit amazed by the way I'd let them rub *the pokeys* for as long as they wanted when they sat on my lap, but then I'd freak if they wouldn't quit talking after forming three words.

The Much-Needed Break

Well, the much-needed break finally came, but it's not what I expected. The nursing home bed that I lie on, the one rigged with deafening alarms that notify the world if I try to get up without permission, the loneliness felt behind that closed door to the colorful hallway. Not what I wanted. The monitors, a wheelchair instead of shoes and the ability to walk, the bar code institutionalizing my underwear, socks, pants, shirts. The assisted bathroom trips and showers. None of this could be classified as a needed break. None of this is a refreshing intermission filled with positive forward movement and growth. But it has all come to this, along with repeated blows from simple truths, before my hardened heart would soften, and my tear ducts would spring a leak. (This paragraph is the original start of this book.)

I'm not a bawl baby, but I can't handle this! The aides who entered and exited my room like ants foraging at a picnic understood. "It's because you're a loving man with a tender heart" comforted one worker.

I was hundreds of miles away from my family, friends, and loved ones. And for over a month while the insurance company, doctors, therapists, and Heather figured out what to do with me, I laid in seclusion. No one could just pop in for a visit. Day by day I pondered my new reality and who I used to be. The crotchety dad. The poor friend and husband. The angry son. *Will I ever bust outta here?*

Only physical therapy and lunch breaks broke the solitude daily. Some days I never left my bed. It was during those lonely days that I felt led to expound on the paragraph above and continue drafting this book. Through self-discovery and hours of endless typing, the LORD began showing me the meaning of my existence through a clearer lens. I had clouded my love with frustration. I had empowered nearly every selfish motive to my own detriment. Deep down I *am* kind and tenderhearted. *Explore these truths, please.*

I enjoy free time when I'm able to get it. I don't mind being alone. But not like this. The occasional date night and dinner out with friends is gone. *Interrupt me with Teen Titans Go! Please!*

A tough guy is not invincible. The barrier will collapse if the proper tool is used against it. Again, the magic my children possess... The night I heard my seven-year-old daughter's squeaky voice on the other end of the line sounding like she had lost her best friend had a dynamite-like explosive effect on my stronghold. Heather tearfully described overhearing my daughter telling her grandma she felt like she didn't have a daddy anymore. No foundation can withstand that kind of attack. It shook me to the core.

Shake your head, Jason. Your eyes are stuck. Look at what you've been blessed with. Never had I been absent from their lives for any length of time. Then outta the blue it happens. No in-depth conversation could explain the absence to a shattered child.

Flat On My Face, Again

Recovery isn't easy. It's not *POOF* and all better. It's fall. Get back up. Take a step. Fall. Get back up. Take a step. One lonely afternoon I began questioning my family's love and true intentions. *Why did my absence matter anyway? You seriously can't miss a dad who stonewalls, barely shows sympathy for a boo-boo, blows his stack without reservation.* I was overwhelmed by my situation, their pain, my shortcomings, and the turmoil caused a hardness to develop. Overwhelming evidence proved they missed me, but I remained doubtful. The fact that I was covered in my kids' most treasured stuffies should have been a telltale sign. They kissed the skin off my face and piled their favorites all over me before they left. For years it had been impossible to separate them from those things, but they freely gave them up. *You can't have that many stuffies on your bed. You'll suffocate!*

But the hand-made cards I had received in the mail, the sad goodbyes, the tears I could hear through the phone falling from their eyes but couldn't reach to wipe away, every ounce of love they continued to show began lifting me out of the trenches.

Cards and balloons, gifts, tiresome-long hugs, the endless rambling of an excited kid may seem pointless to most tough guys, but I've found a new hat to wear: loving with a modest splash of stern. Gentle but respecting the clear line between right and wrong.

All this promoted the first step in rebuilding. Stepping out in faith. Learning to love unconditionally. When the house is chaotic and I seem to be losing ground, the good times, the love, focusing on the blessings that God freely gives is what keeps me from sinking completely under.

The hardest part of recovery is acting on the reminder. Casting off frustration long enough to see the truth and enact it.

I encourage you to love unconditionally because at any moment, the "needed" break you might be asking for may come and turn lives upside down.

Questions

Is a rugged exterior robbing you of blessings?

Is being a "tough guy" worth what you're giving up?

Satisfaction, are you possible?

Is it time to allow an atmosphere of change to refresh your soul? Whatever answers you come up with, ponder what 1

Corinthians 13:13 NIV says, "And now these three remain: faith, hope, and love. But the greatest of these is love."

Chapter 3

SATISFACTION? ARE YOU POSSIBLE?

Who can answer with authority why we as humans want what we can't have, don't have, or shouldn't have? And is it humanly possible to be satisfied with what a person currently has? It seems instead of understanding and embracing satisfaction in seasons of our lives, we begin to question whether anything will suffice. Will I ever find true happiness in what I own? My relationships? Things I've been blessed with? Is there anything or anyone that'll show me the way to satisfaction? These deep questions I've pondered for quite some time. In fact, they've ruled my mind to near detriment. Robbing me of sleep, happiness, and sanity. And the end result of these deep subjects when I try to ignore them? Questioning God's love for me and doubting His promises.

One lonely afternoon while lounging unwillingly in my nursing home bed, I began unpacking the deep subject of satisfaction by audibly questioning, *What's satisfaction, anyway, and who classifies it? It has passed me up, that's for sure. Is this some sick joke?* I know, it's random, but that's what came out. Sometimes my thought bubbles populate so suddenly it's cataclysmic. Most stay in my head but far too many fall out my mouth. Am I alone in this? If anyone heard me talking to myself that day, it must have been alarming.

Some of the Questions I've Pondered

Then a pile of questions buried me in contemplation. Here's a snapshot of where my mind went that day.

1. Should a person always be understanding when the waitress consistently gets the order wrong? After all, am I not the paying customer? Doesn't customer-satisfaction offer me dominance over incompetence? What happened to my patron's rights to fulfillment?
2. Should I trash a defective item to avoid being labeled as a complainer? After all, if I paid for the item, did I not also purchase the right to gripe? Doesn't a warranty afford me the right to scrutinize?
3. Where's the line between demanding constant satisfaction and being content with one's reality?

My mind raced back and forth viciously, enough that I refused to eat that day. *Why now? Where had this disaster of a day come from?* I was faced with drawing the impossible line between complaining and satisfaction, and I wasn't ready. *Put out the cones, warm up the sprayers, the proverbial line must be drawn. Today!* But I wanted to know details before I participated. *Where's the supposed "happy medium"? Who sets the standards? Do I have a say in it?*

I seriously believed for years I had no say in the process. No wonder my thoughts were conflicted.

The Peak of Dissatisfaction—2006

One of the hardest lessons in contentment came when Heather and I bought our first house. At that time, I believed my opinion to be king and yours sucked. Wherever I went I word vomited imbalance in every conversation. Many saw me coming and ducked for cover. Heather describes my behaviors back then as almost manic. I would air my unfounded opinions to the world and expect zero rebuttal.

This is how you will treat me if you know what's good for ya. The world owes me. I'll take a whole lot of this but not any of that. Don't even try it, Buster.

I walked out a huge sense of entitlement and included anyone who'd listen. And if you didn't wanna hear it, I'd slap ya with freedom of speech and enforce my right to defend the kingdom of Jason before you managed to escape. Clearly, I had stacks upon stacks to learn about the subject of satisfaction and life, not to mention respect, but it was gonna take a train wreck of epic proportions to correct my path.

Shortly after we moved in, I voiced my disgust for what I believed the neighbors were like.

"Why in the world did I buy a house right next to the sickeningly-happy 'Jones' family?"

"I don't know, Jay, I think they're really nice." *Add Heather to the sickeningly happy list.*

"Nice or not. Their life is perfect. So is their yard. So is their house. Must be nice. All I do is struggle."

"Oh, stop. We have a nice place. I like it."

What caused me to behave like this in the first place? Not occasionally but continuously for nearly a decade? The answer's quite simple. I had planted a flourishing jealousy garden early on in life and had been watering the snot out of it. It wasn't the new neighbor's fault. Buying a house next to anyone else in the world would have produced the same results. They just happened to be the fertilizer that produced a bumper crop of bitterness, choking out the tiny row of common sense that struggled to survive in the jealousy garden.

The Bitter Taste of Dandelion

Loads of sun mixed with a crisp breeze blessed the spring day when Mrs. Jones sauntered into my front yard for the first time. The fact that she left behind her consistently groomed reality for my unkempt disaster lit my anxiety wick, but her chattiness about her love for flowers as she approached seemed promising.

"I see the tulips and daffodils Carmen planted are doing well."

Happy dance! Mrs. Jones crossed the divide and emerged with a compliment! Then the hammer dropped.

"You gonna do something about these dandelions?"

Music stopped. Dancing ceased. Train derailed. Skies darkened and bitter winds slapped the smile off my face.

This is what I heard…

"You wanna keep your trashy mess on your side of the line?"

How do you suggest I achieve that, Mrs. Jones? Those yellow curses in my yard reproduced quicker than rats in a trash pile. Eradicating them would be like climbing Mount Everest. I knew I'd never reach the summit, so I had previously given up on that battle and let them proliferate. *You got something against bees? This yard is a natural haven of rest and nourishment. Reproduce away my little friends!* Besides, clearly I was at a disadvantage. Lack of resources. Life was against me. The competition was rigged! Anyone driving by the Jones's estate knew they had the lush, golf course greens edged by pristine sidewalks. The mansion uplifted by stately white columns seated on an elegant front porch. Barely aged vehicles gracing the tidy, poured driveway. Should I continue? Ahh, why not? House guests coming and going. Multiple well-attended holiday parties afforded by covet-worthy jobs. They defined the good life! *It's GO TIME, Mrs. Jones! You don't wanna go there with me!* I accepted the challenge, regardless of my chances. *Game on, kids! Let's do this!* I set out to mirror the Joneses. To not only compete and stay relevant but to come out on top.

Wait a second...it was just a comment. Nobody asked you to compete. She hadn't initiated a challenge. The Joneses had merely worked hard enough to get where they were in life. But the headspace I was in expected the same blessings because I breathed the same air as the blessed.

Truth Be Told

Years down the road, Mrs. Jones celebrated my gardening talents. Complimented my taste, asked me for advice, showed my beds to friends. What a humbling turn of events for a supposed tough guy bent on competing. Additionally, I came to realize she meant no harm with her comments about the colorful weeds. I was sensitive and easily offended, that's all.

You Wanna Dance? Let's Dance!

Instead of taking a moment to think, to ponder Mrs. Jones's possible blunt personality into the equation, I raked the life out of the grass, took a flat headed screwdriver after those blasted dandelions, and cursed the ground I sprawled out on. *Maybe now she'll be happy with me as her neighbor?* But the more I hatefully ripped those bloody weeds out, the more they reproduced. I decided to take a different route. Instead of wasting time on a losing battle, I planted a memorial flower garden to honor the previous owner. I crammed as many flowers as I could into the meager and quickly built remembrance beds and then dedicated them publicly to her memory to cover up my horrible intent. But even though I busted my back landscaping, nothing I did seemed to satisfy because I still felt the perceived stink eye from across the fence. Weeks later I heard of a quarry in Rapid River full of flat stones perfect to build paths and borders around the house, and off I went. *Surely, I've found the winning ticket to the superior yard. Sorry about your bad luck!* And with hours upon hours of grueling work, the borders, and paths I built were gorgeous! Skads of passerbys stopped to compliment me of their beauty. Pride swelled my head to explosion when a state senator campaigning for a new seat stopped his canvassing to commend me for my landscaping abilities. *SCORE! I've finally bested the Joneses!*

But then the unthinkable happened…I fell drastically behind in the competition when Mrs. Jones pulled up in her new car. Mine had rust on the quarters. The wheels no longer glistened in the sunlight. And my house was an embarrassment with all the busted plaster and cracking ceilings. I had no time to repair the house while landscaping and working a full-time job. Visitors became scarce because I had no time to chat. I began to realize if victory were to be mine, I'd need to pull out the big guns because flower beds and paths were no longer adequate.

What's the flashiest way to impress the neighbors? If a person needs to ask that question, he or she is obviously on the wrong track. But I found the answer: get a boat! A massive pontoon boat!

Picture it with me: Load up the truck bed, fill the coolers, gas up the tanks. Dump the boat into the harbor and motor to a solitary section. Commence sunning in the middle of the lake while balmy waves splash the sides of the pontoons, offering a warm, hydrating mist. Fling open the side gate and dive into the sweet blue green to cool down. Towel off and grill some fat burgers while slamming icy adult beverages under the canopy. *What else could deliver so much status?*

Hold on a quick minute. Let me bust the myth. What's this chapter about? Satisfaction? You won't find it in the middle of a competition or amassing material possessions.

Satisfaction eluded and so did status. I was still the same miserable guy who had taken a turn for the worse. Mentally and financially. What happened to being a husband, a dad, a child of God?

Had these descriptions lost their meaning? Had a single misunderstood question shoved me off a cliff? Had the presence of dandelions set my world on fire and driven me mad? A person usually senses when he or she has lost control. I knew I had. And at that moment a person is presented with a choice. Keep going to prove a point or simply end the madness because it's wrong. And for a follower of Jesus, it's wrong in His eyes, too. I am who He says I am. Nothing but His approval matters anyway.

Pride and jealousy won the coin toss, and I flushed myself further down the drain. But when Mrs. Jones tossed me a dandelion removal tool, excited to support me in my quest to tame the yellow beasts, it provided the extra water pressure to blast me straight into the sewer.

You Know I Love To Ask Questions

Maybe this all could have been cleared up with a simple question? *What did you mean by what you said?*

Maybe just like me you're good at assuming, too. How about pondering this before continuing…What if I would have stomped over to the Joneses, angrily bloodied my knuckles on their elaborate $2,500 screen door and demanded a financial statement. A completed satisfaction survey. Evidence of some sort of disappointment in their lives. Something. Anything. But also ponder this: at the end of the day, it'd still be none of my business.

Would you consider doing this? Or keep on making a mess like I did?

Too much work for me to correct it now.

I had seen their noticeable successes and heard stories from friends of friends. They were among the lucky. *I bet they're saddled with their own Joneses and are miserable. I bet their competitor has deeper pockets, and it drives them crazy.* I never once thought they might be truly thankful, satisfied, or not in competition. Or were simply good people, wonderful neighbors. *Yup! That's why she had spoken to me the way she did. She's unhappy. Lucky but miserable.*

The Car Guy

Maybe speaking in terms of oil and grease will better express my flawed deductions to the gearheads out there.

Consider this ridiculous phenomenon.

For years the Cadillac wreath and crest has been considered more prestigious than the Chevy bowtie. And with Caddy recently sparking new excitement in the heart of luxury car owners, they seem to be gaining ground by divorcing the old man image and sporting a new aggressive stance. More horsepower, more styling. Look out. And what seems to be Chevy's only chance to compete: the Corvette. Who's gonna win? Who has more prestige? Wait a second. There are more players to consider. Don't forget the Buick Grand National from the eighties. Reportedly pulled from production because one of the Buick models put the Corvette to shame. Sounds like what Chevy did to Oldsmobile in the fifties. Chevy keeps pulling rank and asserting its own relevance among its stablemates. A rivalry has been brewing for years. Yet try as Chevy may, it will never be number one in all areas. It'll always fall short of Cadillac, Buick, many others in various segments. But as usual, outdo or be outdone. That's the name of the game.

Have you ever asked why this happens? What's the actual difference in these cars other than comfort levels and a ton of outdated-in-five-years gadgets? Is it performance numbers?

Full grain Nappa leather? Dependability? Is it the emblem awarding Caddy more praise? Does the wreath and crest exude quality and the bowtie exemplify cheapness? Truth be told, both brands are endowed with miles of cut-rate plastics aimed at saving a buck. Shouldn't we be satisfied with the fact that the vehicle gets us back and forth and keeps us out of the elements?

Have you noticed that the vast majority of humans draw many of their conclusions from societal perceptions? *Hey! Read this review. It must be good because 3,753 people said the shipping was fast, and they love it just because they opened the box!* The automotive industry seems to be no exception.

Is it society's fault, then? Something's worthy of more praise and accolades due to public beliefs? Flawed or not, this is what most often believe. I worked in the automotive field long enough to know not to subscribe to this train of thought. After many years in dealerships and aftermarket parts stores this is what I have learned: Cadillac has just as many issues as its stablemate, Chevy, in every area. In fact, I've always considered Caddy less worthy. Oil chuggers and leaky messes.

Might as well leave that NorthStar oil pan gasket on the counter. Don't put it away cuz it'll be flying out the door before noon. Oh, grab a rear main seal, and while you're at it, a valve cover gasket set and a case of 10w30. Should be an easy upsell.

That's why I chose to drive Oldsmobile, even though that brand was riddled with its own shortcomings as well. It literally comes down to perception.

However, because GM killed off Oldsmobile in 2004, and I had morphed into a crowd-pleaser, I needed a relevant way to boost my socioeconomic status. I knew I'd never look cool in a dated Oldsmobile, so image overtook smarts the day I test drove my first SRX, and I caved. The *I'd never be caught dead in that* dissipated, and I replaced reason with opportunity to one-up my competition. Bad mouthing Caddy wouldn't bring status, I believed driving one would. And honestly, who can resist a luxury car when a person's perceived status is at stake, right?

Comfortable, full of electrical jargon that'll wow the crowd, how could I lose? And that's precisely why the manufacturer adds in all that junk. And to outdo the other manufacturers. That SRX was loaded for its year and had an all-glass roof that retracted way back behind the rear seat! *Sorry, Oldsmobile. Ya came up short.*

Remember the senator complimenting the stone path I was building? *Who cares about him! I've moved up in class without his help.* Rolling into the Keystone parking lot with the top retracted one sunny afternoon, my district manager noticed and walked over.

"Hey, Jay! Didya just get this?"

"Yeah, yesterday. Check out this roof!"

"That's what drew me. What a beauty! Congrats."

"Thanks. I love it."

"What's not to love?"

I climbed the ladder that day. The last time my district manager had graced us with his presence, he had seen me exiting a Chevy Uplander while he climbed outta a tricked-out Lincoln MKS. I had also jumped a thousand points on the cool scale, and I planned to preach to the world the merits of going from a busted Chevrolet to a technology-laden Cadillac. *Eat that, Mrs. Jones!*

My buddies, mechanic friends, previous co-workers all tried to convince me to rethink my choice. But I defended my rash decision.

"What are ya doin'? Those things are nothing but headaches."

"Nah! That's speculation."

Not only were they a headache under the hood, but the all-wheel drive units, alone, were a huge deterrent. I sold the parts, took the money from angry customers forking out skads of dough at the dealer. I couldn't afford the repairs or the maintenance, and especially if I wanted to continue the soul-crushing quest to best the Joneses.

What if the bearings in the transfer case let go? The teardown alone is costly. What about seal leaks? Eighteen dollars a quart, and that's on the cheap side, ya better fix it quick if it leaks. Do the Joneses have oil stains uglying up their pristine driveway? Ah, who cares? I'll deal with it. Sears sells pressure washers every day. Besides, eighteen dollars a quart is cheap for a good impression, fake or not. The grease spots are worth it. Forget about the issues and dive into the possibilities. Oh, the opinions and conclusions people will form of me! Ceremoniously gracing the drive with a phat Cadillac would cement my relevance and shout to the world that I had finally arrived. The Brunette's are doing well. And when Marisa, at seven years old, said she thought the car was "classy", it bolstered my new ego. *See, even a 7-year-old gets it. Don't tell me I'm outta place and inferior.* Never once did I heed the warning sign that my attitude was instilling a materialistic vein in my daughter.

That car is gone now. I traded it for a two door Pontiac worth $3,800. And now I wonder how an inanimate object, a car, can help a person develop a sense of who he or she is? That's absurd.

We Come to Many Crossroads

Deeper and deeper into the black hole called finances we sank, until one day, I remembered that suppressed feeling of losing myself in the battle between true happiness and the insatiable desire of material satisfaction. My heart ached and longed for peace. My guts churned and begged for a truce. *How could I have let myself self-destruct? Where had the joy of being a dad of three beautiful children gone? Of having a wife content with just hanging out with me?*

I clearly remember when this realization hit. I was lost in a vision of self-correction. I was at yet another crossroads. I saw the Jones's driveway to the left. On the right beckoned material possessions loaded down with guilt. Straight ahead was my driveway lined with love and joy. While I looked around in confusion, memories of a spectacular sunset I had enjoyed with my wife the previous night flooded in. My kids, singing and skipping their way down the driveway, then excitedly kissing our faces right before heading inside to get ready for bed, brought tears to my eyes. The intricate blooms and gorgeous smell of the Lily of the Valley sprawling down the retaining wall alongside the driveway warmed my soul. The woman I love sitting next to me on the retaining wall with lips puckered, waiting for a kiss from her flawed man tore my heart in half. I was beyond blessed! In need of nothing more because I had it all.

But what about the unfinished stone paths? What will the Joneses think if I don't promptly finish my projects? What about the unfinished projects inside the house? The trash the neighborhood hoodlums keep littering in the front yard. One more pop bottle and someone's gonna get it! What!? Mrs. Jones decorated for the holidays before me again?!

What's it gonna be? questioned the Caddy as it coughed, kicking an engine light, and attempting to stall.

Not you, too! I'm counting on you. You're on my side, remember?

Then the still small Voice whispered clarity.

The road to the left will rob you of your happiness just like it always has, and if you turn to the right, you'll always be torn. Choose life. Go straight.

But I can't let the neighbors win! I've got too much invested!

The road straight ahead leads to the simple treasures you hold dear to your "tough guy" heart. You know the straight-and-narrow is loaded with blessings from the Father.

Honk, honk! Mrs. Jones' new car swerved around my clunker.

I CAN'T WIN!

Best Late-Night Snack: Saltines

A conversation outside my door snapped me back into my current surroundings. How could I not hear it since the last aide hadn't shut my door like I had asked? Like many nights prior, yet another resident in the nursing home was shouting again. Irritation swept away my peace; it was 11 pm and frustration fired back.

"BE QUIET!" I yelled.

"BRING ME CRACKERS!" an angry male voice boomed. "CRACKERS, BRING ME CRACKERS!"

"Lawrence, you're diabetic and shouldn't have crackers this late at night," lovingly said the desperate-sounding aide.

"DID YOU HEAR ME?? THE CRACKERS!!" shouted the resident.

Where are my crackers? Would God ever send me comfort this late at night?

Back At the Crossroads

Nope. The day had come to choose which path I was gonna take at the crossroads. No more could I dance around the issue. The Lord was asking for my decision. Left to continue in misery, right to what if and constant guilt and shame, or straight ahead to love? *No rest for the weary mind tonight.*

The struggle to decide ended as my two daughters strolled into my room the next morning, hugging and kissing on their exhausted dad who they sorely missed. I chose my family. The wheel that had been viciously yanked right and left all night long had finally straightened out. I chose home, right where I belonged. I chose the arms of the ones I loved and felt completely satisfied. I'm thankful that God used Lawrence the night before to drive home we *want what we shouldn't have*. With my world upside down, the Lord knew I needed a refresher. I never thought an unexplained illness and separation from the ones I had struggled to choose would be the refresher, but it taught me to cling to the words in 1 Thessalonians 5:18 KJV, "In everything give thanks, for this is the will of God in Christ Jesus concerning you." And hang on tight to the Apostle Paul's inspiration to keep going in his letter to the Philippians, chapter 4, and verse 11 in the NIV. "I am not saying this because I am in need, for I have learned to be content whatever the circumstances."

Shall We Continue to Dance?

As far as the competitive edge that nearly destroyed me, it's fading. It hasn't disappeared miraculously. I still gotta choose to be satisfied, thankful, appreciative, or I'll keep dancing like a sizzling egg in a frying pan. But no longer can I dwell on what I can't, don't, and shouldn't have. I'm here to say it is humanly possible to be satisfied in all situations. But you can't let the ad campaigns, the materialism, friend's coercing, public opinion, personal jealousy dictate your life and then expect to find satisfaction. You gotta choose one or the other. But the most amazing choice is being satisfied. True happiness and thankfulness are found in God, not in what a person owns, has, or has been blessed with. When we saddle those blessings with dissatisfaction, we turn our back on the Gift-Giver. And what a horrible mistake. Lives start lacking joy, happiness becomes outta reach, relationships take on water, minds degrade from constant unrest, and sleep...*what is that?*

I gotta ask one more question before you turn the page. How can a person be truly thankful if he or she is never satisfied with the simple treasures in life?

Chapter 4

SIMPLE TREASURES

With the details of my new existence at the forefront, my mind has wandered from one end of the spectrum to the other. Some days it's been back and forth like a yo-yo. Yanked up and down so violently I feel everything upstairs has turned to mush. But since this nursing home bed has held me prisoner, the exhaustion I've felt from self-analysis seems like adequate exercise. Never knowing what to expect, I do know each passing day will require the same determination and routine. Nap when tired, wake-up to minimal responsibilities, eat, drink, exert myself in therapy, sleep a bit more, eat, drink, push the call button, sit on the john. Might sound boring to some, but it takes all I got to do anything other than think and sleep. And sometimes the thinking part is more tiresome than actual physical exercise. *Welcome to your new normal.* All previous activities have abruptly halted since my body has screamed *ENOUGH!* And lately perusing the memories of my past foolishness has become depressing, so my mind has screamed *ENOUGH! Allow me some quiet time with little refocusing on the things that truly satisfy.*

I'm learning how to be satisfied, and I'm beginning to notice how overly blessed I am. There's no turning back now. But as of late, loneliness and boredom has continued to threaten this new realization, and I gotta squash this depression or I'll fall into despair. If I don't, choosing to be satisfied will become one of my top ten dumbest choices.

After Heather and the girls left me in this barely-enough-space-for-me room I'm trapped in, a familiar choice presented itself : waste time and feel depressed or sit up and embrace life and its beauty. Rise above and be successful in recovery or continue sniveling. *Even though harsh realities abound, I will not fill the remaining days, however many they may be, with emptiness and boo-hooing.* Even though I've never been a timewaster, I have spent enough time grieving, *and it's time to move on.*

I'm confused, though. *What should this new determination look like? I'm remanded to the noisiest bed in the building. There's nonstop commotion in the hallways. Residents yell into the wee hours of the night. Visitors are rare, and I only got this wall mounted tv for company. Are there any other options besides boredom and irritation?* I'm vowing not to be labeled as a loafer, yet satisfaction seems out of reach! Heather brought my Samsung tablet, and I could click the seconds away playing games. *That'd be fun.* Until it's not. I haven't switched on the tv yet this morning because it's all the same. Noise. *What in the world am I going to do today? Keep typing on this little phone all the words rolling around in my head?*

I felt the hope and determination being sucked outta me like the green goo on Ghostbusters. But as I sat up and began looking around, I noticed a minute pop of color between the gray damask curtains. I quickly pushed back the drab curtain to reveal a flower petal that had tried to escape its solitude. The sun glistened off the petal like the glitter my girls like to sneak on my forehead, and it sent me into an array of contemplations. *How'd the small pot from the corner of the window land right there? How'd the purple petunia blossom balance the whole pot on the ledge? What does this mean? Did this little flower come to visit me because it knew I was struggling?* Had boredom led me into imagining ridiculous conspiracy theories about flowers and windowsills that were trying to teach me a lesson? *What had my thoughts been reduced to? I'm searching for meaning behind a plastic pot of petunias partially squished between a curtain?! Nurse!!* Lying in a bed *was* getting to me. I had become like Tom Hanks in Castaway. For a second, I laid back down and closed my eyes, but even more thoughts flooded in. I sat right back up and shoved both curtains open as far as they would go. *Make it stop!!* But they didn't stop.

Counting Flowers On The Wall

They did bother me if you know what I mean.

Had I no room for the smaller things in life?

Does everything require a reason for its existence?

Was I ignoring what others so easily adored?

I believe God was using a budding white geranium and a blossoming purple petunia perched in my tiny windowsill to pave the avenue of a new rationale. I began to realize that, even though God has a purpose and a plan for everything, I don't need to understand any of it. I only need to submit to Him.

Travelling this boulevard was bewildering at first. Simply because I'm way too analytical. Without a clear-cut reason, I've always rejected chance encounters, any randomness as a moment where the universe came together. *You only got lucky that's all. And as far as these flowers are concerned, they're a couple of dumb flowers sitting in a filthy window covered by ugly gray curtains. Nothing to see here.* But oddly enough, that's not what began to roll around in my brain as I stared them down. Was I at the start of something novel? *Probably losing my mind.* Taking delight in the finer things? *You're looking for Wilson.* Crazy-to-me notions coursed the neural pathways for hours, and inexplicably enough, to the delicate side of things I went.

Now It's Gonna Get Weird

Have you ever examined a dainty geranium blossom? How about took the time out of your crazy schedule to study the intricate details of its leaves?

Hold on. Maybe you're asking *what's goin' on here? This took a weird turn.* That's how I felt!! Moments ago, if I were reading this stuff, I'd roll my eyes and light the woodstove with these pages. *What kinda pansy nonsense is this?* But before you get worked up and preach tough guys flex their muscles while the maidens faint, I'm well aware dainty and delicate aren't on the approved list for muscle shirts. Indulge me this for a moment. I promise you won't regret it if you let your mind travel to where mine went. Odd as it may feel, there's beauty in God's design everywhere a person turns. And it's worth a look. Besides, to those who find this hokey, have you ever moved past your thoughts to admire intricate beauty designed by our Savior? I hadn't until that day. What a rewarding discovery.

Let's get back at it. Start with the blossom. Examine the detail. If you don't have a geranium handy, Google it and let your eyes marvel as your mind wanders. Look at the veins and the creases. Maybe yours has multicolored leaves with colors that fade seamlessly into each other. Isn't it amazing how such a delicate bloom can survive in a harsh world? No protection, no worries. It flourishes to bring pure joy to those willing to admire God's design. And was created to bring glory to God.

Now look at how many other blooms are on each stem. They're in competition for necessary nutrients, yet they grow united. What simple truths surrounding unity could we gain from the fragile geranium? Unlike some plants that shoot vines to choke out competition, the geranium coincides in harmony.

Remember the Joneses? Maybe they're the same way. They wanna carve out a simple existence without someone threatening their happiness. Be harmonious instead of being outperformed by the neighbor. Why is kinship and coexistence such a difficult concept for many? Diversity makes us beautiful. Imagine white blossoms, white leaves, and white stems sticking out of a white pot. How boring! But sadly, the idea of celebrating diversity threatens many insecure people.

If I'm different then I won't fit in.

You don't look, act, and think like me so you must be a threat.

Our creeping vines of fear reach out to destroy perceived competitors, ruining not only their attractiveness, but also destroying their inner beauty. Gardens that wow are filled with flowers that complement each other not compete with each other.

Back to admiring the amicable geranium. What else do you see or feel? Run your fingers across the petal if you can. They remind me of the top of my daughter's feet when she was younger. Soft and velvety. When my middle daughter, Marisa, would hop on my lap, she always requested a foot massage. Of course, initially, I refused, but after repeated requests, I caved. And then it turned into a cherished ritual. I'm unsure why the silky skin atop her foot impressed me so, especially when touchy-feely anything weirded me out, but I couldn't refuse her requests. Additionally, I'd even oblige rubbing in a little lotion. Completely outta character for me. I hate lotion. The feel, the smell. *Let the girls have that!*

The Handshake

Nothing can erase how polar opposite of masculine I felt when I shook a loan officer's hand after signing papers for one of my bazillion cars. His hands were unnervingly delicate and almost wet. So much so that I nearly yanked mine away in disgust. He had gripped the handshake with his one palm and covered the top of mine with his other sloppy hand. Gross! A man's hands should be rough and caveman, not fancy and elegant. Just not for me.

But that prejudice against lotion led me to be judgmental and ultimately into hate. What if he likes his hands that way? What business is it of mine? And what's the difference among the touch of a geranium blossom, the feel of those chewable baby feet, and the softened-by-lotion hands?

The truth of the matter is clear to me. I may not have enjoyed that handshake or never took the time to appreciate a budding marvel, but I had lost sight of the simple, enjoyable treasures God had blessed me with. And why? Because of my subscription to *masculinity* and what composes a tough guy. *I was enculturated to think that way. Blame it on the world. Yeah, right, Jason. Believe whatever you want, but yer creating excuses to promote your fixed mindset.*

Before the argument surfaces that a person is allowed to like what he or she likes, understand what I mean.

Ignoring the simple treasures is a dangerous habit because it leads to dissatisfaction. Dissatisfaction leads to disharmony. Disharmony leads to misunderstandings. Misunderstandings left uninvestigated ultimately leads to bitterness, rejection, and anger. Bitterness leads to hate. Can't we just live in harmony with others instead of forcing a conformity to our views? Could it be that the banker's silky hands were one of his simple treasures? Shouldn't I just celebrate the difference with *while that's not for me, I'm glad you enjoy it*? Why did I label him so quickly, totally misunderstanding that, in his line of work, rough hands would probably be a negative for him with all the handshakes he does? *It's not always about you, Jason.*

To drive it home in a floral fashion, would I smash every geranium smell-less just because it possessed soft petals? (That one's for you, Mom!)

A special kind of hateful would be required to do something like that. Would appreciating the finer things of God's creation make me a sissy in the world's eyes? Maybe, but who cares. Runaway thoughts also lead to dissatisfaction. Everyone's allowed to have his or her opinions, likes, feelings, as long as they're not in opposition to God. We are commanded to love, not wreck the place.

Mirror, Mirror

Do you ever just look in the mirror without nit picking what you see? I'm sure you've looked in a mirror. You've seen yourself a million times. Some of you might make an hourly habit of it.

But have you really *looked* in the mirror to gain a good visual of yourself? Is there something you dislike? Be honest—but not rude or demeaning, please—someone else will always have better features, straighter lines, less wrinkles. That's life. But ponder this.

Do you think the simple geranium would cease blooming just because a neighboring rose is prettier?

Of course not! It doesn't have that kind of power. But we do.

"That darn Sally. Every chance she gets, she makes me look like a pug. Why do I even try?"

"Don't say that. You're beautiful."

"Just look at me. I need to lose at least six pounds, my hair is ugly and brittle, and my jowls are pronounced." (An actual conversation I've overheard.)

Or if you're the insecure guy who projects his insecurity onto others with hateful, judging words…

"Wow, Sally might need to scrape a few pounds of makeup off. She's trying too hard."

I've learned that discontentment vocalizes when I'm dissatisfied in even the smallest and most insignificant areas of my life. Dissatisfaction will come, and I believe it's healthy to verbalize it sometimes, but be careful. True happiness comes from contentment with what God has permitted in our lives. Without a tangible love for the LORD Jesus Christ, where thankfulness is evident in all things, the simple treasures will be ignored, and discontentment will ruin things in a quick hurry. In the case of the mirror, continual fault-finding will lead to self-loathing, jealousy, and a critical spirit. At that point, I wish you all the best. But it won't stop there. Unfortunately, this list is inconclusive. Besides losing yourself in all the chaos of discontentment, you'll rob yourself or possibly others of faith and trust in God. And don't get me started on friendships.

Is it worth it?

A rosy life full of perfection was never promised. It was in God's original plan before sin entered the world, but you know the story. But look at this truth: even roses have wound inflicting thorns. Some may consider thorns an imperfection and others may consider them a perfect design. Which means not everyone will appreciate a rose for its every feature. Some florists remove these imperfections to attract a larger crowd. But it's still loved. Is the Florist trying to remove some of your thorns?

Take this advice: keep focusing on what God is doing and has done. Disregard the flower you wish you were, and flourish as the one you were created to be. As soon as I focus on the fact that I'm not a rose and just a plain geranium, discontentment leads to root rot.

Maybe I'll fit in if I become part rose and part geranium.

Don't do it. Hybrids are not a part of the plan. Each of us is different, and we all have individual value. Striking beauty. We'll flourish if we learn to be content in the garden where God planted us.

"I praise You because I am fearfully and wonderfully made; Your works are wonderful; I know that full well." Psalm 139:14 NIV

But why can't a geranium become a rose? Scientifically it's possible. I'm convinced a scientist could graft a rose onto a geranium and eventually prune away the original plant once the rose begins to thrive. But why would you wanna do that?

Smash The Mirror

I had a friend smack me upside the head with the truth so hard one day that I didn't know if I should cry or check her hand for broken bones.

"The grass is green, but you want it to be blue. But it's green. No matter what you say, think, or feel, it's never gonna be blue."

Yeah, well, I planted bluegrass. How's that grab ya?"

I'll never be Mr. Jones. I'll always be Jason. I gotta quit trying to become a rose because I certainly don't look like or smell like one. Maybe I'm a petunia. (More like a Venus fly trap.) And once I put forth the effort required to discover who God designed me to be, I'll develop a finer taste for the simple treasures, a well-rounded contentment, and a complete sense of myself *without* having to rob styling cues from the neighbor. And my wife will enjoy the man she married because she didn't marry Mr. Jones.

I've been continually looking for simple treasures since that white geranium and purple petunia served me up a platter of truth. I stop by the floral department and admire the beauty. I drink in the various scents and admire the textures of the assorted leaves. Smell the herbs and spices before sprinkling them to the simmering pan and thank God for creating them. The sunsets come alive. Songbirds impress me with their melodies. Even an ant's marching pattern is noteworthy.

Throw off the noise and distraction and soak up the orange, pink, and yellow hues of a sunset. Write out a card to a stranger in a nursing home, knowing that it might be the first bit of mail in an awfully long time. Smell the roses every chance you get.

Unbelievable Grace

When I was given the option to either be miserable in my surroundings or be thankful for the small things, it was an overwhelmingly difficult decision to make. But it goes hand in hand with satisfaction. Just like the previous chapter's last question, *how can a person give thanks if he or she is never satisfied*, I had to make a choice. I could've easily lost myself in all the pain, became yet again a completely different person, and rode the tidal wave of anger into another dark era of my perceived bleak existence. But thankfully God had initiated a plan, giving me a way out of that temptation. He sent my mom and son the week prior with a dinky geranium in full bloom, a similar-in-size petunia top heavy with color, and a miniature cross which read, *I can do all things through Christ who strengthens me* to rescue my inner peace superhero style.

You know, the good LORD works out His plans in ways we'll never fully understand until we stand before Him. If we would only trust Him, He'll provide simple treasures that'll pull us through the dark times. Especially during those seasons when we feel like *I can't do this alone.*

During quiet reading and reflection time, which I hold so dear, I have discovered immense truths. And now without blinders hampering my view, the evidence is all around that God loves His children more than we know. Luke records the words of Jesus pertaining to the flowers He graciously created for our enjoyment. "Look at the lilies and how they grow. They don't work or make their clothing, yet Solomon in all his glory was not dressed as beautifully as they are." Luke 12:27 NLT.

Will you be on the lookout for the simple treasures in your life?

Chapter 5

I CAN'T DO THIS ALONE

Heather and the kids' first tearful nursing home trip was bittersweet. It was way too short but desperately needed. After they had left I remember thinking, *I can't do this alone*. The thought of being abandoned frightened me. And then angered me. *Why is this happening?* Even after quickly accepting the truth— they had to go home to their lives; they couldn't stay here—it failed to comfort or console. I knew each of them would've pulled up a cot right alongside me and camped out until I was able to go home. And then the macho tried to take over. *Quit yer boo-hooing. You don't need them. You've got this.* I was split right down the middle. The partial comfort from accepting they couldn't stay worked only half of the time. But the other half, loneliness cuddled me like the kids' favorite stuffies.

My health condition had demolished the chance to ride home with them. Everybody knew it. No one except a skilled facility would be able to give me the care I needed. So, they tearfully left without me.

Good Thing I've Had Practice

Both Keystone and Carquest had sent me to many out-of-town training classes when I worked for them; short breaks from the family had become commonplace. And refreshing. Many of the Keystone trips were to Minnesota for PPG paint class and were several days long. *I've got an idea! When the family comes to visit, it'll be like I've returned home from class. And when they leave, I've traveled back to class. That'll work! See! You were moanin' and whinin' for nothing.*

But the nursing home and paint class had nothing in common. Nor did any of the other classes I had attended. The nursing home was going to offer drastically different training. It would test my faith, expose the weak side of my bull-headed nature, and impart desperately needed coping skills.

A few days after my family had departed, I was reading in Joshua about the discouraged Jews crossing the Jordan river before marching around Jericho. Joshua had quite the feat to pull off. He needed to encourage the weary folk, pump them up to cross the river, and take possession of the land God had promised to their forefather, Abraham. I can only imagine how powerless they felt. Alone. Tired from wandering for forty years in the desert. But Joshua, being the strong and courageous one, jumped up and ordered, "Go through the camp and tell the people, 'Get your provisions ready. Three days from now you will cross the Jordan here to go in and take possession of the land the LORD your God is giving you for your own.'" Joshua 1:11 NIV. *Who the heck is this guy telling us to get excited? Don't you understand what we're up against?* I felt the same way. The river I had to cross is obviously impassible! Then out of the blue my phone rang. It was my mom with a Joshua pep talk.

"Good morning, Honey. I wanted to surprise you and just show up, but I couldn't keep quiet. I signed Dylan out of school, and we're headed down to see you. We're almost to Marinette, so we'll be there in a little bit. Is there anything I can bring you?"

I needed the boost in morale! Being without my family had started to exact high dividends from my determination.

Dylan was spastic the entire visit. He had no idea how to contain his excitement for traveling instead of attending class. The excessive amounts of junk from adoring staff really didn't help the hype, either. He scribbled ridiculous pictures while blurting odd kid noises and scattered an entire stack of post-it notes all over my corkboard.

The bizarre phrases he wrote on those notes…

But the charge he got outta writing a million little notes was worth letting him do it. His silliness was his coping mechanism, hoping to bring his dad some joy in the only way he knew how. I fought back the irritation and let him be. Trust me, I would have rather visited with Mom, but he desperately needed his dad.

Tears stained my face as I watched them leave. And this time seeing family leave shook me to the core. Their departure dug a deep hole in my soul that began clouding the joy of their visit. After they disappeared, I whipped the curtains shut to block my view of the visitor parking lot and just sobbed. I couldn't imagine myself watching Mom's taillights illuminating the darkened sky while remaining composed. The sobbing continued long after their shadows had faded in the hallway. I had worked hard emotionally to stay together during their visit for the sake of my boy's stability, but I couldn't hold the goo in anymore. I watched as part of the castle walls I had built came crashing down.

For days I sulked and remained quiet, observing the rubble from the massive walls. *How had they fallen so easily? And stayed down? Who's gonna clean this up?*

Stupid Wonderful Picture

And then it hit me. The picture of my children Mom had placed on the dresser was to blame. The one of my kids glowing with pride over a homemade pizza they had joyfully put together. The pizza, the kitchen, the night was a mess, but they loved every minute of the adventure. I had tearfully stared at that picture, sometimes for hours, every day since they had left, and it had made a mark. From my bed it was completely out of reach; not even my handy dandy grabber could reach it. I wanted to hold it. Examine it. But I refused to ask the aides to grab it because I'd look weak. But from where it sat, that picture continued to magically ward off the unwanted every day I stared at it. Building anxiety and fear of the unknown were no match for the smiling faces shining through the acrylic protection. Surprisingly my courage returned, and my demeanor brightened. Even though cards and letters, a couple of stupid balloons, a few plants and figurines, reading material, my tablet, the tv were present to comfort me, they were all inanimate objects. Not people. The wonderful aides were there, and I loved them all, but I longed for the familiar personal connection. Somehow that silly picture battered the ugly walls and emerged victorious. I wish it would've popped the balloons while it was at it. That would've provided adequate entertainment in the battle!

In Time Of Need You Were There

One of the many hats I wore at Carquest was inventory correction and management. Each morning we'd receive a daily truck full of parts for inventory replenishment. For the most part, shipments were smooth, but if mishaps occurred, the mending process oftentimes became disastrous. Track down the forever-missing check in sheets, find and record the tote number the missing part was supposedly shipped in, research the truck run and which warehouse the part or parts had come from, call in the long and shorts to the main warehouse. None of it was fun, but the worst part was breaking the news to an already irritated customer that his or her car would be down for yet another day because of a missing shipment. The process stunk. I dreaded every bit of it except when I got to call the distribution center because Miss Sally would answer 90% of the time.

Sally was a Rockstar. She could make the worries of this world disappear. She was the no-nonsense type of warehouse wizard, and I could count on her to investigate any and every issue *as long as* I respected her efforts *and* accepted her discovery. *I can investigate this issue for you, but don't feed me any nonsense after I come up with the answer. Your store is not the only one this distribution center services. Keep that in mind.* Her blunt and straight-to-the-point demeanor won me over, and we instantly clicked.

Well, one day, Sally walked into my room at St. Joe's Hospital. She was holding a card and two get well balloons. Since I had chosen Marshfield Clinic to investigate the oddity of the onset of my disability, Sally could visit me because she lived and worked nearby. She certainly didn't seem like the balloon type when I chatted with her at work, so it was kinda shocking to see her there and with a present. I was extremely excited to meet her face to face, but I gotta come clean. The moment she darkened the door with those blasted helium bags, I plotted their demise. There was no way I was gonna tote those curses around. I already stuck out in a crowd with uncontrollable, sporadic muscle spasms head to toe; I didn't need a colorful billboard supporting my awkwardness. *Look at me and my get-well balloons! Aren't I adorable?*

Ditch The Airbags, Please

I've never really enjoyed balloons, even from childhood. Except maybe to explode the smile off somebody's face when I eradicated their joy with a single clap of the hands. And for those wicked behaviors, I believe I finally got my just comeuppance. After Sally had left, what seemed like every nurse in the hospital flocked into my room to congratulate me on my balloons. I tried to grin in tolerance, but instead I blurted, *those balloons gotta die!*

I should've kept my mouth shut. Immediately my nurse, Donna, grabbed the balloons off my rolling cart and placed them just outta reach, ensuring their safety.

"Remember the bed alarms!" she remarked as she exited the room.

I was discharged the following day to the nursing home. Public transport was on its way, and Donna began packing up my belongings.

"What do you wanna keep? I'll put the majority in this plastic bag. Whatever you don't want I'll toss."

I seized the opportunity.

"I'll take the cards, the shampoo and toothpaste, the socks. Leave the balloons for the trash."

She gathered everything, stuffed it in plastic bags, and situated me into a wheelchair and put all my possessions on my lap. But left the balloons sitting in the corner. For a moment. Piled high with junk, I had to wrap my arms around it all to keep things from falling off my lap.

And then Donna seized the moment.

On the way out the door she grabbed the balloons, shoved them between my left hip and the arm of the wheelchair, and jeered, "These'll keep you company, Jay."

She had taken a cheap shot, and her grin confirmed it. And when a transport nurse wheeled me away, Donna called out, "Best of luck, Jay."

Fate began to whisper its truth. The balloons had become permanent. However, it doesn't end there. The payback gets worse.

After transport left me in the lobby to wait for the bus, I sat loaded to my chin with personal belongings and those stupid attention getters by my side. As people entered the hospital, nearly everyone in the ten-minute wait commented on those cursed balloons, and how thoughtful it was that someone blessed me with them. They didn't say it in passing, however. They gathered around me. Doted over me. I faked so many smiles that day I think my face still bears the lines. But as they applauded Sally's kindness, my fake smiles turned into a sinister grin as my thoughts became evil.

The next person who says a single word about these stupid balloons is gonna witness me savagely shredding them with my teeth! That'll show them how nice they are.

I was enduring a public shaming at its worst. Luckily for the balloons public transit rolled in only moments later. But for me, as the driver wheeled me toward the bus, the wind-blown inflatables kept smacking me in the mouth every time I attempted to answer his questions. And there wasn't a single thing I could do about it until the driver finally removed the mountain of possessions off my knees. Picture this: I was the only guy strapped into a wheelchair on a loaded transport bus with all his worldly possessions stuffed in plastic bags heaped onto his lap, sportin' *hopefully you recover balloons*. No wonder my nerves were malfunctioning. I finally gave up the battle with the balloons and kept my head down, letting them mock me the entire trek across town. And unbelievably, those stupid curses lasted the full month I stayed in the nursing home, offering a daily reminder of the ridicule I'd endured. *Note to self: respect the balloon!*

Would You Give Me That Picture?

Staring at the picture of my kids became my new morning ritual. It seemed to have mystical powers, so I searched for missing details. I replayed the scene over and over in my head. Tried to remember their looks, their shrieks of joy, anything that happened that day. Marisa's publicized hatred of cheese brought joy instead of irritation. What had annoyed me previously, Marisa's incessant whining about a single morsel of cheese touching her lips, the flour from floor to ceiling, the pizza sauce smeared into the cloth seats, had become my solace. It was the inspiration I needed to stay connected.

I've never enjoyed talking on the phone. It's because I answered phones all day at work. But after staring at that wonderful picture, I purposed to keep my phone charged up so I could call home more often. I drained that battery more than I ever had because I couldn't hold out much longer on my own. I needed constant contact. And even though constant in-person support wasn't possible, Heather began to realize that some kind of rotation had to occur if I were to stay strong.

I woke up to my girls hopping onto my bed and snuggling me one morning. Can you imagine the shocked expression painting my face? Such a beautiful sight to wake up to instead of that picture. *Wake me up that way every day*!

I sobbed like the kid who had just witnessed his puppy being clobbered by oncoming traffic. (Sorry so dark. This happened to me.) But that morning they were tears of joy. A rare commodity for this guy. They overpowered my stubborn-streak, and I openly embraced the odd feeling.

Oh, you're taking my birthday away? Here, you can have it. And empty my savings while you're at it.

Realizing where I'd previously placed my value seemed to afford the breakthrough. A short visit with Mom and Dylan? Bonus! But surprised by my ladies? Tears should fall.

Shortly after the girls slobber-bathed my face and Heather readjusted my spine with her death-grip hug, they slowly walked out of the room. Not wanting to leave me to start the three-hour voyage back home, they stepped in and outta the room, disappearing for a moment and returning for another goodbye a few seconds later. They did this several times, and it was brutal.

But then there was silence.

I Really Do Miss Them

At the deafening moment of quiet, our 10th wedding anniversary trip to Vegas rushed in to break up the silence. The 5-night, 6-day adventure had been packed full of exploration and excitement. We strolled the strip, admired the architecture of as many casinos as our legs would carry us to. Spent hours poolside soaking up the desert heat. Searched out buffets and restaurants, stood in line for an hour for a chance to enjoy Carlo's Bakery. I mean, Cake Boss, right? Why not? We rented a triple black Challenger with only three miles on the clock. Hit 90 miles per hour toward Red Rock Canyon and blasted through Death Valley. Visiting Vegas for gambling and drinking wasn't our plan. I think by now you've gathered I'm dreadfully honest. Neither of us had been anywhere but Michigan in years. *Go West, Friends, go west!* We filled our time so full that missing home would mean we're having a dull moment. I remember dragging myself down the ridiculously long hallways of the New York New York hotel at two, three, and sometimes four a.m. after nearly eighteen hours of sightseeing. But on the fourth day we crossed the threshold of a novelty store and *WHAM!* Tears streamed down my face as I pictured my kids and the thrill they'd get if I bought them a treasure from out West. I remember turning toward Heather with springs a' flowin'.

"The kids would love this."

"The tough guy's crying?! You miss the kids. Aww!" And then she teared up.

What am I gonna do in Marshfield if I had crumbled so quickly in Vegas? Heather was with me then! I knew the challenge would be brutal, but I also began to understand that I'd hafta draw on the recent visits from loved ones and the pizza photo for strength. And end the confinement with my head held high. It became my new goal. *I am strong. I am capable. I am love.* I'd never attempted such a grand scale task before, but the nurses and aides supplied daily needs. I was well taken care of, even if my mind reasoned otherwise. The phone calls, incoming mail, the drawings and pictures left by the kids, those crazy post-it notes, they'd have to pick up the slack. I had a new goal that I would achieve. Regardless…

Why's There Gotta Be Difficulty All The Time?

It didn't take long, however, before I was plagued with trial after trial. Resident's friendly faces along with the staff's tenderness helped to some degree, and for that I'll forever be grateful; but the debilitating pain from physical and occupational therapy, the unquenchable nerve pain even at rest, the ever-changing symptoms, they began to overrule my new positive mindset. Loneliness swept over me like a tidal wave. Anger ripped up several of the pictures the kids had sent me. Bitterness burrowed like a chigger. The physical therapist, Sam, let me wheel back to my room after one session, and I slammed my bedroom door multiple times before calming down. And then despair began banging on the door. *Give me something other than the current reality. I'm not gonna make it alone.* And eventual defeat came the day I woke up in the hospital. Again. And when the discharge nurse stopped in a few days later to inform me that no nursing facility closer to home would accept me as a resident without a solid diagnosis, I lost all hope. This meant one thing: I wouldn't be leaving any time soon. A low blow gut punch right to ol' breadbox. I began shouting obscenities and word curses over the situation and nothing consoled. Even the nurse worked to comfort but eventually silenced the nonsense I spewed with a sharp rebuttal.

"You aren't listening to me, Jason. You won't make the trip home without excruciating pain, so get it outta your head that you're going to up and leave. You're in worse condition than you'll admit, and this foolish rant isn't helping things."

Extremely difficult to accept, but honestly speaking, events like these truly happen for a reason. I heard her message but didn't let on.

Luck Or Divine Appointment

The day I met Sam, my physical therapist at the home, was a serious stroke of luck. Hmm… It seemed almost as if every person I had previously met, the ones cheering me on, had been sent by Sam as a tie-me-over until he could get to me. He was a hope builder through and through, tough as steel and completely unbendable. His suit of armor deflected every negative statement I initially threw at him, and it magically transformed them into useful and motivational tools for my toolbelt. And I believe his armor was magnetic, too, because everyone wanted his attention. Staff, residents, visiting family, and eventually, me. But as firm and unrelenting as he was, no one had a bad word to say about him. Management sang his praises. Residents lit up when they heard his name. Even the crabby old dude who stared me down every session eventually broke the silence.

"It looks like you're crying a lot. Must hurt, hey? Sam's good at what he does. He helped me."

And then I never saw the old guy again. I believe he sat there, recalling how hard he had struggled, and that was his way of showing appreciation for Sam. *If that old cuss made it, then so can I. Gotta push!* But Sam had the exact opposite of push in mind. The goals he set were slow and steady.

Rush the progress and damage potential. Run a marathon and not a sprint.

Unfortunately for me, sprint was all I knew. The box full of high school 1st place ribbons for dashes and sprints…*take that, Sam! It's in my blood.* But he refused to honor a mad dash to the finish line. His calculated plan involved tried-and-true steps toward increased range of motion. He gently directed me in his plan and awarded space to dry up the tears when I veered off course, but then led me back to where I needed to be. Slowly trust crept in, and I stopped defying his plan and started applying myself to his coaching. Determination reactivated on that longer road to recovery, but it seemed more stable and weirdly, clear sailing. Because when setbacks, roadblocks, uncontrollable tears would threaten my endurance, I had learned to combat them with an unshakeable grit.

Concealing tears and pushing past the target shows tenacity, but, in many ways, it's unwise.

Here's The Rub

Ya can't be next to a guru without philosophies rubbing off on ya. Answer me this: will your tenacity reinforce good behaviors or develop bad habits? Each situation is different, and some circumstances require brute force, but weigh the options against the outcome. I'll give ya a moment to deliberate.

Tough guys. Take a seat, please. Quit flexing yer muscles. No one's looking at ya.

You Can't Run AND You Can't Hide

Trust me, before the above revelation hit, spite powered the rage furnace and only a pansy would accept a hand cupped to his butt to tenderly lead the way. Unfortunately for a know-it-all like me, the rage-filled muscle responses resulted in severe pain, which led to more public displays of weakness. Continuous waterworks. Defeat and hopelessness. Until I surrendered, dread for upcoming therapy sessions strapped me to my bed, but Sam would barge into my room with sharpened lopping shears and sever the banding. He wouldn't accept any defeat. He would briefly remind me of the progress I had made, and then say, "I'll be right back. Be ready". But he never left until he had put the gait belt around my waist. And that was code for *now you can't refuse me.* I knew I had to sit up in preparation for his return because, if I didn't, he could grip the belt and drag my sorry backside to the therapy room! And guess where that stupid belt is hanging. In my closet because Sam sent it home with me to serve as a reminder of past determination that would pave the way for new beginnings. I'm telling ya. The man's a guru.

But just like a kid obeying one request and resisting another, I fell back into hiding the pain responses until the waterworks again betrayed me. From the beginning he said some discomfort would be normal, but unbearable pain needed to be announced. A grunt seemed adequate but he'd immediately question.

"You displayed a pain response. What number would you give it?"

"Oh, that was nothing. Probably the spot…"

And I'd ramble on about a previous injury until he stopped me with a refocusing question.

"Oh, ok. But in relation to what we're working on. How'd that exercise affect your overall discomfort?"

He knew I was bluffing. And when I wouldn't answer him honestly, he'd calmly end the session.

"Great job. We're done for today. I'll see you tomorrow at 10. Oh, and do you want a hot compress or something else for the pain?"

"No, I don't want anything for the pain."

Steam poured outta my ears as pride fed my words, but he just ignored my response. I needed the pain relief, but I wouldn't relent. Later that night, I was writhing in pain from ignoring Sam's direction. My evening nurse, Wendy, was passing out meds, and she lovingly offered me a pain reliever. I snapped at her and cupped my hands over my face. Sam had blown off my hateful remarks, but Wendy wasn't having it. Her face reddened and every bit of her 5-foot stature came alive.

"You need to reconsider your thoughts on pain medication, Jason. It'll help you get through the therapy sessions, and you won't be this miserable. If you don't take them because you're too stubborn, your heightened pain will limit your therapy."

"And become an addict? No thanks!"

The time had come to surrender once again. Her rebuttal made sense, but I needed time to think. It was sound advice and I eventually latched onto it. Three days later while dangling at the end of my self-knotted rope, I accepted the extra support.

You're Certainly Not Alone

Undoubtedly Sam provided excellent care, but he wasn't the only one. Congress needs to create a Congressional Medal of Honor for nursing homes, and then head to Wisconsin to pin the entire staff. These facilities run on a ridiculously tight budget, causing a shortage in staff and so much more, but, even then, the staff at this establishment always went above and beyond. Toward the end of my stay, I loved wheeling down the corridors to wave at other residents who had left their doors open. As I observed the loving staff pouring out compassion on the rest of the building my joy became complete. Whether they were kicked, scratched, bit, punched, had poop thrown at them, were cussed out, had discovered a recently deceased resident, they all recomposed themselves and pressed on. This takes guts, folks.

Sometimes I believe we forget to pay homage to the ones who cultivate these environments of grace and mercy: the strong director who's invested heavily in his or her staff. *Do your job, and I promise to do mine. Give and take but respect the delicate balance. Remember what we're here for.*

The day I rolled into the home toting those blasted balloons is when I met the director, Terri. We briefly chatted that day, but I had quickly forgotten about her. Day after day someone new would darken my door, so to remember them all would require a deep personal interaction. Some offered the basics; they fell by the wayside. Others became overprotective and cemented a memory.

If you need me to wipe for you, I'm willing. Don't be embarrassed, we do it all the time. Just pull the call string by the toilet; I'll be right out in the hall.

How does one forget a person like this?

The Terri Bomb

The memorable day started out like any other, sharp pain radiating into both hips and scalding sensations torturing my feet. Crank up the heat in the hot tub to searing and then jump in but don't ever get out. That's what my feet feel like daily. And because the nerves won't calm down, the muscles from the soles of my feet to both hips spasm, causing intense pains as my muscles jump and bounce to a spastic rhythm. Somedays I could lead the marching band with my big toe tapping the beat.

11 a.m. that day I had my first occupational therapy appointment. As the therapist introduced herself, she excitedly wheeled into my room a huge contraption loaded with wires. Never seeing the machine before, I knew my normal therapy was about to change. But as she sang the praises of the "new" technology and stickered me full of electrodes, a glimmer of hope flickered on the horizon. Physical therapy had been grueling, so I welcomed any alternative at that point. *You wanna hook a battery charger to my nipples because it'll take my mind off the foot pain? Hook. Me. Up.* And when she said studies had shown it had offered patients up to six hours of relief from chronic nerve pain, say no more. Surprisingly it worked for me. It lowered my pain to tolerable. *What a wonderful day it's gonna be!*

I felt the old Jay was back for at least six hours, so I figured I better make the most of every minute of freedom. An aide caught me dangling my feet off the bed. As I changed into my Superman t-shirt, I swung my feet back and forth.

"You're chipper today! It's great to see!"

"Help me to my chair. I'm going to lunch."

It was rare to see me in the dining room, so every staff member commented as I wheeled by. The lunch ladies loaded my tray with extra cherry Jell-o and slipped a couple mini chocolate bars under my napkin. I was the king of the castle. And the glow continued into the afternoon, even when Sam popped in to announce his intentions for therapy that afternoon.

But the ship sunk about fifteen minutes after Sam revealed his plan. Slowly but noticeably the pain came back. I suffered through a grueling therapy session, after which Sam wheeled me into the dining room. I told him I wanted to go back to my room, but he leaned in and whispered, "Stay out here. It'll do you some good." *How could he be so cold? Parking me smack dab in the middle of a packed mess hall while I'm sobbing.* The heat from my anger dried up the tears.

Residents at my table asked a few questions, trying to distract me from the pain, but it didn't help. One lady put her hand over mine, hoping to console me, but that didn't work, either. I choked down a couple bites, and then wheeled like a madman down the nearest hallway. *All I need is silence right now!* And when an unfamiliar hallway presented itself, I wheeled to the left and sped toward the end. The hallway opened to a dead end filled with workers engaged in a staff meeting. They split like a school of fish attacked by a shark when they saw me coming in hot. And right in the middle stood Terri. I nearly plowed a few aides as I attempted to slow down. Humiliated because they had witnessed my continuous sobbing, I swiftly wheeled around and headed back the other way, completely ignoring their kind and consoling words. By the time I arrived at the intersection of the nurse's desk and the hall leading to my wing, rage had replaced embarrassment. I was livid with Sam, the workers, the onlookers. Everyone. And to make matters worse, another group of aides stood at the station watching me reach the turn.

"Oh Jason, can I give you a hug?"

"I'd rather not."

"Are you ok? Is there anything I can do?"

Before I could wheel away, loving arms wrapped around me. And on came the waterworks again as she squeezed me tight. The entire length of the hallway back to my room I was met with kind regards. The fight-or-flight sensation kept me amped up, but, as soon as I clawed my way into the bed, my arms gave up. *I hate being gawked at and doted over. I'll be fine! I'd be better without all that sappy stuff.* Bitterness overwhelmed me, yet, strangely, their sincere concern intrigued me. *How could strangers show so much compassion, and why am I craving that attention?* The softer side seemed to have gained strategic ground. *They have proved their love by taking care of me. Why not show them love?* And amongst the confusion emerged a startling thought from outta nowhere.

What if the wrestling in my nature is a direct result from my decision to draw closer to God?

I had spoken here and there about my faith in God, and how it would carry me through; yet I had continued to bounce back and forth uncontrollably. How many people do this on a regular basis? Act as if God is unreliable. He says, "Fear not, for I am with you," but then He asks, "what's your name, again?" Know the truth: He doesn't bounce back and forth. I'm the irrational one. Luckily, God is long-suffering and patient, and He had plans to prove Himself faithful. Again.

The Ticking Is Getting Louder

Seconds after I slammed the door and dragged myself from the wheelchair into bed, a knock at the door shut me up. I nearly yelled *go away. Leave me alone!* but instead polite *come in* fell outta my mouth.

"Hi Jason, it's Terri. Do you have a minute?"

She nervously rounded the bathroom wall that blocked a straight-shot view to the doorway. Then another knock rang out as soon as she started to talk.

"Can you give us a minute, please?" Terri asked of her employee.

The Explosion

"Do you believe in God, Jason?" Not at all what I expected.

"Yes, I certainly do" immediately left my lips. "No doubt about it."

"Great! I gotta admit; I was instructed by God to pray with you sooner, but I was afraid of what you might say or think. On the way home from work last night, God, again, reminded me that He asked me to pray with you. So, when I saw you in the hall earlier, I knew I had to do this. My heart started pounding hard, but here I am. Do you mind if we pray?"

Tears gushed like a fountain as I agreed to her request. I was baffled. Her boldness knocked the proverbial legs right out from under me as I bowed my head.

"I gotta tell you something first before I pray. Whatever you are working on right now, keep working on it. People need to hear what you have to say. You preach the Word of God without fear. Don't you add anything to it or take anything from it. You hear me?"

Well, how could anyone sass a woman like that? She dealt me the truth better than a Vegas blackjack dealer could dole out a deck of cards! She had no idea I had started jotting down thoughts that led to the writing of this book. How could she have known other than God? I hadn't told anyone, not even Heather.

"Yes, ma'am" I uttered as I wiped away the nasal outflow brought on by excessive tears.

"Ok. Let's pray, Jason. My beliefs include laying hands on the one I pray for. Are you OK with that?"

Again, how could I argue? She could've beat the prayers into me, and I would've agreed. And as she lay her hands on my shoulders, she began to fervently pray like an inner-city Chicago preacher I had witnessed while on a mission's trip with a church in Indiana.

That Wild Church

Before we move on, I gotta relive that church experience for a moment. Mom spanked the foolish outta me every time I horsed around inside a church building. *Sit still, pay attention, we're here to learn.* But that place…there had to be thousands in attendance, and even as a child I remember chills coursing up and down my body as intensely spiritual folks praised the LORD. I'm convinced Mom would've mowed me down if I had jumped and waved and carried on like they were that day! As an adult I can appreciate their mode of worship. To praise my Heavenly Father with uplifted hands is such a spiritual high for me.

During The Explosion

No one else was raising a hallelujah with Miss Terri that night, and still she portrayed the mirror image of that preacher all the same. She sought the Father's grace on my behalf without a moment in between. Although it's familiar to me now, back then I was stunned to find myself calm and reserved by the time she declared amen. I had an astounding sense of peace that I couldn't shake, and the shame and guilt for not trusting God had come and quickly went. *Hallelujah! God had not forgotten me!* Even in the middle of nowhere, God had followed through with His promise to never leave me nor forsake me. Not only that, but He had dropped a prophetic bomb which fueled my desire to pen these words.

The Aftermath

Along with a myriad of other thoughts after the Terri Bomb went off, I realized the source of my loneliness: I hadn't turned to the One who had promised to never fail. He is the only Source for true inner peace. *Of course I can't do this alone!* It's easy to lose sight of God's blessings and dwell on the hardships, but it's a personal choice to fall short when we have the Solution within reach. But we're human. We're gonna fall short. We are called to abide in Him, to grow the relationship out of a pure love for Him, to remember loneliness is a choice. The King James version of 1 John 4:19 KJV says it best, "We love Him, because He first loved us." Just abide. You're never alone.

Because I'm a selfish human who loves to throw pity parties for myself, I easily lose sight of the truth that we have all we need in the One who cares for us. I don't mean to offend, but sometimes we lose sight of God because we're too self-absorbed. *Dry it up and press on. No human being can provide the acceptance we need.* Trust me, drop to your knees, and vocalize an apology to the One who's always faithful. *LORD, I need You more than anything else.* And then believe it. We've gotta trust that Romans 8:28 NIV is the Word of God. "And we know that in all things God works for the good of those who love Him, who have been called according to His purpose." If you claim to know Him, or maybe you don't, He says we all have a purpose in Him. Being that the Father can't lie, we have a true purpose in life. Don't believe me? Chew on this verse in Jeremiah chapter one verse five in the NIV, "Before I formed you in the womb I knew you, before you were born I set you apart; I appointed you as a prophet to the nations." Granted, He said this to Jeremiah the prophet, but those who put their faith in Him are called by Him. And to further drive it home, Ephesians 4:11 NIV says, "So Christ Himself gave the apostles, the prophets, the evangelists, the pastors and teachers." We gotta allow no room for doubt in our love for God and His love for us because He literally starts us out on the straight-and-narrow headed toward blessing after blessing. But we gotta choose to stay on that path because something so simple as human loneliness can yank us off it. Why is this so important you ask? Because the world is watching. Terri mentioned the moment I had arrived at the home, she knew I was someone special. She noticed a God given glow. And without that glow, the pathway grows dark, and others might miss the route. We gotta illuminate the path for those seeking God's salvation, even through our own dark seasons.

From that point on my viewpoint changed. It was no longer about me and my loneliness. Yes, I was in uncharted waters, but I'd have to muster faith like Peter and get outta the boat to be able to walk on the treacherous waters toward God. I'd need strength, peace of mind, personal forgiveness, a tough guy's persistence, and a Godly love; all the fruits of the Spirit to carry me through. God was requiring me to be fearless in Him and run toward Him, even if my legs wouldn't work.

"Have I not commanded thee? Be strong and of a good courage; be not afraid, neither be thou dismayed: for the LORD thy God is with thee withersoever thou goest." Joshua 1:9 KJV.

In the middle of Wisconsin, on a county road leading outta town, I found myself in the heart of an insurmountable challenge that had produced the unexpected. I had landed smack dab in the middle of a lesson in wholehearted trust in the only One capable of delivering me to the promised land. If I wanted to go at it alone, He'd let me. But He also showed me why His presence and love are enough. His grace is truly sufficient.

Will you put your faith and trust in the God of the universe who doesn't lie, never gives up, always follows through? Or be haughty and rely on earthly things that'll always disappoint and ultimately leave you lonely? Haughty? What is that?

Chapter 6

HAUGHTY? WHAT'S THAT?

I've gotta be transparent regarding my true nature. I bet you can't guess it. Ready?

I love using big words.

Sorry, folks. Or to fancy it up…constituents of the proletariat. I didn't mean to get you overexcited and then pop your balloon with such a boring reveal.

For the past twenty years I've lived out this motto: if the English language is littered with a colorful plethora of terminology, then why not incorporate a deluge of pigmentation? Sounds acceptable. Right? A bit nerdy, maybe, and admittedly annoying, but I refuse to cease and desist. Everyday verbiage bores me, so I sling in a little spice. But the aggravating part for me is having to explain the definition. I'll try to keep the color at a minimum.

Come on, now. Context. Misinterpretation is misread context.

But have you ever noticed that adding too much seasoning and flowery word choices leads some into haughtiness? You know the type.

Prim and proper meet self-absorption.

They're usually to the letter and have a specific way to cross their t and dot their i. Strait-laced I am not. Ask my mom. Or my wife.

Hold the spoon closest to you when it enters the bowl, carefully scoop the contents in a movement leading away from you, with shoulders squared and posture straight, lift the spoon to your mouth. Do not slurp or lean in. Return the spoon the same way and repeat the process. Leave the spoon in the bowl when you are finished with the handle pointing to the right or position it on your empty plate on the right-hand side.

I just said I'm not dainty, prissy, yet I'm cognizant of proper etiquette while primly consuming lobster bisque? Quick! Somebody slap me!

It's A Black-Tie Affair

For extra cash in college, I Clark Kent-ed into a waiter/server at local black-tie events hosted at the university. Black suit, tuxedo style, with corresponding bowtie. Pressed white pleated shirt and black, silky pleated pants.

A dapper young gent I was. A genuine hottie. But let's remember…a suit doesn't change the guy. I, eye-rollingly—not a word—suffered through etiquette classes because a Milky Way and Mountain Dew on a Friday night was hard to come by for a defiant poor guy like me. *Stupid parents make me work for college tuition. So dumb! And wait just one minute!! No one said we had to exercise to work here!* Because management didn't want servers embarrassing them by dumping the chow into the laps of the prudes, they forced us to bulk up through daily aerobics. *Sweat to the oldies,* or in this case, opera, *or give us back the suit. And it better be well pressed and clean. Now, SCRAM!* The excessive daily pushups weren't exhausting; learning how-to put-on airs was. But the smell of Benny's and junk food propelled the crazy train. *Forget tuition, Ma!*

I also took a job selling concessions at college sports events, and one in the cafeteria changing the 900-pound milk bags in the bulk milk dispensers because I consistently fell into the red each month. Consequently, I let the chips fall, as they say, because I felt slighted. *Use all the red ink ya want.*

Anyway, elegance seekers are fine by me. *If you wanna pay four hundred bucks a plate for six crumbs of pilaf and a splash of caviar, knock yourself out. Serve up the one-inch square chunk of chocolate cake—the French name depicting "exquisite" escapes me—with forty-five drizzle marks of ganache adorning a three-foot plate. Go for it. You earned the right.*

But give me a break already. You know how many times a guy's gotta walk back and forth delivering dessert when the plate used for less-than-a-lick of sugar is bigger than his head? *You mean to tell me I gotta make 73 trips before the fat lady sings? There's no way!!* I began to despise the wealthy. I was the kid who kicked cow patties in muck boots just to see how far the splatter would fly. Exquisite? No thanks. I belonged in the barnyard. So, slurp the soup and elbow up the table. Life shouldn't be so rigid!

But I guess through all that training, I had never noticed the haughty label that I had glued to my forehead. I pictured the prude who crabbed-out disdain for pouring ice water on her left as opposed to serving from her right as the one with the problem. That's what described haughty in my dictionary. Not my behaviors. *For the love of word play, I gotta be the one displaying haughtiness? No way.* For those who are unaware of my past, arrogantly superior fit me like a wet suit on a dolphin trainer. You know the type I'm describing. *It's raining, Sir, you'd better run for cover with your nose held that high in the air or ya might drown.*

I loved to assess the competition, pour on the charm, and then one-up ambush ya when yer back is turned because I can do all things better than ya.

Remember this? Preteen I determined to outdo my dad in every way, shape, or form. Well, it became a life-consuming sport by eighteen. Mortared, pasted, glued, cemented, welded. Whatever word you wanna use.

The Kaleidoscope

It turns out, I developed a hole in my retina, and it's still there. And go figure, it's in the left eye, the side that houses most of my medical mysteries. Don't be too alarmed, though. I hear macular holes, as ophthalmologists verbalize, are quite common. It only obstructs my vision, somewhat distorting the images captured by the retina. Objects droop, half of the visual disappear some-days, and light refracts into a kaleidoscope of colors. No biggie. I've got my very own circus mirror, that's all.

How's this happen you may be wondering? I'm not quite educated in the optical world, but I remember hearing stress, cancer, a trauma, blunt force blows to the head are listed among the possible causes. And since fear of what I'd find curbed researching root causes and lasting effects, I chocked it up as yet another stroke of bad luck. Weird that I'd have bad luck, right? Scarce treatment options other than monitoring exists, so I've concluded the array of symptoms currently plaguing my body should take precedence over an eye that hasn't fallen out yet.

Hmm. Which one is top priority? A few vision changes or my legs won't work. Brain…ignore the eye problems.

I'm convinced I should've asked an eye guy if a haughty spirit could cause the macular hole. And considering how cocky and arrogant I've been, I'm quite surprised this all hasn't resulted from a blow to the head.

Pardon Me. I'm Prone To Stupidity

To the kid in 8th grade who bloodied my nose and blackened my eyes on the bus because I sprayed cologne in your hair and taunted that it would mask your stench:

1. First, I do apologize. What a scoundrel I was to you, and I don't think I sought forgiveness. So, I'm doing it now. Rather late, I know. I'm a slow learner.
2. You're off the hook. Your fist rearranged my nose cartilage judiciously, but I developed this vision impairment a good twenty-five years after your lesson in kindness, and it reminded me of you. No worries. All is well. Carry on.

P.S. I could use a few more broken noses to drive the lesson home. Are you available?

Well, What Is It?

Numerous tests confirmed the big C is not a contender at this point. And I haven't bumped my head or been punched in a very long time. Can't recall a major trauma, either. *What about the stress surrounding Jess' death? Where does this leave the puzzled diagnostician?*

"For now, we'll pin it on stress."

Shut yer face. I'm not stressed. Says the haughty guy who can't accept his own faults as a possible reason for his unexplained eye condition.

Well, how does that grab ya? It grabbed me around the throat! Especially when I began to realize that self-induced stress without the desire for repentance leads to physiological symptoms and signs. Get a load of this. Proverbs 14:30 changes things. "A heart at peace gives life to the body, but envy rots the bones."

At the time of macular hole diagnosis, I was warring with certain family members, with myself, my neighbors, with God. I had overworked myself to the point of collapse chasing a dream of opening a hometown bakery while continuing to work full time at the car dealer. The list goes on. *Who needs rest? When do I have time for any of that?*

The Yellow Ram

The day I noticed the irregularity in my vision, my ten-pound water head—as my wife lovingly calls it—was throbbing. I blew off the skull knock because headaches were frequent while working for the dealer. And who wouldn't get one? Exhaust fans are capable protection against noxious fumes if the guys decide to switch them on. Too many vehicles idled in that garage without proper venting of the fumes. Daily. Summertime wasn't an issue; lift the doors and let the fresh air flood in. What about winter, pinheads?

Here's a valid option, guys. This neat little black tube is called an exhaust vent hose. And those plates in the garage floor are magical doors. Lift the plate and slide the hose into the opening, and you'll see amazing stuff happen! Come with me over to this groovy, life-sustaining switch. When lifted to the upright position, the suction fans leap into action and magically swallow the carbon monoxide monsters whole, rocketing death forcefully to the moon! Then we'll live happily ever after while our lungs dance free among the pristine oxygen and carbon dioxide molecules.

How's that for condescending and haughty?

Quite often I'd slide the glass parts window closed to somewhat escape the smell and noise. I tried to remain even-tempered, laughing and joking with the guys because I liked them. But that day my headache intensified the irritation, and the tech's prolonged blasting of the truck horn threw me over the edge. They loved to honk the horn in every vehicle they drove into the shop. Every one of them did it. But they also chased fellow employees with cars as he or she walked across the parking lot, stretched tape across doorways so your face would distort as the clear tape ripped out your facial hair. They stuffed packing peanuts in your car vents and greased your door handles. They were brutal. One day one of them took carb cleaner after my legs as I sat on the john to do my business. I started hollering and stomping my feet as the chemical soaked my pants and bare legs. But he didn't stop. And then came the match. Nothing surprised me after that.

"Quit blowing that horn, you jerk!"

The parts window banged shut before he rolled down the driver's window to boast in amusement. Ear cupped to lure me in, he expected a scuffle, but I waved my hand, shooing him away while wearing a scowl. I should've known what he'd do next as I laid my aching head back on my desk. Have you ever stood inside an enclosed metal building with a truck horn sounding continuously? It reminds me of the ear-piercing tone of a civil defense siren set off blocks away.

My manager looked up for a moment. No wonder he was partially deaf.

I cradled my head in both hands because every noise felt like a jackhammer to the skull. Searing pain lingered over my eyes and spread into the middle of my forehead. Moments later another honk rang out as the overhead door raised and a white Dodge pulled inside. Anger shot outta my eyes as I glanced at the truck and put my head back down. The wind from the opening door swooshed in and rattled the glass, causing me to look up again. This time I wasn't prepared for what I saw.

"Ok, now that's not right!" I blurted out after lifting my head.

"What's not right" questioned my manager.

I didn't answer. Too busy trying to rationalize what I saw, I got up and mumbled under my breath, "when the Ram came in, it was white." I moved toward the window and opened it to gain a better view.

On second glance, the truck had appeared yellow. And that's what I saw again. A weird shade of mustard. Panic raced blood through my veins and my head thumped like the moment after slipping a nitroglycerin tablet under the tongue. I frantically blurted to an uninterested manager, "that Ram that just pulled in is yellow."

He squinted out a glimpse, refocused on the screen ahead of him, and continued to henpeck the keys.

"It's white, Jason" he calmly stated.

"Well, no kidding." I snapped. "You asked what wasn't right and I'm telling you. Do ya care if I skate out early to find an eye doctor? Something's not normal with my eye."

"I coulda told you yer not normal. You don't need a doctor for that" he teased.

Harsh sarcasm and coarse dispositions from his coworkers for nearly twenty years had seasoned his nonchalant attitude. Rudeness wouldn't shake him, and neither would vulgar language; he shrugged everything off. And if a person wanted a direct answer and not a joke, he'd have to work hard.

"Well, what is it? Do you care or not?"

Out the door I darted after securing his yeah whatever.

The Search Is On

Eye care had never been a top priority for me, so when I needed an immediate exam, I had no idea where to go. I could direct you to all the auto parts stores and repair shops in town. I wheeled outta the parking lot and took the cut across road between the dealerships and the post office that led to the four-way stop in front of our local Shopko. I jerked the wheel into Shopko's parking after seeing their optical sign, jumped outta the car, and sprinted toward the door.

Would I go blind if no one could fit me in? Why had the truck appeared white one minute and yellow the next? An hour's not much time to figure this out. Why's this happening to me? Is there something majorly wrong? They better squeeze me in. I don't have time for this!

The vision dude I saw at Shopko Optical agreed to an impromptu examination but abruptly ended the visit moments later. He determined the issue was far more than his department store practice was equipped to handle, and thought I'd fare better with an ophthalmologist guy he knew across town. He suggested seeing him as soon as physically possible.

The news had pulsed amongst coworkers before I had left the parking lot at work, so numerous inquiries met me at the door when I returned. And with those inquiries came a bunch of nonsense that quickly annoyed. One tech asked if my eye had popped out. Another suggested if he slapped me hard enough, it'd jar the sense back into my head. One questioned, "will you get to wear an eye patch like a pirate?"

Some were concerned and others didn't much care, but I feared the worst yet couldn't let on. But their tomfoolery revved me up. Instead of kindly responding, I sarcastically brushed off the questions.

"Will your whole eye turn black?" asked a concerned coworker.

"Of course not. Why would you ask such a dumb question? Will your whole eye turn black?"

The demeaning and mocking response curbed further questions from that individual. And when another nearly kissed me while invading my bubble to get a close-up, I sprang backward and barked, "ya can't see it from looking into my eye. Pfft. They're still dilated. That's not the hole."

Sympathy has always tasted to me like a turd sandwich, so I wanted no part in it. When another coworker tried to console I quit discussing the issue with everyone. The one that angered me the most: *it must be hard being so young and horrible things like this keep happening to you. I feel so bad.*

Either they're oblivious or they need fresh gossip for the water cooler. And I won't be supplying their juicy bits to spread. Eventually they quit asking and started avoiding me. Even my manager closed off small talk. I had become despondent and unapproachable, a know-it-all in the eyes of everyone attempting to understand my situation. But what did they know, anyway?

Why don't you record yourself and play back your absurdity? You'll find your support is useless, and I don't need it. Is it gonna fix my problem? No, it won't. So, leave well enough alone. Please.

Watch Your Mouth, Sir

Identifying arrogance as one of my many flaws wouldn't manifest for many years, but I applaud the specialist in Green Bay who spoke out against my obvious behavioral issues. He had discovered a macular hole with excessive fluid buildup that threatened the integrity of the surrounding tissues. He said he could inject a gas bubble into the affected area to sorta glue the hole shut until it healed, or he could monitor it for a few months. The fluid would possibly recede on its own and heal the affected tissue, or it would get worse. Time would be the determining factor but either way I'd have permanent damage. Distortion. Clouded or blurred vision with normal peripheral. Color changes. None of this sounded good, but I accepted it as my fate. All was well until he finished with these exact words, "if it's not medical, it's emotional."

His gut punch alluded to personal stress and a negative outlook. Constantly revving up the rage furnace. The tests showed no other signs pointing to a medical etiology, so only one common denominator remained: situational stressors. I knew I couldn't argue, but his comment made me so angry.

A Sunday School verse comes to mind right now. Romans 12:21 NIV, "Do not be overcome by evil but overcome evil with good." Friends, family members, coworkers had questioned my attitude daily. Many reasoned against my logic, but it always ended in a fiery crash.

They know nothing of my pain. Or the level of daily rejection the world has subjected me to. The universe is against me.

Proof of the world hating me has been evasive, but I was wise to the hidden games of the cosmos. *Why are others so blinded to the truth?*

Maybe my Sunday School teacher should've backed up in Romans 12 to verse 16 in the ESV and had us memorize it, too. "Live in harmony with one another. Do not be haughty but associate with the lowly. Never be wise in your own sight."

As a result of the specialist's gentle rebuke, I stormed out of his office offended—after he was gone, of course. The few steps to my car were filled with childish rants.

I don't need him or anyone telling me anything about my life. That dude needs to get off my back! What gives him the right to judge me? He knows nothing about me.

How many times have you heard that ridiculousness outta a proud person's mouth? That exact moment I needed to hear Proverbs 11:2 ESV. "When pride comes, then comes disgrace, but with the humble is wisdom."

While I wasn't in the right frame of mind during the first visit, the second proved to be fruitful. For a minute. After reviewing the results of a repeated exam, the specialist turned in his chair, took off his glasses, and leaned in. "You have gotta deal with the stress in your life." He must have seen the drastic color change in my face facilitated by a skyrocketing temperature. "Take a minute and hear me out before you get overly upset."

Although others had attempted to drill through the coarse exterior and failed, his sharp boldness breached the outer shell. Intrigue cracked the innermost layer when he said, "Unless you clean up whatever is weighing you down, you'll continue losing sight, possibly complete vision loss in the left eye." It was a lofty goal, but no longer could I instigate and promote strife. I needed to be a mediator for peace. To toss haughty and cocky out the window and speed away. To kill pride and to quit using blunt honesty as a cheap source of entertainment. The unfamiliar change looked promising, especially after absorbing the speech from an unexpected motivational speaker.

Sadly, although these events made huge cracks in the tough guy foundation, resurfacing pride resealed the gaps and anger, along with bitterness and resentment, troweled in the mortar needed to renovate the selfish empire. But regardless of the rebuilding efforts on my part, God in His faithfulness kept knocking on the door of my heart, seeking to restore a loving relationship with me. But I kept shutting Him out. I'd open the door for a second, take heed His teachings, but then, like listening to an irritating door-to-door salesman's pitch, I'd slam the door in His face the moment I didn't align with His requests. And what did that finally award me? The signature required to authorize the destruction of my pride.

Throughout the Scriptures lie numerous verses describing the hatred God has toward a proud and haughty spirit. Nevertheless, repeated warnings go largely unheeded worldwide. Disrespect for His holiness abounds, and we think none of it is our fault in any way, shape, or form.

Unfortunately, like most who won't self-correct, with every sledge-hammer strike against my foundation supporting the fortified walls, I responded with bitterness, resentment, and anger—my personal choice.

When God Gets Your Attention

I stumbled on Proverbs 16:18 NIV while lying in this bed, asking God to bubble to the surface everything that displeased Him, and I nearly did a backflip in astonishment. "Pride goes before destruction, and a haughty spirit before a fall." This Proverb had me written all over it. But it's an ugly sweater to wear.

Here's a heads up for you, the reader. Throughout this book you'll find countless examples of my haughty lifestyle. But since my vision serves as a constant daily reminder, I thought it was the best example to share in this chapter. If you don't have something to serve as a daily reminder, please write down Proverbs 6 verses 16-19 KJV on a notecard and keep it handy. It'll inspire you to choose wisely.

"These six things doth the LORD hate: yea, seven are an abomination unto Him: A proud look, a lying tongue, and hands that shed innocent blood, an heart that deviseth wicked imaginations, feet that be swift in running to mischief, a false witness that speaketh lies, and he that soweth discord among brethren."

Each one listed will ruin your testimony, lead people astray, and damage your relationship with the LORD Almighty if you don't recognize and destroy them.

Does pride rule your life? Are you haughty? If so, you my friend need an attitude adjustment before it's too late. Trust me on this one. Pride enthrones you and dethrones God, and that's a recipe for disaster.

Chapter 7

ANGER: MY PERSONAL CHOICE

Of all the human emotions to choose from, electing one that portrays strength and dominance would be the best choice for a tough guy, right? Why not use anger? It powers the muscles, gets the heart pumping. Win win.

But there's arguments all over the web against emotional dominance, so is it immoral to employ anger on a regular basis? Should one even exhibit emotional dominance over another, and especially when the situation warrants an anger response? Is resentment and hate the only outcome produced when anger is employed as a dominant emotion?

Oh, my! Those are some troubling questions. They can't be answered plainly with a yes or no. *I give up already. Maybe there aren't any positive benefits associated with being angry.*

A person can't possibly be cheery every moment of the day. And in every situation. To be angered regarding what God deems as injustice is our job as Christians, yet Proverbs 15:1 ESV says, "A soft answer turns away wrath, but a harsh word stirs up anger."

How does one softly inform someone he or she is being an idiot?

And besides, tough guys can't be soft. They'll be overpowered and lose their reputation.

Keep The Questions Coming

I can't stop there. I gotta keep asking more questions. Afterall, I struggle with anger the most.

Will anger produce predictable outcomes if carefully executed? *Maybe I should thoroughly think this through and express my anger in a civilized yet demanding tone? Get my point across with a firm, do it again, and (fill in the blank).* Employing anger gently, will it still be powerful enough to mend and shatter relationships?

And if James 1:19-20 NIV instructs against it, "My dear brothers and sisters, take note of this: Everyone should be quick to listen, slow to speak and slow to become angry, because human anger does not produce the righteousness that God desires" then why do we have it as an option on the list?

Should I strike it off the list as no longer an option because Ecclesiastes 7:9 ESV instructs "Be not quick in your spirit to become angry, for anger lodges in the heart of fools"? Or is it still permissible because Paul tells in a letter to the Ephesians, "In your anger do not sin."

Man, I'm so confused!

Who do I listen to? Solomon or Paul? James or Jesus in Matthew 5:22 NLT? "But I say, if you are even angry with someone, you are subject to judgment! If you call someone an idiot, you are in danger of being brought before the court. And if you curse someone, you are in danger of the fires of hell."

What's a guy to do?!

I've struggled for years with the appropriateness of an anger response. All I heard repeatedly from people at church, teachers, coaches, my parents, friends, my family was that I had an anger problem.

Why are you so angry, Jason? What happened to you that made you harbor so much resentment?

I've admitted being a fuming mess countless times, but I've never afforded anyone the chance to delve into the truth of the matter. One elementary teacher endured full vent after he gently inquired of the nature of my short wick. *What do you care? You're just gonna tell me I need to straighten up and not listen to a word I say!* And in the mid-nineties, such behavior awarded a trip to the principal's office and a phone call home. I guess yelling at him in the middle of class was an unacceptable anger response?

I Hate Being Wrong

I predetermined at an immature age the world to be apathetic toward my feelings because I kept hearing the same message.

Everything you do is wrong, Jason. Go lay down by your dish.

But what everyone was trying to say to me: *I genuinely care that you're upset, but you may not speak to me with such disrespect.* My indignant nature never allowed this to register. If they wouldn't give me what I wanted, then it was none of their business why I was angry. And my actions, responses, rebellion proved that point daily. Very seldom did I self-correct, and this lasted well into my thirties. My mom, however, had an uncanny way of breaking through the disrespect before I left the nest. It's called a wooden spoon. Yes, I am proud to say I'm a wooden spoon survivor.

Bring On The Stories!

I love examples. Something tangible to grab a hold of. But I gotta slim things down. My editor said I'm wordy. (Insert smiley face. He's right. Sorry.)

Mine and Heather's wedding day proved to be one of the happiest days of our lives. I remember keeping myself calm and reserved amid the chaos because a remarkable event was unfolding. When little issues would surface, I'd squash them to keep Heather from getting worked up. It was her big day, and she had found her Prince Charming. (Insert barf face emoji. Is there one for *what a load of crap?)* I vowed to stay grounded just for her, but with a faulty thermostat, that proved difficult. Especially when tux rental misunderstandings popped up. Half the guys don't have them. Their shoes don't fit. Shirts are missing. Pants are too tight.

Things simmered down after a while until we got to the ceremony. Then I discovered ten minutes before it all started that the best man had forgotten the rings. Then my mom and my mother-in-law tussled in a silent feud. One of the bridesmaids was found a drunken mess on the deck outside the hall. After the ceremony another bridesmaid rolled down the hill and grass-stained up her dress right before pictures. Then one of the groomsman's pants fell down on the dance floor in full view of the guests. My best man disappeared from the reception at seven to drive around in his Neon SRT4. All these mishaps compounded with the fact that it was the hottest September evening on record, and the location we had rented decided air conditioning wasn't an important feature for a reception hall, still didn't make me snap. *WHO CARES?! It's all about my beautiful bride.* And when nearly every guest remained outdoors until it had cooled down, and Heather worried her reception would be remembered as a flop, I reassured her that everything would be fine. Surprisingly, I remained composed for my bride's sake. Nothing bothered me because I was genuinely happy. My day to realize a dream of true happiness and personal delight had finally arrived, and nothing was gonna wreck it. No one was pointing fingers at me or accusing me of any wrongdoing. Everyone appeared satisfied with me on our happy day. The black cloud had finally moved out.

But even on my happiest day I had let anger take the helm because past grudges and resentments had crumpled invites to specific family members and friends. I relentlessly buried any attempts made by many to fix past discrepancies before the wedding, so I wouldn't have to invite them. But then afterward when the videos reminded that those individuals weren't in attendance, anger along with resentment drove bitterness deeper within my soul. Looking back at the scene, I was just as angry that day as any other day, I had just suppressed it for my wife's sake. Had I been sincerely happy, not a single past hurt would've clouded the joy that should flood from such an event.

Excavating

Unearthing truth is one of the most brutal journeys for an angry macho to embark on because trips down memory lane usually become a painful replay of hurtful times instead of a recounting of joy. Wonderful memories get rehashed as past disputes. Frustration and pain bubbles bitterness to the surface every chance it gets, and the reminiscing turns toxic. I've learned that all memories come with a bit of hurt and pain, and many hardships give way to humor after the fact.

It wasn't that bad. Could have been better. Could have been way worse. Maybe next time I'll do this or that instead.

But an angry person replays memories with a payloader full of pessimism, and somewhere in that pile of steaming poo is a drop of pleasure. The memory always revolves around a negative, and a happy event for the average guy turns sour as the resentful person works to spin the recollection into a poor-me session. Because in his mind the world's waging an ongoing fierce battle against his happily-ever-after, and no event, flawless and wonderful as it may have been, will ever be remembered without its defects.

Have you met this kind of person? Of course, you have. You point out the sweet scent of the rose, and he points out the wilting petal. You speak of Nana's ninetieth birthday bash reuniting the entire family, even Aunt Joan who's been estranged for ten years, but he points out how Aunt Joan's been avoiding Nana all these years. Regardless of how many arguments you present, how many harsh words you employ, how many avoidance tactics you engage, this angry person will continue to spew negative at every turn. No one can reach this person with the truth. How do I know? Because that was me.

You're So Cold And Guarded

At the start of our relationship, Heather recognized I was guarded and searched for an opening in my walls. She toiled endlessly to promote positivity and sway my discouraging demeanor. To build trust and show that she genuinely cared. She'd leave little notes here and there saying she loved me. She'd pack a candy bar or a pop for a break at work. Pick me up my favorite country cd. Order me French fries covered in gravy. She'd give little tokens of appreciation and allow me to release my painful baggage. A few weeks into dating, she began speaking of herself as a "safe place". Reminding me that "it's not going anywhere because it's me you're talking to." But even though I loved her with all my heart, and she proved over and over her love was true, I refused to let her in.

It scared me to think I could trust her, and that made me hesitant to leap off the cliff. I had trusted no one. The day we met, all it took was to look into her eyes, and she cast a spell that softened a portion of my heart of stone. But weeks later I felt an obligation to protect her from my past. She seemed too innocent, so she obviously wouldn't fully understand. And then I felt the need to protect myself against her naivety in case she secretly meant to hurt me. All these deep-rooted beliefs caused me to hold her at arm's length.

She describes it like this: I'm holding my hand on her head and she's running toward me but can't get anywhere. I suppose when I'd say things like, *don't try to fix me. You had a perfect childhood* or *what would you know about a rough life?* it'd be like slapping her across the face.

Looking Back

I wanted her to love me but leave it at that. Take me as I am. Be good with us, regardless. But when we vowed *for better or for worse*, she believed the unresolved situations making things better or worse were what the vows referred to. *Can't just leave them be and ignore them. Sometimes our paths lead us into crazy circumstances that we can't control. That's for better or for worse. But refusing to self-correct and choose a different path when the correct option is clearly available—not what our vows meant.* She wasn't gonna stick by me for better or for worse and hope I'd quit making things worse. That's asking too much. *If you desire through-thick-and-thin, troubles or merriment, yer gonna hafta quit the drama and heal from yer past. With my help.* That's what kept her going. Her thick-and-thin. I could be sweet and kind, and she knew it, but sweet and kind would only last so long before happiness gives way to breakup.

Surrendering to her world and the flowery happiness that I didn't understand would require me to give up my anger, along with many other things. *Yeah, no. I'm not thinkin' that'll happen anytime soon.* I paved the relationship with heartache after heartache, but she kept steadily working. She saw a man that she could bring home to Daddy. One who Mom would fall in love with. One who Dad would say, "I'd be glad to give you two my blessing."

Man do I love her more today than I did back then. The woman I married was a saint, but now she's a gladiator who's earned her scars.

Because Heather intrigued me with her good girl persona, I decided to let down a few guards. I held her hand after a couple months of going out with her. I even decided to kiss her. But I held a few reservations. The world still wanted to slit my throat, and Heather lived in that world. *Ask me to meet yer folks, and I'll put up a fight. I'm not ready for another wading pool of uncertainty, and they'll dump me into the deep end.*

Little did I know they would accept me as another son. A welcomed addition to the family.

Why could one family be so happy and mine be completely dysfunctional? They're hiding something. They gotta be. The shocking reveal will come. Wait for it. Wait for it.

But it never came. They were the average, loving and quirky family that I'd always longed for. However, I continued to believe they had an angle to work, and I'd soon discover it. The implosion of my family kept me angered and skeptical of any happiness.

Heather continued to reassure me that her family meant it when they said, "Love you, Jay. Hope to see you again soon. Maybe for dinner tomorrow night?" She knew I was overly skittish to accept, but reasoned, "Ya gotta eat, right? Mom makes the best hash. Just come." I obliged because I followed Heather around like a lost puppy. Truth be told, Clare does make the most ridiculous hash. I don't know how that woman accomplishes a remarkable delicacy with just potatoes, chopped pork roast, onions, and salt, but that stuff's currency! You don't need ketchup and put down the salt and pepper! And those fried eggs on a Saturday morning…

While dating Heather I lived with my mom after my parents divorced. And because I allowed the tension surrounding their divorce to define my character, trivial things would set me off. Too much noise in the house. No string cheese in the fridge. The cat needs attention. If anyone intervened, I'd rant until I hammered my point into a weapon and used it to induce tears. I'd verbally abuse anyone who disagreed with my foolish rage. Because I never physically harmed anyone, I felt justified in the verbal misconduct. Involve me in any argument and I'd go straight for the jugular. Evidence was all around that I was out of control, yet the castle walls continued to fortify with each fight I instigated.

The Cliff

And then I fell off the cliff because no one would engage with me the moment rage flickered in my eyes. I became even more combative and cowardly, and I took to mistreating inanimate objects.

My love for cars back then was at its peak. It was common to see at least three cars of mine in Mom's drive at any given moment. *Full disclosure—it's because I wrecked one right after another.* But because of that obsession, I had become a self-taught back-yard mechanic. A surprisingly good one at that. Every weekend I had off, I'd load up the garage with brake jobs, cv shaft replacements, tune-ups, whatever the wind blew in. The extra several hundred bucks a weekend helped feed my obsession and buy more tools. Eventually, easy jobs turned into rusty disasters as word spread that I wrenched for cheap. But it all ended in a fiery crash one day. One evening as I tried to put the axle nut back onto the stub shaft of a Bonneville, I noticed the threads were mushroomed from hammering it out of the seized wheel bearing housing. I had previously warned the Bonny owner to get the rusty wheel bearing replaced months prior or it'd become a disaster, but he kept jaw-jackin' on how he'd get it to me rather than actually doing it. Cherry red I heated that shaft, pounded the arms right off my shoulders, drenched it with rust penetrant. Five hours of frustration finally separated the disintegrated mess from the car and onto the garage floor. I filed the threads and reattempted setting the nut. No go. Back and forth I went, filing and trying the nut, until finally I lost all self-control. I grabbed the nearest wrench and whipped it across the garage. At that very moment, Heather had stepped out of the house to check on my progress. The wrench sailed past her face and stuck in the drywall. Then the sheer terror of what I had done set in.

What if she had stepped out a second earlier? It coulda connected with her temples, and I would've killed her, the woman I love, because of a messed-up thread pattern.

I was so furious that I started punching the fender of the car repeatedly until I bloodied my hand. Heather went back into the house without saying a word, grabbed her things, and got in her truck and left. I'm surprised she stayed with me after that.

When she left, I completely lost it. *What had I done?* Cuts would heal. Grease would wash away. But the rage I portrayed not even Heather could diffuse. Sadly enough, even after that stunt, I sunk even further. A few weeks later I threatened to run a family member over with my car after a heated discussion. Gravel flew from the rear wheels as he jumped outta the way before the rear bumper caught his knees. A split second and I would've seriously injured or killed him. *Agree with me, give me what I want, or I'll write you off and move on. There're no second chances. Even you, Heather.*

Discovered Etiology

Many things contributed to my explosive personality: the troubled relationship between me and my dad, the perceived black cloud raining misfortune, my catastrophizing attitude, never fully getting my way. I was wildly selfish to the detriment of my relationships, my jobs, anyone I encountered. Blaming my upbringing and the situations I always found myself in became a sport, and I warred with my own conscience daily. There was never a moment of peace.

Unfortunately, this is all too common with kids who know it all. Everything makes them angry, however, don't scold them when they prove themselves wrong because you'll be wasting your breath. They all seem to build their own truths, and that's all they will listen to. I don't know about you but lies make me angry. And that's all I'd feed myself back then.

As a child, I thought Dad would rather work than give me any attention. And maybe I had a lot to do with that because of my hateful attitude. But not being able to see past my selfishness, I began to resent him for his absence. And I pushed him away. Convinced myself he was just too mean to like. Formed an opinion and dug the divide.

And what's a dad to do when he can spend quality time, and the child rebels or rejects every effort? No matter how hard he tried, I would twist his words or efforts into a poor me situation. And I believe that's where my black cloud mentality emerged. As an adult I acknowledge the stress he had endured and the rebellious streak I had exhibited. I fully understand that's where his *why try?* attitude came from because he eventually quit trying. I currently experience the same defeat as my children gang up and chant what feels like *you don't own me*. Who wants that stress? Especially after an exhausting day at work? I'd rather tuck my tail and run for the hills. I'm sure he would relate if we ever got the chance to talk about this. Life for my family in the early eighties and nineties was usually tense because of money, lack of jobs, my parents' own childhood struggles, usual family drama; but I sought to lengthen the list of woes by driving a wedge.

I won't accept the entire blame for our poor relational outcomes, however. I picked sides between my mother and father at an early age just to drive that wedge in further. And by the time I realized the gravity of my mistake, it was far too late. I loved my mother deeply. She dragged me kicking and screaming through my childhood years. Wore herself out trying to keep me on the straight-and-narrow. But so did my dad. Maybe not as steadfastly as Mom, but he worked outside the home. I longed for a relationship with my dad. To learn from him. To be just like him. And that he would spend time with me and love me for who I was. Yet I kept these realities to myself because I was too invested in the empire of Jay. And to undo all the mess I had created would be far too challenging for a kid, so I wrote it all off as a loss as soon as anyone spoke of my shortcomings.

The Hostile Environment

I've come to observe…

When presented with a hostile environment, even the most determined to succeed struggle to thrive. Love is completely abandoned the moment the seeds of hate are cultivated. Why should any person try when no matter what he or she does is attacked, scrutinized, or doubted?

And when kids feel they're forced to choose sides because they cannot find peace in the home, they choose to position themselves with the party with the most common ground. Could be a parent. Could be a gang. Hopefully, it's a positive role model. As a young child, I developed my own set of choices, but as a teen to early adult, I cemented those choices. Many times, both my parents self-corrected, but I never forgave. But many times, they didn't, and I forgave. But continued unrest led me to choose sides as an adult, as well. I didn't want them to fight, and especially over me, but I also thought admitting my faults would be like cutting off my own legs. And if I did that, I couldn't run away and hide. Lose-lose.

All this contributed to the angry young man I grew into. And when everything began to calm down between my parents and life returned to a new normal, I initially chose not to accept the new reality. *I'm not wrong, they are. I'm not wrong, the world is. I was robbed of happiness. Who's gonna repay me all that I lost?*

What I had actually lost was myself and what I was meant to be.

Put Out Wildfires

Wanna breed anger like a wildfire? Never admit when you're wrong and refuse to apologize. I'm living proof, as many are, that anger, if left unchecked, will consume you. Hebrews 12:15 NIV coaches, "See to it that no one falls short of the grace of God and that no bitter root grows up to cause trouble and defile many."

Fights, disagreements, arguments pop up everywhere, but it requires the art of emotional intelligence instead of emotional dominance to wisely diffuse a disagreement. We must offer the same grace God gives us when we disagree with others. I know my parents taught me this truth. Did they model it flawlessly? No, but they taught it. And that's what matters. Furthermore, no one can blame his or her parents for every choice he or she makes. If parents teach their children to follow God's mandates, and their children understand, then the responsibility falls on the child. Keep guiding but keep teaching. Eventually the child will have to choose.

Let me reiterate in a simpler way. My parents taught me right from wrong. I understood and felt personally guilty when I sinned. They failed to follow their own mandates occasionally. But my conscience performed flawlessly. When I suppressed my conscience and went against God's rules, I personally chose to disobey, thereby excluding my parents from the punishment I rightfully deserved. Their shortcomings are between them and God. And if they repent, I must show them grace like God shows grace to every one of us. No exception. My parents didn't force me to act the way I did. They continued to lead and guide with multiple flaws. But in no way were my behaviors a reflection of my flawed upbringing. My behaviors reflected my choices. I may have based some of those choices on my environment, but it's a dangerous line to dance on if one continues to blame his or her life outcomes on others. A person's surroundings may largely influence decisions but cannot be used as a crutch for wrongdoing.

Not For The Faint Of Heart

Breaking the mold of past indiscretions is grueling work. Break a habit on the first attempt. I'm sure you won't succeed immediately. But it's even harder when children are involved. They soak up information, habits, seemingly everything they shouldn't, so be careful what habits you exhibit. Many are wildly contagious.

Can you name a few tumbling rocks that have cracked your foundation when they hit?

Go! No, Don't Go

After I nearly struck Heather with a flying wrench, lots of uncertainties surfaced. You know the weird skies before a tornado? The freight train sound and hail serve as a possible warning. Sirens were going off for Heather, and many of her friends warned her not to put up with me. And then the tornado touched down in our relationship when she took the advice and questioned her ability to hold on.

I knew this bomb was coming from the beginning of our relationship. I called it! You planned on hurting me, so why did I even try? No wonder I felt your friends weren't worth the effort; they planned to turn on me the first chance they could get. Yet another group of friends to write off and forget!

Weeks went by, then months, solidifying the building grudge between me and Heather's friends. I blamed them for destroying our relationship, and I stewed in it for months. But the part that infuriated me the most, without Heather, I couldn't function. I moped around the house. Cried more than I cared to admit. Ceased all activities except playing with my stupid cat. And when Grandpa threatened to blow her head off for digging her nails into the clearcoat of his triple black 69 Lincoln Continental, I dug a rut in our driveway and laid rubber for as far as my Olds had the power to. I ended up downtown driving past Heather's work. I wanted to talk to her, but, when I saw she and my sister were having lunch, anger overtook my common sense, and I sped away. "Forget her. I'll never be happy, anyway."

Obviously, Heather and I weathered the storm. We're still happily married, even though life has required us to fist fight our way through endless drama. Our relationship and marriage have fallen on treacherous ground numerous times over legitimate issues, but we've continued to work them out. Several times before our marriage, I broke it off with her, but each time I ran back. Or should I say sprinted. And every time she welcomed me back, forgiving me and loving me even stronger. I don't know how she does it, but she is one tough woman.

The LORD Builds The House

Heather hasn't fixed me. She's unable to; I still struggle with anger. One evening recently while at a support group meeting, I melted into a sobbing mess while discussing my past indiscretions and battles with anger. That night I felt like I had finally given it all to God, and I no longer needed to beg Him for a resolve before it cost me every wonderful gift He had blessed me with. I had told Him how angry and exceedingly unhappy I was too many times. I had admitted that I had no idea how to fix it but had kept taking it back and trying. Everyone who had tried had failed. *How was I gonna fix it if all else has failed?*

The answer is quite simple. Only with God's help. I'm powerless on my own. Just like with any flaw. He showed me that I'm the problem and source of my own unhappiness. I had to quit catastrophizing, complaining, blaming everyone else. Realize my childhood was interesting not terrible. Keep reminding myself that Mom and Dad did the best they could. Forgive. Forgive. Forgive. Deny the temptation to be self-absorbed, reject the victim mindset, and listen only to the voice of the Spirit. Because in the moment, He will provide a way out if I ask. I gotta walk away from the situation knowing that God is handling it. End of discussion.

And when I did all this, I had no clue who I was. I couldn't recognize my old self anymore. I had enveloped myself in a caustic world centered around sinful anger that was distorting my true reflection. I had lived outside of the real world and had created a whirlwind of anxiety and fear. And none of it had an ounce of familiarity anymore. As scary as it appeared at first, I couldn't let the new reality terrify me, or I'd shrink back and be consumed again. I would have to employ the patience I had prayed for. Use the tenacity that had empowered the miserable drive for self-destruction to turn the wheels of love. Keep pressing into God because the reward would absolutely be worth the fight to stay on course. And always use anger under full control. Always.

Take this advice from a recovering rageaholic before it's too late.

Analyze in what ways you use anger for the sake of yourself, your family, and others around you. Refuse it full reign, or you'll be cleaning up the kingdom after extinguishing the blaze. And regardless of whether you douse the flames, or some other method facilitates the quenching, know that anger's devastating path is horribly wide when wielded inaccurately. Take Proverbs 19:11 ESV with you before you meet Louis in the following chapter. It's better than my advice. "Good sense makes one slow to anger, and it is his glory to overlook an offense."

Will you control it? Or will you and the ones you love become anger's next victim?

Chapter 8

AND THEN THERE'S LOUIS

Anyone who's been hospitalized might agree when I say being in the hospital is like being incarcerated. I've never been jailed before, surprisingly, so I feel somewhat outta my league referring to an incarceration; but for those of you that've sat behind the bars I'm speaking of, I'm convinced you can relate. There's no rest, no privacy, no dignity. Every moment is invasive. There's constant monitoring. Want a reprieve from restrictions? Dream on. The only sweet beacon of hope: the faint smell of freedom overwhelmingly stifled by the surrounding stale institution air.

Life in a hospital bed is a cruel sentence.

Well, Saint Joseph's Hospital in Marshfield was no exception. It was loud, unrelenting, and prison-like. During the first stay, isolation from roomies was the only thing that had shielded my sanity, which caused it to feel somewhat like solitary confinement. Most wouldn't describe the constant influx of nurses, doctors, transporters, lab workers, therapists, and insurance folks as isolation. And because the third floor bustled like the pedestrian-packed streets surrounding Sears Tower in Chicago, my chance for peace and serenity presented as strikingly thin. But being a guy in his middle thirties who had begged for a break, I guess I'd learn to acclimate? Yet, regardless of the continuous commotion, exhaustion along with the stiff cocktail of pain medication effortlessly drowned out most of those memories, painting the scene a voiceless blur. I was rather content.

Except for the biggest complaint: the heart monitors and tests. The electrodes by the pallet loads. Stickers, one right after another, kept removing patches of chest hair from my skinny frame. *Can't ya reuse those things or take a razor and spare me some agony?* I remember thinking Cardinal Health must have amassed a fortune from my chest alone. Miles of wires covered my body from top to bottom. I resembled an electrical grid powering a small village in Croatia. A fancy power grid, mind you. We all know what I'm talking about here.

The *modesty* gown.

When I first arrived, I modeled that gown with pride. A genuine hottie adorned in the drab pattern with the stretched-out pocket in front. Paired with florescent yellow gripper socks, *look out Tyson Beckford; this guy's gonna show you a thing or two.* But eventually I lost my runway status to the 37th invasive test, and all that remained were my golden slippers.

Even though I had been arrested by the fashion police and lost my wardrobe, I had gained so much in the process: my own personal symphony. Bed alarms sounded when I moved too much. A beep here and a tap-tap there rang out as numerous monitors reported my every cell function. The periodic clicking of the iv-pump intermixed with the buzz of the sequential compressing device comforted while it worked to squeeze warm blood through the veins of my immobile legs. That concert was the only company I needed. After the second day I started humming along with the familiar tune of the orchestra just to drown out the boredom. But then more meds kicked in, and it all mutated into a blurry hum that I can barely recall.

I Don't Wanna

Initially I willfully submitted to the numerous requirements and demands of every professional who entered my room. But the willingness faded quickly as the days dragged on. The incessantly busy environment and my nonstop pain began to work harmoniously against compliance. I became ornery when insomnia joined in, and then unmanageable.

You know that moment when your firm grip on reality is slipping through your fingertips, and you feel the urge to detonate? Yup, I had reached the precipice, and I was ready to take the plunge. Regardless of the loopy juice being pumped into my iv, exhaustion and pent-up rage yanked the ball valve and forced me through the sewer grates. A suspicious and argumentative spirit replaced the trusting and cooperative nature, and a growing bitterness root quickly shot up and choked out respect.

I've always protected my mind and body with plenty of sleep. When I'm in bed, don't wake me until I'm good and ready or I'll hulk. I wanna feel refreshed and ready when I conquer the world. Sound decisions and a clear mind spring from adequate rest, causing a healthy determination to flourish. Strength to persevere through a health crisis would only be birthed from sufficient rest. Success requires a balance.

It's alarming how quickly imbalanced I became. And it should be obvious by now that I didn't have much to start with, but I began basing all my beliefs and observations of reality on uncontrolled emotions. I thought I knew best, and the staff was plain incompetent since they misunderstood my rash outbursts. None of the doctors and nurses knew the real me or understood my situation.

I begged to have the monitors removed if they weren't gonna produce any real results. I requested the physical touch of a toilet seat but was given a bed pan and a portable urinal instead. Called for a walk around the room but was permitted to move only during tests ordered by the doctors. And because

I had lost most bowel and bladder functions more times than I care to admit, every request for normal self-care was largely disregarded. Torturous symptoms and the relentless hospital hum began to destroy my will to succeed. And the nonstop refusal from the staff wasn't helping.

I'm Human?

Desperate attempts like these are classic human traits. We feel we aren't gonna survive, so we claw and scratch to get what we think we need. The average person reacts precisely the same. Am I right? And when someone once said to me, *what? Jason Brunette's human? No way!* I released a sigh of relief. *I make so many mistakes. Wow!*

Have you ever noticed hindsight reveals loads of truths? Writing down my errors and painful observations has been shocking. If you choose to do the same, guard your heart. Scrutinizing can go wildly wrong, or it can be a bucket of gold.

At The Beginning Of The Rainbow

Here's the pot I found at the beginning of the rainbow.

St. Joe's was filled with some of the most incredible people in hospital history. Completely unnoticed health care professionals busting on scene to save the day. And nationwide most remain uncelebrated because of our human tendency to dwell on the negativity of why we were locked up in the first place. They generally float by undetected unless they're rude or fall short of our expectations. But after further review of both good and bad, I've decided that St. Joe's shines like a constellation in the sky. And they deserve a shout out. My hometown hospital has continuously left me with a horrible distaste for health care, but there's many there, too, who deserve recognition. During a crisis people need their diagnoses spoken in a straight-forward and supportive manner. Kindness and a measure of grace sure is helpful. And sometimes it's hit or miss. I have been an intolerable patient at both places, but I've received wonderful care, nonetheless.

Bring Them In

I hope you love stories and examples as much as I do. Let's honor a few of the staff members with some of the ways they impacted me. I changed the names, so everybody's safe!

In walked Matt one day, a bit over average in height and generously muscled. His easily identifiable military haircut and take-charge attitude pointed to prior military service. Not gonna lie, he intimidated me. Straight away I knew I was no match for his poise or brute strength. Luckily for him, the intimidation brought me into submission at first. I honestly feared upsetting him; I thought one afternoon he'd rip my arm off and beat me with it if I failed to extend it properly while he replaced the iv. Yet amid my unfounded fear, I began noticing a softer side. The qualities of a big brother swooping in to protect his weaker sibling. I felt fully assured of my safety while he was nearby. Truthfully, judging by his biceps, if I were to fall, one arm would be sufficient.

Later he proved his strength when repositioning me in bed without breaking a sweat. I felt like a toddler being scooped up and flipped around. His notable honesty and dependability won my trust in a time where I felt I couldn't place my faith in anyone. And what cemented that trust was the afternoon he plopped down in the guest recliner, clasped his hands behind his head, and allowed me to word vomit my fears, complaints, and anxieties without judgement. Gently he disproved my poor logic, rebuked my analysis firmly yet lovingly, and fortified my outlook with a new, positive mindset. He became a true brother to me that day because he was honest in word and deed. Practiced what he preached, as they say. Prior to that, his joking seemed coarse, and I had viewed his big brother actions as bullying, but I was sensitive and skeptical, thinking him incapable of gentle and consoling words.

His kindness was more brain shaking than a slap to the head! Skepticism had made the impenetrable walls slippery, treacherous to climb, but somehow Matt scaled effortlessly and went full tactical. Disdain and insensitivity never surfaced. Empathy and understanding owned the mission. He personified tough guy seamlessly, yet he was approachable and tenderhearted. And when he proved that day that it's possible for a tough guy to be tenderhearted, a major crack in my foundation rang out as I sobbed. Marking the beginning of mourning the old me. What a life lesson Matt had taught! Nurses aren't afforded much time to console. There are charts to complete and iv bags to replace, but Matt reclined in that bony chair until my tears had dissipated and hopeful sentiments started coming out my mouth. And the only insensitivity from him that followed was the dart-like tendency when administering my daily Lovenox shot. I'm convinced a dart board must feel unloved when someone launches a dart at it. It's gotta hurt. Pull the arm back and *thud!* A total disregard! Well, that's how I felt. Laid out on the bed belly exposed, I swear I could hear the impact noise a dart makes when it connects with the dartboard when Matt gave me that shot. *Boing!* Poised like a dart league champion, he'd release the yellow missile while cracking a huge smile. Anyone who's experienced these shots understands the immediate sting and abdominal tensing brought on by the heparin as it slowly seeps into the belly fat. It's almost evil. And with a satisfied-meets-sinister look when I'd squirm after he'd jab me, I'm persuaded that he drew far too much satisfaction from it. But the crazy truth of it all, you gotta pinch belly fat to inject the solution. I'm unsure of how he pinched an inch while simultaneously injecting with toes behind the line. He did it so fast and almost hands off.

Even though Matt flew up the rungs of the Best-Nurse-in-the-World ladder, he did have stiff competition. Nurse Donna. She deserves more than an honorable mention. *Put your hands together for the nurturing mom type. Everybody loves a big brother, but moms steal the show.*

When tears stained my pillow, she'd change the pillowcase, hand me a tissue while offering a gentle embrace, and lower my head onto the fresh support.

The perfected mothering touch award goes to... The nurse offering the gentle pat full of love and concern. To the woman with the warm embrace absent of awkwardness.

Nurse Donna was a true mom in every sense of the word.

But don't be misled. The brush strokes on this portrait I've painted aren't just delicate and dainty. Donna knew how to fling paint. Especially when the canvas called for a huge dose of reality. Remember Mom's reactions toward her unruly child? Immediate. Signaling to the child one thing: you'd better straighten up or else!

Mama loves ya but don't think for a moment Mama won't throw down if ya refuse to self-correct.

"Don't you dare entertain those thoughts, Jay. They'll find out what's happening, and if they don't figure it out here, you take it further. You hear me?"

The moment she released her rebuttal, I wanted to salute sarcastically with a *loud and clear*, especially since I had just demanded the on-call doctor to leave my room only moments earlier. And right in front of Donna. But I refrained. She didn't deserve an ounce of disrespect. No matter if the doctor's flowery hinting, supported by a condescending tone, had made me angry or not. Who cares if every test had come back inconclusive? She kept encouraging me to keep my head held high.

"You know he's frustrated too, Jay. Your case is quite complex. Cut him some slack" Donna reassured.

"Don't tell me you're on his side!?"

"That's not what I said."

"Yeah, well, I can't do this anymore. I refuse to be a pincushion for somebody who obviously should've never passed the licensing exam. Just discharge me, and I'll deal with it at home. This place is a joke."

"Don't talk so stupid!" She swore in disgust and passionately continued, "You can't do that to your wife and family. How do you expect them to take care of you when you can't even stand up or walk? You can't hardly leave this bed, and you wanna pin that on your wife to handle? You're not safe to go home and you know it!"

The whole time she chewed my butt, her paging phone rang off the hook, but she ignored it and kept riding me like a steed.

"I understand you're angry but come on! The guy I first met was a whole lot smarter than the guy who just spoke." Donna's phone had never made it past one ring, so when the ringing ceased, and she was still cracking the whip, I knew I'd pushed her too far with the invitation to my pity party. Halfway out the door it rang again, and this time she stabbed the answer button and blurted, "What do ya need?!"

Shame and remorse flooded in before I lost sight of her, but a few seconds into contemplating my brash outrage, she reappeared with her pointer finger extended and commenced another forceful rebuke from the doorway.

"And another thing young man!" Her voice elevated; I knew I was toast. "Don't you ever buck the nurse again! The only thing I'm trying to do is help you. Keep that in mind."

I had picked a fight with a mom who took no guff. From no one. I scrambled for an apology, which she quickly accepted, but out the door she went before I could get too involved.

Hey, Jack wagon. Watch your mouth with Donna! Check. *Think it through before spouting off.* Check. *Don't mess with a mom.* Double check.

But Donna wasn't alone in asserting authority over an unruly and defiant patient. One evening I had tripped the alarms because I wanted toilet time in the actual bathroom, so I decided to get up on my own. Every nurse except Matt disapproved of me leaving the hospital bed because they couldn't hulk me off the floor if I collapsed. Bouncy and weak under any pressure, they knew my legs were useless without two people holding me up. And no slight against the women nurses, but if there was a chance I'd become dead weight on the floor, bathroom visitation would be ruled an unnecessary hazard. Instead, the wonderful invention of plastic alternatives replaced obliging a want with an imminent risk. Who was the one in charge? It was Sergeant First Class Jill on the night shift who met my defiance with a plastic urinal in one hand and a catheter in the other. She wasn't tolerating any nonsense and was now demanding a specimen.

"You can't hold it, Jay, just because we won't bring you to the toilet. Sit back down, please."

I hadn't relieved myself for a while, and I didn't care. Their guidelines were hokey. I wanted bare bum to cold seat, and because the nerves controlling my bladder sensation were malfunctioning, I thought I could use it as a bargaining chip. As far as I was concerned, I could hold out until it forced an exit.

"You can use this urinal, or I can cath you. There will be no trips to the bathroom tonight. Will you be needing my assistance, or would you like me to step out?"

Say no more after the word "catheter". I'm convinced I'd rather lick the hospital room floors clean before I'd be a willing party to urinary catheterization.

A word of advice when you have a drill sergeant for a nurse... *don't pull rank or she'll likely weaponize a plastic tube.*

The following evening when I pushed the call button because I couldn't reach the plastic curse she had left on the rolling cart, I expected to hear Nurse Jill's commanding voice. But hope sprang eternal when it wasn't her over the speaker. The familiar chill to one's backside from a cold toilet seat tickled my fancy, and I thought I was all set. *Tonight's my night!* If you remember, the nurses on night shift were mean bullies who rarely rewarded their patients, so I usually avoided them. But unusual bladder urges changed my mind that night; I couldn't hold it. Wet sheets or call for help?

Nurse Cathy towered in the doorway moments later, challenging the summons. She was half a foot taller than Matt and had broader shoulders. Picture the cartoon villain, looming in the shadows and then emerging into the light. With one glimpse of her stature, I nearly lost continence and immediately regretted my decision. Too late. I was about to be crushed like a criminal being held up by the throat by Robocop. *Should I beg for forgiveness or quietly plead my case?* I timidly began explaining the urgency of my situation, but before I got it out, she had wrapped a gait belt around my waist, hoisted me outta bed, and set my feet on the cold floor. You know that moment when you win a prize at the fair? The bells and whistles going off and the bewilderment on the faces of those around you? The bed alarms were sounding, all the monitors hooked up to me were chiming in, and I think there may have been fireworks in the background.

Your wish has been granted. But here's some fear of the cyborg's next move, and a bit of trembling to go with it. You can't hide, and by the way, you asked for it.

Scared and seeing stars from the blood rushing, I allowed elation to fuel my quivering limbs to the facilities. *Who cares if I'm only going to the restroom? Body... ache away.* Every slow and painful step reminded me that I had broken free from confinement. And freedom was all that mattered.

When she plopped me onto the john and then stepped out, I heard the chains fall off completely. The colors and contours of the drab bathroom came alive and transformed into a glorious art gallery. The stifling smell of antiseptic tickled my senses like I was walking right down the middle of a botanical garden. As exhilaration coursed my veins, discomfort and frustration fled like a startled thief in the night. I began to run my hands across the grab bars and sink basin like an infant handling a new toy. The change of scenery—a dismal bathroom of all places— began to breathe new life into my psyche, and I longed to extend the joy for as long as possible. This may sound completely ridiculous, but I've always cherished my freedom. Send me to prison, and I'm positive I'd lose my mind. I'd be that guy digging at the walls and planning an elaborate escape every second of the day. After I avoided the pull string for nearly fifteen minutes, I finally yanked the cord signaling for help and ended my reunion with freedom. And the thrill of the moment? Shattered like a mirror under pressure. Two well-appointed nurses competing for space in the crowded doorway presented themselves. To make matters worse, the positioning of the bathroom left a clear-shot view to anyone in the hallway if the main door stood wide open. So, in full view of a packed corridor, they yanked me off the toilet, dabbed my manhood with a wad of toilet paper, and hiked my drawers halfway up my chest. I think I went into shock from the wedgie cutting off circulation downstairs while they dragged me back and what felt like tossed me into bed. It took the better part of an hour to remove my Jockeys from their lodging as I envisioned the raiding team wreaking havoc on other unsuspecting rooms. For the remainder of the night, I refused to even glance at that call button and resolved to hold all bodily fluids until the morning. I didn't see either of them again after that night, but somehow the entire staff had heard the story, and they continued to remind me of it for many days to come. I'm glad the embarrassing events that evening provided ample amusement for the staff. Especially since there's nothing better to talk about in a hospital, being such a boring place to work and all!

Back At The Home

One morning between the first and second visit at St. Joe's, my body became almost comatose. The night before it happened, I kept waking up to a surge of electricity pulsing from my left hip down to the ends of my toes and then back up to my hip. Each time it pulsed, both my legs would jump, systematically bend, and jerk toward my chest, and then fall limp onto the bed. Without warning this continued all throughout the night. Good luck sleeping while your legs are doing their own acrobatic stunts without your permission. While this happened, I became nearly hypothermic and overwhelmingly tense. Absolutely nothing made sense that night. My entire nervous system had been malfunctioning, and no one had a clue what to do for me. Have you ever felt completely helpless, and then had to make a decision in that helplessness? *What are the doctors gonna say this time? Oh, he just made this up. Add it to the symptoms list and send him back to the home.* Instead of causing a scene, I decided to lie there and endure it. For hours I dozed off and on in between the repeated cycles. But then the sun rose and toughing it out got yanked from the choice list. When the morning crew found me somewhat unresponsive during check in, they called 911. I guess my blood pressure kept bottoming out, I passed out several times before the ambulance got there, and my eyelids fluttered violently but wouldn't open. And then I convulsed vigorously. The paramedics whisked me away from the teary-eyed aides minutes later. Off to St. Joe's again, but this time to the Oncology and Observation wing on the eighth floor.

I woke up the following day to my dad standing over me, asking how I was doing. I hadn't expected to see anyone, so you can imagine my surprise; I perked up as much as I could the moment I saw him. And honestly, the stamina I had before the accident has never returned, nearly every activity exhausts me now, but by the grace of God, He has healed me of the convulsions and spasms I just explained. In the follow up to this book, *A Road to the Left: Behind*, I'll be sharing my healing experience. You won't wanna miss the explanation of this miracle granted by God.

Dad couldn't stay long, as was the usual custom with anyone coming to visit. Life must go on. He gained reassurance that his son was gonna live, wished me well, and drove back home. And then fear stepped in and began rattling me with all the mysteries of my existence for hours after Dad had left.

What if those episodes continued to repeat themselves? How many times will people travel to see me before they get tired of the same old thing? Would the doctors keep ruling my condition "unknown", and I continue to get worse? I'm probably gonna die here.

The Light Of The Truth

Good thing I had my phone nearby because news travels fast. Message after message and calls one right after another flooded in, and I spent several hours struggling to respond to everyone. The last visual my optic nerve transmitted was the nurse plugging in my phone as I drifted off to dreamland.

Fourteen hours later I woke up to a parasitic draw of eleven vials of blood at 4:30 a.m. Irritation nearly forced hateful remarks out my mouth, but to my own surprise I remained silent until *yeah, you, too* confirmed her *have a good day, Mr. Brunette*. There's something to be said about waking up to a boba tea straw being jammed into your veins at the butt crack of dawn and remaining composed. Those phlebotomists must have nerves of steel to be able to jab a sleeping person while completely unaware of the outcome. I'm shocked only the patient bleeds!

Unnerving silence surrounded me after the vampire left, and I hoisted myself toward the switch to turn on the light over the bed. As I did, I knocked the call button apparatus off the bed. *Now what?!* I pulled the sliding table closer to me and leaned to grab the dangling button. Couldn't reach. The table slid out a bit, and I slammed forward into the siderail. A quick stabbing pain in my arm revealed that my IV tube had gotten stuck on the other siderail and was now stretching to the limits. I fought to reposition myself on the bed for another go at it. Switching on the light was imperative because I wasn't about to lie wide awake in pitch black room. And since all the commotion had caused so much pain, there was no giving up now. I pulled the rolling table even closer, released the tension on the IV tube, and pushed off the bed with all the strength I could muster. I had to reconfigure my face almost in the center of the table, and stretch my left arm past its limits to be able to reach the buttons. This time I grabbed it and fought to roll back over. Physical therapy? *Don't need it. I just completed a planking session with my face. Top that!* It's quite the feat to reach items on the floor without falling off the bed when a person is hooked up to as many leads as I was. I guess in some ways stubbornness pays off? I flicked the light on and noticed my Bible on the other end of the rolling cart. And the package of animal crackers I had saved from the previous day's lunch. Life was about to improve!

Do animal crackers brighten your mood, or am I simply weird? I can't express what those little treasures do to me. It's almost as if they possess a magical wand. Tick me off and then hand me a package of animal crackers. TA-DA! I morph into Prince Charming with the Orbit gum girl's smile. Well…close.

As I devoured every last crumb, I mumbled "I'm up now" sort of like an inspiration and an excuse to read the Bible that kept calling to me. At home I had a horrible track record when it came to reading God's Word, but here it's read or stare at the walls. I opened to the end of Genesis 27 and beginning of chapter 28 because that's where the binding is somewhat coming apart. *Don't know where to read? Let a book open itself and start there. Disregard. That's horrible advice.* But oddly enough it opened to where Jacob's is described as a troublemaker, he's enduring hardship after hardship, God's still blessing him through it all. And why? Because he put his faith and trust in the God of Abraham and the Fear of Isaac. Through trials and suffering, he continued to look to God as his Provider and Strength. Fitting passage for my life up to that point. I devoured the ensuing chapters like I had the tiny bag of animal crackers. Hours seemed like minutes as I studied, but then the fun stopped with the announcement of dreaded news.

The Roomie

"I'm sorry, Jason, but you're getting a roommate. I never thought they'd make you share this room, but I just noticed a name above yours in the computer. Maybe he'll be nice?"

Her sympathetic tone didn't help; I was completely shaken the moment I heard the word "roommate". Right away my mind ran wild with questions. Insinuations. *What's he gonna be like? What if he snores? He's probably rude and judgmental. Just like some of the crabby people I've met at the nursing home. No matter how many times I've smiled at some of the folks, they just glare. Now I gotta get it here, too?* My discriminative mind raced with dreadful conclusions as I waited for his entry. *I haven't been through enough, so let's splatter another colorful bucket of cowpies on the situation.* And just like trusting a kid with watercolors while the parent takes a quick breather, valuable lessons are on the horizon. Don't ask me how I know this, just trust me.

That's exactly what happened with Louis. He whipped color from one end of the room to the other the moment he busted onto the scene. Think of the busty opera lady announcing her presence with an obnoxiously pronounced high A. For several hours.

"When the heck do I eat?! I haven't eaten since breakfast you know. Do you take my order?"

The canvas Louis began to masterfully paint unfolded around two in the afternoon. The silence I cherished: history the moment his transport bed crossed the undefined threshold.

"Sir, we have to wait until we get the doctor's orders first, then you can eat."

Desperate to get her point across, and apologetic for startling me, his nurse whipped the curtain closed with a quick, "so sorry" and went back after her unruly patient. I tried to fit in, "No worries. Good Luck!" before she drew the curtain, but Louis drowned out my encouragement with a shout.

"Take that *blank* thing off me, I'm hungry!"

"I have to get your blood pressure. You need to calm down so I can get a proper reading."

I could feel *my* blood pressure soaring as she battled the irate elderly man. In all the commotion I had failed to catch a single glimpse of him, but I knew by the agitation in his voice, clearly, he was feisty. Intolerable. Probably crotchety. And snores. My unjust punishment had commenced, and in the form of an unknown, unseen crabby old man. And my only protection? A thin curtain. On and on the battle raged for an eternity. He'd shout, then the nurse would squeak in between his bellers. It was a mess. In between his shouts she managed take his skyrocketing blood pressure and announce it to the doctor she had on the phone. I overheard 184 over 92, and it changed every time she ran the cycle after that. The chaos had everyone in a tizzy. I was indignant over losing serenity, Louis wanted a cheeseburger, and the nurses couldn't find a way to settle the old man down. Yet, as frustrated as I was, I could feel a building compassion for his situation when I heard his vitals. He was dancing on thin ice with soaring blood pressure at his age, and I wondered if I should try to calm him down. Louis went silent as the nurse slammed the door behind her. My hope for solitude soared briefly and then bottomed out. The barrier between us unexpectedly tore open to reveal the mystery man in all his feistiness. Startled and irritated again, I believed the black cloud had returned with a vengeance.

"Hi! I'm Louis. What's your name?"

Lou's nurse reappeared and mouthed her apologies to me, but the frail, age-torn old man kept forcing communication as she attempted to squash it.

"We need to get a new reading. This is a different machine. Relax."

"What was your name?" He yanked at the closing curtain, asserting his curiosity.

"Jason. My name's Jason."

"Who the heck is he?"

Frustration tried to upstage curiosity, but determination fueled the old man as he pleaded with the nurse for what his ears failed to report.

"Jason. His name is…"

"I'm hard of hearing, you know. Who is he?"

The nurse impatiently shouted my name several more times, but Louis shook his head and muttered, "still don't know what she said" and decided to revive the dinner battle.

"Where's mah *blank* dinner?! I told you to get me food!"

The curtain fluttered shut and the first act with Louis ended. The commotion continued behind the scenes, but I found myself chuckling while pondering the exhibition. He seemed spunky but scared. Rattled. The sparkle in his eye was fierce, but I could sense something worked to douse his fire. He wasn't the stereotypical old cuss most people would label him as. Only after a few ensuing shout matches between him and hospital staff did I overhear the truth about him. He was hungry, scared, alone, and worried. He hadn't eaten a decent meal since the previous day because his wife had fallen ill, and his anxiety for her well-being explained his elevated blood pressure. My heart began to break for his situation.

True Love

A patient's needs are top priority while in they're in the hospital. Especially when the needs are dire. But Louis kept pleading for someone to care for his wife during the first few hours it took to get him squared away. The more the staff ignored him the more he ramped up efforts. He fiercely fought back no matter how many times the staff explained he must come first. He started thrashing at the curtain, throwing sheets and blankets off his bed, sent his wheeled cart violently into the wall. They finally relented and one suggested they let him call his wife. During the commotion one of the nurses peeked her head around the curtain to check on me. Before she uttered a word, I shot her a smile and said, "I'm all good. Take care of Louis." Those words must have registered as gold because her face brightened, and she shot me a smile back. The compassion-smitten nurse whipped the curtain closed, and then I heard the bedside phone rattle as she picked it up. After the beeps from dialing the worried man's phone number had ended, she handed the phone to Louis.

"I'm in the hospital. Yes, I'm in the hospital. Listen to me! Did you eat today. I want you to listen. I tell you all the *blank* time to listen and you don't. That's the problem with you, you don't ever listen to me!"

His voice thundered as he spouted his harsh love through the phone lines. *I wonder if his wife is hearing impaired as well. What a home life that must be!*

"You need to eat today and call Emma."

I could sense the irritation building as he continued to plead.

"No, I don't know Emma's number. Look in the book. I know it's in the book. No, I don't know where the book is. I will talk to you soon."

I'm assuming he jabbed the receiver at the nurse, but I saw him lie back on the bed. It must be instinctual to check if the person is still on the other end of the line because the nurse pressed the phone to her ear and kept saying hello. Does everyone do this? I often find myself doing this after my kids hand me the phone. But to the nurse's surprise, Lou's wife was still rambling away on the other end of the line.

"Yes. Uh-huh. Yes. Ok. Ok. Wait a second…No. Ok. Yes, Ma'am, I'll tell him."

She finished the conversation and reached for the curtain to lessen the gap she had hastily left. And as she drew it shut, she glanced at me and pushed out a long sigh of relief.

When the number one goal of healthcare professionals like her is providing the best care possible, sometimes their day gets hijacked by utter chaos. No one knows the outcome of a single situation until it arrives, and sometimes uncertainty produces frustrations, hardships that breed doubt.

Am I even making a difference? How long can I endure such stress? Why did I join the medical field?

Why do I mention this? Because I've overheard conversations most thought was private. It's gotta be a natural response after enduring situations like what I had heard. That circus event had my blood pressure and heart rate up, and I was lying down outside the circus tent doing nothing! Picture what these professionals deal with in one eight-hour shift. *And then stay for a double.*

We gotta cut them a little slack. Celebrate their career choices even when they seem a little edgy or curt. Because no matter what these nurses and doctors must be feeling, they barely utter a complaint in the heat of the battle. It takes all kinds to run a hospital, and we desperately need these heroes, faulty or not. Nerves of steel, man!

Stick Around For The Side Show

I gotta admit something. I had enjoyed the craziness on the other side of the curtain, and I wanted it to continue. Mostly because I was bored, but also because Lou was so fiery. *What else ya got, Little Buddy?* And the show continued moments later.

"Louis, I'm Terrence. Can you tell me your birthdate?"

"My what?!"

"Your birthdate."

"You want my birth weight?!"

I busted up laughing, but the food service worker, strait-laced and collected, paused for a moment, and then continued, increasing in volume as he spoke.

"No, your birthday. What day were you born?"

"Yeah, I like corn!"

The starving guy's voice boomed with delight. I lost all composure at that point. Terrence began to waver in professionalism as he grumbled and then redirected.

"NO, LOUIS, YOUR BIRTHDAY!" Not once but twice he yelled. "YOUR BIRTHDAY!!"

The smile dropped off my face as Terrence yelled. I was tempted to press the call button to report his unethical behavior, but, luckily, a janitor walked into the room, and her presence must have diffused Terrence a bit.

"May I have your date of birth, please." He had an unsettling calmness to his voice as he requested again.

"Oh, 7, 4, 18."

As Lou was sharing his simple answer, the cleaning lady peaked her head around the curtain and witnessed my dumbfounded look. I don't remember what she attempted to say to me because I cut her off with, "Did I hear him correctly?"

She let out a weird laugh. "I believe you did."

"That would make him nearly a hundred!"

That dude's almost a century and is still kicking and screaming like that?! After the dust settled and poor Terrence had finished shout-reviewing the menu with Lou, I marveled at the old man's alertness. A few minutes into the intermission the curtain flew open again to reveal Lou's vitality. *Let the side show commence!*

"I don't need this blasted thing between us! Who are you and where do you come from?"

I wish someone could've recorded the shock that covered my face the second he demanded my credentials. *This dude's quite bold.* From that moment on we engaged in an awkward yet richly rewarding shout-conversation for nearly an hour with no interruptions. And I find it fascinating where his mind went, and how thankful he was. But his inquisitive nature attracted me the most. At one point he turned my attention to the billowy clouds dancing outside our window. He considered himself lucky to still be able to see how beautiful and majestic the clouds were. He detailed the wind patterns that brought them together, pointing out how fortunate we were to be so close to them, and that the wind tied them together like a sidewalk that he wished he could walk on. It was at that juncture that I no longer saw a feisty old man and a freak show; I began to see a wonderful man still a kid at heart. A man who seemed lost and broken without the love of his life but was nonetheless adoring the beauty around him with an absolute stranger. Instead of dwelling on the grim reality of being in the hospital, he stared out the window at what obviously had interested him his entire colorful life. *Maybe he had dreamed of becoming a meteorologist? Or a storm chaser? I could learn a ton from this guy.* I wasn't really expecting a lesson from Lou, but I think God had other plans because I still ponder the deep impression he had made on me. Besides, I couldn't have escaped the conversation…the bed alarms would've sounded.

"I will be 98 on July 4th, you know. I got two more years to go." And with that comment a heavy sadness seemed to have descended on the room.

"Two more years?" I misunderstood the mood change.

The love I felt for him is indescribable. But before I could pry, he thundered out a subject change.

"You ever in the military?" I attempted to respond, but he couldn't hear. "Army? Navy? Marines? Air Force?"

Without a pause for my reply, he drilled me. And to address his earlier frustrations with his wife, it's no wonder he felt like his wife never listened to him because he barely left room for others to respond.

"You can't trust those Japs! I would take a German any day. The Japanese were slimy *blanks* and downright mean suckers."

Whoa, Little Buddy!

He educated me like an old school marm. *Don't speak up or disagree. He'll cut a switch and whip the truth into you!* I just listened.

Not every bit of the conversation was commanding, however. He began telling a story about the road to Alaska, and how he had a major part in its construction. The work he detailed was grueling and dangerous; it saddened me when he spoke of all the lives that were lost in its construction. But his riveting description brought me to the scene and generated a deeper respect for what most guys my age would take for granted.

Man could Lou tell a story. I imagined myself back on grandpa's lap, enamored by his tales. The only things missing were a tobacco pipe puffing a savory scent, a ferocious flame devouring a birch log, and Old Yeller curled up next to the rocking chair. But what really excited me about the story: the kids and I had watched a documentary on the History channel about the Alaskan road not two weeks prior to my hospitalization. It was almost as if I was reliving the film with one of the characters pictured! How had I been so lucky to be able to piece together more of the that historical event? But as quickly as the topic had arrived, it sadly disappeared just as fast, and was replaced with a prior sentiment. "Boy those clouds are nice."

"Where are you from? Marshfield? I should expect my son anytime soon. He is about two to two and a half hours away. Where are you from?"

"Not from Marshfield, no. I'm from…"

"Wausau? Merrill? Rhinelander? Where?"

I absolutely hate being cut off, so I completely understood Terrence and the nurse's annoyance. But Lou wasn't being disrespectful or rude. I pointed upward with my index finger, hoping he'd give me a moment to spit out Michigan. He blurted out a few more northern Wisconsin towns, and then I interjected Escanaba.

"Oh! Eksanaba!" A smile cracked his face. "I have been there. What about Gladstone?! I love it there!"

His joy made my heart sing. *I knew I liked this guy!* He began describing his favorite fishing spots along the bay in Gladstone for a quick second, but he stopped short, blurted "gotta wee wee", and then disappeared behind the curtain.

Our conversation ended, and I never saw him again. I did overhear many of his conversations with the hospital staff, however. None of them were positive. Lou was dying of cancer and sliding fast. He spent the rest of his time next to me either sleeping or constantly wheeled back and forth to tests and procedures. And then one day he never returned. I wanted more time with him, to talk to him, to enjoy his company, but I knew he needed rest.

How could a man as decrepit as Lou, dying of a metastasized cancer at 98, be a single bit joyful with the beauty of clouds and wanna share it with me? And loving the scene so much that it brought him to tears. How could he be so thankful with the impending doom crouching around the corner?

My heart ached for Lou. He owned my thoughts for days, and his words were a jackhammer pounding away at my tough guy foundation for months afterward. But what struck the hardest? *I could have easily disregarded him because he was invading and ruining my peaceful hospital stay.*

The warmth from his company had crept into my heart. His beautiful soul had softened a portion of it. I was experiencing true compassion for a stranger for the very first time. With no regard for me and my circumstances. Only him. His situation.

His stories. God in His abundant mercy opened my eyes to my critical nature and showered me in blessings. Again.

Lessons After Lessons

So many lessons come to mind from that experience with Lou. But one that continuously rolls over and over in my mind is: *don't blink, it could all be gone without notice.*

One minute I was battling my way to the top of the success heap, and the next I was bedside to a 98-year-old man dying of cancer. Neither of us strong enough to stand on our own two feet. I was in my middle thirties and fully reliant on care from others while he was in his late nineties lamenting the same.

Listen to me. If you spend the majority of your time worrying about yourself, your tough guy appearance, your bank account, your societal status, whatever's robbing you of the day-to-day joys and blessings of life, you'll ultimately miss out on the little things. The simple treasures. The actual rewards.

Let me say that again. You. Will. Miss. Out.

But it's also very important to reject the free ticket to board the regret train. Listen to 2 Corinthians 7:10 NLT. "For the kind of sorrow God wants us to experience leads us away from sin and results in salvation. There's no regret for that kind of sorrow. But worldly sorrow, which lacks repentance, results in spiritual death." Picture how lonely Lou must have felt when those he had expected never came to visit. So very often I hear of children leaving their parents alone in hospitals, nursing homes, assisted living facilities because life has them tossed to and fro. Or their parent's illness is too difficult to deal with. Or maybe the whirlwind of success is too loud, muffling all cries for help, for love, for a moment of your time before it's too late. Please understand I don't want you to get lost in a feel-sorry moment for Lou. But I simply appeal to self-examine. No one's exempt from this type of neglect. And without a moment's notice, your chance, opportunity, occasion might be ripped away. Develop the kind of sorrow God desires that'll lead you to repent.

What about taking your boy fishing because he loves it?

What about noticing and complimenting your daughter in her favorite little dress? The one she twirls around in, hoping you'll take notice.

The affectionate hug that your spouse longs for but won't interrupt you to get?

The list is lengthy with instances of flat tires and outta gas scenarios when we refuse the miniscule yet invaluable lessons in everyday life. It's not *wham* and life's a mess. It's usually gradual. Slowly derailing every day. Ever so slightly nearly undetectable until it eventually snowballs into a disaster. Life becomes way too hectic and the chances of spreading joy become slim. But it need not turn out this way. Catch the moment and celebrate it. Be present. Ready to make someone's day because the hours are fleeting and so is the chance. I'll get to that tomorrow may never come. Ask any elderly person how he or she got so old, and I guarantee you'll hear, "in the blink of an eye."

Who's Your Louis?

What about you? Are you the tough guy type who wouldn't converse with a "Louis"? I never wanted to. Guys like Lou had nothing remotely useful to me. Ouch!

And look at it this way.

Why would I give this guy an ounce of attention if my 6-year-old practicing ballet moves in her frilly dress never mattered?

What's the difference between a stranger and a family member in God's eyes? Maybe you do give your children, loved ones, friends the time of day but think twice about being kind to a stranger. Why? I've been this guy all my life. I don't gotta be buddies with everyone, but a little kindness goes a long way. Maybe that's why Jesus commands us in Matthew 22:37-40 to love our God with all our heart, soul, and mind and then love our neighbors just like we love ourselves. I believe it's because He knew it would breed unity. A love for fellow humans. A celebration of diversity instead of a discrimination for differences. And honestly, I can't imagine ignoring my own personal needs, so if I can take care of myself, then I can love God and others. It may not be easy, but it's doable. I just gotta make the choice to do it. Besides, why would I wanna miss a single joyful moment? Don't we as Americans preach the pursuit of happiness? Helping others, loving them for who they are, supporting them through a difficult season creates happiness. It feels soul-cleansing.

Maybe, societally, our definition of happiness is somewhat skewed?

I believe that I've missed so much because I've done so little of what really matters. I've let the fleeting moments sail by and then blamed the outcome on its fleeting nature. As out of my control. *It is what it is.* But that's not true at all. Fleeting moments should be seized and cherished not blamed due to my own lack of judgement.

Are you your "Louis"? Your soul's crying out for attention, but you bat it away as silly. Could it be that you're trying to live up to everyone else's expectations and it's destroying the real you? Maybe you're missing out on the beautiful blessings because you're competing with your world? You've got your very own Mr. & Mrs. Jones living right next door.

Or maybe God is your "Louis" and you easily let your relationship with Him slide. Competition with the world has become your god, destroying your peace, robbing you of your quiet time with God. Yet Jesus continually knocks at the door of your heart, gently asking you to reconsider. *What's He saying to you right now?* Maybe you don't have a relationship with Him at all. I'm here to tell you that it's never too late to find the pathway to peace in knowing Jesus. I've found rather recently that if I seek God first, my day is brighter and easier. Not easier in a sense that nothing goes wrong. The peace I have in Jesus walks me through the issues with ease. And what does it mean to me to seek God first? Literally waking up and saying, "Good morning, God. What do you have planned for me today? May You be glorified throughout my day."

Maybe this sounds crazy to you. It did at first to me as well. Until I tried it. And nothing has been the same since. Additionally, when aiming to please God instead of myself, the trials and lessons become bearable, and my mind quiets in contentment as I enjoy the true peace of God written about in Isaiah 26:3. The Berean Study Bible puts it this way. "You will keep in perfect peace the steadfast of mind, because he trusts in You."

Before you slam the book shut and scream *NONSENSE*, know the truth. The trials and hardships haven't stopped coming for me, and I continue to fail miserably. I haven't been perfected yet, and I don't have it all together, either; whatever flawless-personality absurdity your mind may cook up about me is false. That will all come when I meet Jesus face to face. But the more resistant to lessons and trials I become, the more misery it will bring. And if I utter *what would you have me learn from this?* rather than screaming out *why me?* my life will be more enjoyable and peaceful.

I'm living proof that the more you buck the nurse, the harder she works to straighten you out. It's ok to be wrong. Doesn't feel good, but it's ok. But it's dangerous to fight the truth. Especially God's Truth. John 14:6 NIV Truth. "Jesus answered, 'I am the way and the truth and the life. No one comes to the Father except through me.'" That means I can blaze my own path and suffer the consequences or do it God's way and reap the rewards. I could fight the truth, be a know-it-all, but eventually I'll discover God's Truth cannot be denounced forever if inner peace is what I'm looking for.

Reflections

Louis may not have had all the answers, but I learned so much. I'll never forget that sweet old man. I'm saddened to think before my illness I would've never spent quality time with a man like him, but I'm profoundly encouraged that God graciously put us together, affording me the opportunity to learn such valuable lessons.

> *Don't blink if you're gonna be obstinate. You will regret it.*
>
> *Don't waste a single opportunity. They may stop coming.*
>
> *Grab all the love and kindness you can and pay it forward.*
>
> *Be a day maker, the LORD provides the avenue. Divine appointments are special.*
>
> *Cut ties with unnecessary thoughts and judgements.*
>
> *Admire the insignificant things. There are simple treasures in every blessing.*
>
> *Walk on the sidewalk in the clouds, even if it's just in your imagination.*
>
> *Point out beauty with complete disregard for ridicule that may come.*
>
> *Focus on the blessings and refuse to word curse any less-than-ideal circumstance.*

Maybe by the time I'm his age, I'll be wise. And I'll use the distant memory of the tough guy foundation as inspiration from the past to keep loving others as myself into the future.

Before you turn the page to focus on the blessings, listen to Job 12:12 NIV. "Is not wisdom found among the aged? Does not long-life bring understanding?"

It may not always be the actions of the elderly that demonstrate wisdom, but the experiences shared from a life full of lessons can be worth its weight in gold. My advice: seek wisdom from God from the situations He allows you in because it may surprisingly lead you into a brighter tomorrow!

Chapter 9

BLESSINGS

I've often pondered the meaning of *blessings*. Being a word guy, it's a commonly used word. I study meanings just for fun, and blessings is an interesting word. It seems to be interpreted differently depending on the circle you're in. *Bless you* when a person sneezes. *God bless America* circulating across the country on banners and t-shirts, spoken by many. *Bless this food for which we are about to receive* as *Grace* or *The Blessing*. What's the meaning of all this? Why do I repeat *bless you* when someone sneezes? Why have I been so blessed? Where does it all come from? Do blessings come from a positive vibe? Karma? Do they come from escaping a negative lifestyle to promoting peace and love instead? Always being one of the "good guys" with adequate amounts of meditation and a splash of "spiritual" chanting? I hardly have the qualifications to speak on this subject, so where can a person find the answers to the questions I've asked?

Tired Of Examples?

I'm gonna share some examples of blessings in my life because you guessed it, I like to dole out stories. Or blab. Whichever way you classify it, really.

If you recall, I mentioned my wedding day as one of the happiest days of my life.

If my wife has access to this book, I'd better say that!

Not true. I've never been one to sugar coat anything. Words, non-verbal cues, body language. But truth be told, it was the biggest blessing from God I had ever received. Another event rivaled that happiness, however. Well, came awfully close in comparison. It was the December day when our three kids spent their last day as foster kids and woke up the next morning as part of the Brunette Bunch. Only parents of triplets would understand the joy AND sheer terror of going from none to three in one day. It's not for the faint of heart, and I'd recommend months of preparation in mental fortitude alone. Zero to three is a jolt of lightning, a complete shock to the system. And especially when the ages are just-turned two, just-turned-three, and recently-turned-seven. Our two girls are eleven months apart and polar opposites. Blonde hair, blue eyes. Brown hair, brown eyes. Keeping them from nonstop biting and pinching each other was a full-time job. *Rip off the Band-Aid and suck down the Mountain Dew cause these little monsters never stop.* Yet from the beginning they were blessing after blessing.

I'm sure you've figured out by now that I loved to complain about my entire life, and that nothing had ever worked out for me. I mean, nothing. I always had to fight for a job, a raise, to hold a position I deserved. Keep friends in my personal life, at school, at work. I had to beg for a loan under fifteen percent interest. Find reliable cars while maintaining at least a twenty in the billfold and $500 in the bank. Remain in the good graces of my family while focusing on my unfocused dreams. I had perfected turning the unending list of woes into a pity party invitation. *Hang tight. I'll send ya an invite.*

The Invite

You're Cordially Invited

For: Jason's a Victim Party

Date: Always & Never Gonna Change

Time: Now's a Good Time. Bring Gifts

Place: Wherever You See Him, Feel Sorry for Him or Else

Given By: The World. It's Against Him

Told Ya Kids Possess Magic!

Yet, all that fighting for something to go right mysteriously disappeared when the opportunity to adopt our kids surfaced. Our charming but becoming-dilapidated three-bedroom castle passed the rigorous state inspections on the first try. The only check mark we got was the hot water being too hot. Wait, I think we had a dead battery in one of the fire alarms. Oh, and the broken storm window from a 5/8ths bolt chucked at the house by a wanna-be thug fourth grader wanting to impress the group of hooligans he was with. *Turn down the dial on the water heater, run to the hardware store for a 9-volt, and pop out the storm window. Anything else?*

And because clothes donations, toddler beds and a crib, diapers and toiletries, food box after food box were dropped off for weeks, we had become a fortified bunker to rescue three souls from the crosshairs of abuse. And remember the begging for a loan part? Not this time. We met Connie at the credit union. *Forget the cosigner and high interest rate. Put your hands together for Milly the Montana. She's number 31 in the car collection. She's super nice!* Anything that pertained to the adoption of our children worked out seamlessly.

In John 1:16 the passage speaks of receiving blessing after blessing because of God's abundant grace. And in Psalm 40 verses five and six it speaks of how blessed we are when we trust the LORD, and His wondrous acts are far too numerous to count.

Do you ever reminisce God's goodness, or are you like the ungrateful me mailing out pity party invitations? Numerous blessing came, but because of my downturned outlook, I missed the cherishing-them-enough memo to store them away for later recall. Even some of the mind-boggling ones seem hazy.

Blessings From Out Of Town

Moving ahead to closer to current, I nearly destroyed the memory of several blessings in Marshfield after arriving home from the nursing home. My health had taken a major dip and the seizure-like convulsions that plagued my body became relentless. My two girls and Heather grew weary of comforting me because nothing appeared to help. Dylan had abandoned the project to chase after a soccer ball. One evening the Holy Spirit intervened with the truth I had been overlooking. While I was lying on my air mattress in the living room, Makenna graciously asked me if I wanted a bowl of ice cream. I barked out a rude response, and she walked away shoulders shrugged in defeat. Before I came to my senses to apologize, one of my favorite aides from the home came to mind. And reminded me that I had learned the little blessings in life shouldn't be ignored.

Kaylee Loves Ice Cream

No matter what mood I possessed, my favorite aide, Kaylee, harassed me until I began to smile. When she first started doing this, it irritated me, and I gave her the cold shoulder. Try as I may I couldn't dim the sparkle in her eye. That glimmer wasn't easily ignored; I succumbed to her fiery personality and quick wit by the end of her second shift with me. I was no match for her and began to warm up to her charm. She reminded me of my niece, Emma, so I felt I should give her a chance. But what drew me the most? Every time I broke the rules and did something I was instructed not to do, she'd say, "Well, that was stupid of you. Maybe you shoulda listened." *Don't sugar coat. Tell me what you really think.*

Because the nursing home was at full capacity and the place was short-staffed, I rarely left my bed unless for appointments or physical therapy. If you remember, I couldn't get outta bed and into my wheelchair alone, so leaving my room took a ton of work for me and the staff. Yet everyday Kaylee had one goal in mind: get me out of that uncomfortable bed to escape the mundane-depressive life of the home. Most of the residents were sixties and up, but she refused to let me act like them.

"You're too young to be here, Jay. I'm gonna get you up, maybe take you outside or something. You can't lay around like the old dudes down the hall. I can't do it today, but I'm coming in early tomorrow to bust you out."

Earlier in the week, she was telling me of a local farm store up the street that *has the best soft serve ice cream in the world.* My hope soared when she mentioned busting me out. *Maybe the day had come for me to escape.*

As promised, Kaylee swung open my door and demanded to "get a move on" because she wasn't gonna wait for no "slow poke". We had places to go, people to see, and ice cream to eat. I had never really enjoyed ice cream before the home because I'm a label reader. *Don't get me started on carrageenan or any other emulsifier.* But let me get started on telling you something else: if you ever get to Marshfield, you need to look up Weber's Farm Store at 9706 County Road H in Marshfield, Wisconsin. They have the most fantastic ice cream in that little country store.

If you do stop at Weber's, notice that it's on top of a little hill. And if you follow that hill a short distance back toward town, the nursing home is on the right. Kaylee pushed me up that hill in the blazing heat in a wheelchair to get the ice cream. We didn't take a car. And then pushed me back down the hill past the nursing home to a small nature park and zoo. And as we chatted while I admired the beauty around me, she gave me a tour of the zoo. *What an immense blessing this is!* To my knowledge and judging by the way she reacted when I mentioned anything religious in nature, she didn't have a relationship with Jesus. But to have so much love and compassion for a complete stranger? Wow! *LORD, in the name of Jesus, I ask for a blessing on Kaylee. Reveal Yourself to her as faithful, and may Your name be praised for the kindness she has shown so many. Amen.*

I dare say there were too many wonderful blessings to list while in Marshfield. I'd need to write another book titled *Unearned Grace* which would barely scratch the surface on how God has faithfully taken care of this rebellious guy. But for now, the story of one blessing after another doesn't end at that nurturing and supportive facility in Wisconsin. Hop over the state lines to Minnesota, but before you do, here's a snapshot into the events leading up to the adventure at Mayo Clinic in Rochester.

Let's Panic A Bit

Trying to get accepted as a patient of Mayo Clinic felt like what I imagine running for a political office in the United States would be like. No detail of my life, insignificant or not, was left unearthed. Every bit was analyzed, scrutinized, and questioned. If you've been to Mayo, you understand that they piece together your entire life story before issuing a simple eligibility determination. The anticipation and fear of rejection wore me out. And when the acceptance letter arrived, and I had my first appointment scheduled, I began to work myself into a tizzy over the details. The long ride from Gladstone to Rochester. The hotel costs. The gas money. The worst anxiety: the coming pain from the long car ride. Don't report me, but on the way back from the nursing home we folded the second-row seats down, and I stretched out from cargo hatch to center console of my mom's Trailblazer. Not safe at all. And far from comfortable. Can you imagine the pain that would've come from being launched in a crash while being punched in the face by the 79 airbags promising to cradle me like a baby? Yeah, not smart. Tinted windows had hidden me when going to local appointments when I got home, but I couldn't travel seven hours to Mayo like that. Even with cushions and pillows to offer support, it wouldn't be safe or comfortable. Every turn, stop, slow down, slight acceleration would cause muscle tension. Muscle tension for more than a simple maneuver and for extended periods of time—outta the question. I could hardly flex my left ankle without bringing on a muscle spasm. Without sedation, I was convinced I'd never make it.

A few worry-filled days passed, and I finally vocally broke down about the trip. My concerns were busting out; they had overwhelmed me to the point of despair. I decided to call my dad.

"I checked on flights, and there's no way we can afford upwards of seven hundred dollars." Dad knew of the horrors of me traveling as luggage in the cargo hatch.

"Is it that much?!"

"Yeah, that's the cheapest I found. I don't know what I'm gonna do cause I gotta go. And I don't think I can ride in the car that long again." By then tears had stained my face and my voice began to wobble.

"Don't worry about it, Son, I'll see what I can do. I'll call you in a few days. When do you go, again?"

"Three weeks."

Defeated, I smashed my face into my pillow and sobbed. The enormous weight of mine and my family's life flipped upside down felt like a sixties Lincoln Continental parked on my chest. I saw no way out. Both my parents were recovering from their own financial woes. Friends, family members, strangers had already overabundantly supported our family; I couldn't expect or ask for more. Mayo appeared to me like a mirage in a desert to a parched lone survivor, yet I was trapped and couldn't take another step toward the oasis.

Heather shook me awake from a nap a few days later.

"Jay! Get up. You might wanna call your dad."

"What do you want? Why are you shaking me?"

"You need to call your dad. He tried calling you. Is your phone off? When you didn't answer he called me. He found you a flight."

"He did WHAT?! What'd he say? He can't afford that!" I flew off the handle, blurting out questioning absurdities. My angel wife has grown immune to my outbursts; she calmly replied and left the room.

"Call your dad, Jay. I don't know any more than what I just told you."

Talk about being blessed! To have a wife like mine. Just an ounce of her demeanor would be life-changing for me. And to be so smooth. The ensuing conversation with Dad revealed my Uncle Ed knew of a business owner with a private jet with a seat with my name on it. The only one question asked by the owner: does he need a ride back each time?

Hop A Puddle-Jumper

The first flight to Mayo was over in a flash. Uneventful, comfortable, and the scenery was gorgeous from up there! The wing against the stunning blue expanse. The earth below resembling a patchwork quilt. Rivers and lakes carving out the landscape. Breathtaking! I remember thinking flying on a private jet was the way to go. *I need to get me one of these!* My wife's cousin, Amy, had been given the green light to accompany me while Heather followed with our friend Myra in her Toyota. Amy and Heather planned the whole trip right down to the perfect timing of her arrival with ours in Rochester. After landing, the pilot handed Amy his card with instructions to call for a return flight.

After all that kindness, one might think that benevolence had the power to defeat my stubbornness and create in me a willing spirit. Nope. Remember King Saul and how stubborn he was? How lesson after miserable lesson was required to crack his ridiculous nature? My life story seems to align in comparison. Especially the part where Samuel says in 1 Samuel 15:23 KJV, "For rebellion is as the sin of witchcraft, and stubbornness is as iniquity and idolatry. Because thou hast rejected the word of the LORD, He hath also rejected thee from being king." When I read this passage recently, it struck me with an overwhelming conviction to change. Too bad I hadn't read the story before I made the next choice.

Stormy Weather

The grueling yet fascinating week at Mayo ended in a whirlwind, causing us to forget to call the pilot for a return flight. Heather urged me to call the moment she remembered, but, because I didn't want to be a bother, I foolishly pressed my wife into letting me ride back with the girls instead. In my defense, I've never been someone who appreciates last-minute plans. I gotta have things mapped out with plenty of notice. That's actually why I wouldn't call him.

I stubbornly rode in the back seat of Myra's 4Runner with both feet resting on the center console nearly the entire trip home. The girls asked numerous times if I needed to stop or reposition, and I'd just shrug them off. *Nah. I'm fine. Keep going.* There was no other position for my legs to be in because the SUV was loaded to the headliner with tons of luggage. I was miserable. That horrible ride felt like a decade in a go-nowhere job surrounded by scorpions that kept stinging my legs and feet without provocation.

About a week of sleep and way too much gabapentin, Motrin, brandy, and cigarettes later, I finally admitted my err in judgement. And the worst part of it all? I had been scheduled to return to Mayo. *I'm gonna have to swallow my pride, admit my foolishness, and humble myself. Pick up the phone and explain to the pilot why I hadn't called. Hopefully he'll fly me back there.* His card haunted me every time I glanced at it. I grabbed the card, contemplated tearing it in half, but tossed it onto the table, instead, just as Heather walked into the room. *Busted!* She watched it bounce off the table and hit the floor. As her eyes met mine, she mouthed some dreaded words.

"Didya call the pilot yet?"

"Don't need to."

She left the room but not before I saw the blood boil through her cheeks. I swear there was steam escaping her ears.

It's Pointless

How does one reason with an idiot? I had my reasons and she had hers; they just didn't align. And when that happens, the man is usually right. Wrong. I don't think there's a stubborn man alive who can outreason a logical woman. As men, we get that absurd *I'm right* mentality even when we know we're way off base. And what do we usually do with it? We don't use it as a blessing, that's for sure. I know God blessed me with good sense and a bit of wisdom, but I curse myself by cultivating stubbornness. Don't agree with me, guys? Hear 2 Timothy 1:7 NIV and apply it. "For the Spirit God gave us does not make us timid, but gives us power, love, and self-discipline." Hear it in the English Standard Version, "for God gave us a spirit not of fear but of power and love and self-control." Yeah, argue with God. Only fear of losing the upper hand drives stubbornness. Self-control and self-discipline don't include cultivating bull-headedness. Quit making the woman you love miserable.

It took until the following day to come to my senses; I dialed the pilot's number.

"I will need to check with the company what the schedule looks like and will call you back. It will be within the hour."

No questions asked. No condemnation. Just professionalism. *What a guy!* Within the hour as promised, good news rang out. We'd be flying out again on Sunday at 5pm, accompanied by another person being dropped off first in Green Bay. His details were short and to the point, leaving so much to the imagination.

Load 'Em Up, Boys!

Let me tell ya, it's an interesting event to be *loaded* into a plane. The first go around I focused on preoccupying my time with relaxation techniques and calming exercises. But the second trip proved to be totally different.

The plane that had whisked me across state lines was quite small, with just eight seats and enough head room to stand up. A regularly ambulating person would have had no issue in the boarding area, but for a guy like me sportin' a wheelchair, it felt like ramming me through the eye of a sewing needle. The jostling and sudden shifting motions hurt a bit, but it was the fear of being dropped that set panic into overdrive. *Good luck shoving a wheelchair up the stairs!* I had to be loaded into the plane once again by a rickety metal contraption called the runway.

I imagined the guys loading me saying something like this... *Here, Jason, sit on this tiny seat, hang on real tight, and we'll launch you into the plane. Guard your teeth.*

Obviously, they were a tad bit gentler, but I was a hot mess. Being scooted along the flimsy runway on a miniature seat too small for a toddler while maintaining a death grip on the flexing rails that separated me from safety and certain death, *not cool.* Maybe I'm overdramatizing this a bit, but imagine your legs don't work, and you're being hoisted off the ground about ten feet by a couple of strangers who are loading you like cargo into a plane. Add severe nerve pain and uncontrolled muscle spasms into the mix, and then try to think logically after a near-death experience involving heights. Not a good combo.

How'd I do this the last time?!

"Jay, you're ok. Let go of the rails and just let them slide you. You're gonna be fine. I see that you're scared, but it's gonna be fine, Bud."

Dad appeared double through all the tears, but I released tension on the rails and slid closer to the opening. *Dad's a mind reader.*

"These guys know what they're doing. You're safe. The plane's safe. You can do this, Bud."

I'm tearing up as I type his loving words. It was very comforting, and obviously I got through it. Moments later I found myself safely herded like cattle into the plane, buckled into my seat, and an oxygen tube crammed up my nose. My heart rate had spiked, and I was gasping for air.

While we waited on the pilot's arrival my parents offered their last goodbyes. No one knew what kept him. After about twenty minutes of waiting, a small door on the hangar flew open, and he approached the plane.

"Jason, we'll be on our way shortly. She's running a few minutes late."

She? Why's a guy's brain seemingly programmed to assume an unknown person is always a guy? Is it just me who thinks this way? I figured a male employee or some executive, maybe even a kid, but I had never thought my travelling partner would be a woman. Not that it's a big deal, but my people skills up to that point revolved around cars and engines, bearings, and grease. Lots of grease. Anxiously I began begging my brain for a chick subject to chat about for the next thirty minutes. I felt trapped. Set up. And I kept coming up short. The mystery lady climbed up the steps, goodbyes rang out yet again, and the dungeon door slammed shut. *Welcome dreaded moment. Brain, do something!!*

"We'll take good care of Jason" she said before the pilot closed the door. Puzzling.

I had never met this lady before the flight. *Maybe the pilot had filled her in?* Unlikely. The fella walking out of the hangar with her looked familiar; I studied his face while the lady buckled herself in. Then it hit me. *She's the owner's wife. Finally, the subject I had begged for! Now I can directly express my gratitude. She appears to be friendly and pleasant, easy to talk to. Everything's gonna be alright! I'll find a way to connect.*

We Have Lift Off

As the plane reached altitude, we found ourselves lost in conversation like the best of friends. Her gentle questioning about my disability felt neither invasive nor uncomfortable. And oddly enough I explained without hesitation.

I wish all conversations about my disability were like the one I had with her. Some inquiries have felt cold and investigative. Others judgey. I've learned the hard way that sensitive topics, overall, are too uncomfortable for most to remain engaged in. Right in the middle of the interrogation, many have either lost interest, walked away, or worked to change the subject, leaving me to feel shunned and almost shortchanged. *Yeah, I've heard too much. All I wanted was enough info to spread the news, but I really wasn't interested in how you're doing. Hey, the sun's pretty bright today, eh? It was super nice to see you. You take care now. Don't follow me. K?* This isn't true for everyone. Calm down.

Our conversation never side-stepped to awkward. Many chances to feel inferior presented themselves—my clothing, my disability, getting a free ride not once but twice from the lady sitting in front of me, flat broke and jobless. *Yer poor. So poor.* None of this mattered because her kindness calmed my nerves, relaxed my fears instead of feeling condescended. Furthermore, she encouraged me to stay strong in stature, build a rock-solid faith in God, and become lion-hearted for my kids. *Thanks for not coddlin' me.* Clearly her faith and love of family mattered the most, but she employed firm yet nurturing mannerisms. A growth mindset.

And the most touching part? We took turns confessing our love for God, and how He had rescued both of us from seemingly impossible situations. There's a whole lot to be said about sharing testimonies of God's faithfulness with a stranger. You're gonna walk away—or wheel in my case—with a pile of faith! And catch a load of this: she mentioned the flight to Green Bay had been up for debate. At the last minute she decided to join me. She saw it as a divine appointment to strengthen mine and her faith. And our conversation became her confirmation.

Man, You Ask A Ton Of Questions!

Many people have said that I ask too many questions. I guess I'm nosy, inquisitive, love to have all the details before planning. I gotta know more. This is no different. So, I ask you again, where do the blessings in our lives come from? *Chance encounters? Karma? As a result of good mojo, froufrou positivity? Perfect attendance? Great behavior?*

Nope. None of that. Only a loving and compassionate God could orchestrate the sending of blessings in our lives. He deserves the glory for everything, great and small. These wonderful and cherished benefits are a clear testament pointing back to His promise expressed in Deuteronomy 31:6 to never leave us nor forsake us. Far too many blessings get written off as *this is what I deserve* and *I worked hard for that*, leaving God in the dust and elevating human merit. I've come to realize that, when I put God where He rightfully belongs—far above my own comprehension—I begin to see clearly my Higher Power is in control of everything, and crazy good things start to happen. This control-of-everything includes the blessings I receive.

I'm not saying we gotta work for God's grace and blessings; there's nothing we can do to earn either of them. He freely gives and He freely takes away. But we do gotta continue to build our relationship with Him on His principles and standards and not ours.

God Doesn't Wanna Pick Up Your Laundry And Fold It, Too

Get married once and leave your clothes on the floor right next to the hamper. You know full well it'd take just two seconds to pick it all up and do right by your spouse, but you don't wanna. You'd rather leave it lying around the base of the hamper. (I'm preachin' to the symphony AND the choir here!) Later that evening you catch a reprimand, hopefully a little grace, but, nonetheless, your spouse gets irritated. Why behave this way? You love your spouse, right? You wanna please him or her, correct? Then do the right thing. Bend your silly little behind over, grab those stinky grunders off the floor, and toss them into the basket with the love of Jesus in your heart. And I guarantee you'll receive a blessing. Peace in the home. A kiss at night instead of an eye roll followed by a cutting remark. Joy in the morning. It'll be there, I promise. But honestly speaking, you gotta do your part. Ya can't just expect yer spouse to be good to ya while ya show half-hearted love back. Same thing goes for God. A person can't just cry out, "LORD, save me!" in the dark seasons and then expect the one-sided relationship to produce anything good. *Pick up yer laundry for cryin' out loud!*

Worldly Blessings Smell Like My Son's Dirty Socks

It's easy to take our focus off God and His marvelous blessings and fix our eyes on what the world deems as a blessing. But trust me, they don't align, and reek like my son's dirty socks.

Do all teenagers' feet stink? I attempted to research the topic but nearly lost my supper at the thought of it. As soon as you think the smell is over because you've Fels-Naptha-ed a fist-sized hole in the strands, three steps inside a shoe and the house clears out again. *The happy dance never lasts.*

But God's blessings are richer and sturdier. They're meant to last. And they never smell like the tank below an outhouse. So don't be fooled or lured into Satan's trickery because that's just what it is. Temptations abound to draw a Christian's eye away from the truth and onto fleeting good fortune, but there's only One blessing who matters: our LORD and Savior Jesus Christ. God first. All else second. No other gods before Him.

"Set your minds on things above, not on earthly things" Colossians 3:2.

Folded Laundry

In my case, God drew me closer to Him through a series of undeserved blessings. He showed me I had been tossing them as filthy rags around the hamper. *Pick that up and let me wash them clean. Then I'll neatly fold and arrange it if you will put it away nicely.* I'm still baffled at His goodness. And when I speak of all the silliness I've perpetuated, many who never knew the old me say *Oh, stop. You shouldn't be so hard on yourself.* And without prideful boasting of how far I've come, I remind each and every one of them that he or she has no idea, no clue as to how far down the rabbit hole I had gone. *God has done mountains of laundry in my life.* But I'm forgiven, and praise Jesus, He's made up the difference through the finished work on the Cross. I'm learning how to keep the floor around the hamper clean, both in real life and spiritually.

Never Forget

It's imperative to never forget where I've come from and how easy it is to mess up. How comfortable it is to allow an overflowing hamper. But examining past mistakes tends to keep me grounded because it's a constant call to humility. It teaches me to realize I'm forever one moment away from blowing my testimony and grieving the LORD. If I allow such complacency to set in, then ungrateful will whip my blessings in the trash and I'll become entitled. At that point, even God's blessings are unimpressive. It's that easy to stray, folks.

Regardless of the season I find myself in, I'll trust Him because of His faithfulness, His mercy, grace, and justice. *Grab your hat, and jacket. Put on your shoes. I invite you to come along with me!*

Before you move on to discovering God's perfect timing in my life, check out the encouraging words of Paul in his second letter to Timothy, chapter two and verses eleven to thirteen in the NIV. "Here is a trustworthy saying: If we died with Him, we will also live with Him; if we endure, we will also reign with Him. If we disown Him, He will also disown us; if we are faithless, <u>He will remain faithful</u>, for He cannot disown Himself." The world can blame Him all it wants, or its surroundings, anything and everything, but we can never truthfully deny that all favor comes from the Father above. James attests to this in his book, chapter one and verse seventeen, "Every good and perfect gift is from above, coming down from the Father of the heavenly lights, who does not change like shifting shadows." He sees fit to bless and then does. He shows grace and gives strength in our times of weakness. He calls to us from exactly where we are in life and chooses to use flawed and broken people in His remarkable plan. Why not surrender to the Sovereign LORD and live in the shadow of His love? Enjoy an interesting life filled with troubles, trials, yet be blessed in every recognizable way through His mercy and grace within His perfect timing.

He's taught me another valuable truth worth shouting from the mountaintops: dwell on the issues and lose sight of God. Dwell on God's goodness and lose sight of the issues. Take 2 Corinthians 12:9 NIV at full face value and be strengthened, "But He said to me, My grace is sufficient for you, for my power is made perfect in weakness..."

What better blessing can a person ask for than to hear over and over from a faithful God, *trust Me. Go rest for a minute. I've got this...*

Chapter 10

PERFECT TIMING

As I lie on this air mattress, the same one I've been on for months, asking God day after day why my paths have led to this moment, He seems to have answered me with a question.

Do you believe in my perfect timing?

What a riveting question! *See! Even God asks tons of questions!* The answer is *No, LORD, I kinda don't. Being unable to freely exercise my own wants and desires doesn't seem like perfect timing to me. You wanna show me why I should?!*

And then the hateful spewings started. *What's the meaning of all this? I'm in my middle thirties with a revolting nervous system. Now should be my time to shine. Or so they say. The world preaches prove your worth before it's too late, but it seems like I've missed the window of opportunity. The ship has sailed. The parade has noisily marched right on by. My nervous system has declared war and has left me with the inability to swim after the ship. March in the parade. Open the window of opportunity back up, please, or I'm destined to be another tax on society.*

And I've come by these sentiments honestly, so why not inquire, right? The leading events in my life seemingly prove this point. I'm now a menace. A monetary drain. And there's no way around it.

I 22. I…22.

Bingo! What'd I win?

Not money, that's for sure. *Who wants money anyway? I busted my backside for that green junk and look where it got me. Nowhere.* The prize I won is being largely disregarded and stared at. The prize basket is loaded with hurtful remarks and condescending tones.

LORD, tell me why I shouldn't make defeat my anthem? All I ever hear is how I'm not good enough, not by a long shot. And now the jury has deliberated and closed with "Thanks for all your hard work and dedication, but the court has decided to take a different approach."

Disability.

What else do you wanna pile on me?

Back to Mechanics

Every car is prone to breakdown. We've already discussed this, so why do I speak of this again? Because it's a great way to recognize the need for perfect timing. *Better catch it before it breaks!*

How do I know this? Because I handed technicians the oil and filter, the repair parts, day in day out, month after month. After a service, I'd send lucky and not so lucky customers packing while straightening stacks of twenties in the cash register. *File that workorder under complete. No up sales for the bonus check off the Smiths or Mrs. Jones.* Those workorders ticked me off. I needed that bonus check. *Put me in the service department. I bet I could get the upsell.* Cars came and went but mine sat in stall three with half the top end removed, waiting for parts. And unfortunately, the night before it had landed in that stall, four hours were lost replacing the tensioner that had nearly took my head off the moment I opened the hood to investigate a noise that had been going on for weeks. As soon as I picked myself up off the ground, I cursed the day I bought that pile of junk. *Stupid Oldsmobile. Shoulda bought a Ford.*

I had ignored the warning signs. The perfect timing before it broke.

Check This Out, Ma!

What about this perfect-timing scenario?

Work, work, work to the point of exhaustion. And as proud as a kid with a half-ripped scribbled-up coloring book page.

Wow! Did you see how much I got done? I built Rome in a day! They said it couldn't be done!

But nobody applauded. And nearly every time instead of others' vocalized admiration, I'd hear my sad voice instead questioning. *Wait…what? That was tonight? I'm way too tired to leave the house now. Why'd you guys plan it for tonight? Guess I'll pout over here on the couch with my other friends, Loneliness and Anger, while you rude jerks go enjoy life without me.* I believed my friends held the only key in the universe to a fulfilling life and would never let me touch it. *You have no say in the matter. You just keep working like a good little boy.* They had foo-fooed my emotions and had refused to acknowledge the Colosseum I had brilliantly thrown together. *Ya'll better recognize!*

What did I continue to get instead of *wahoos* and *congrats*? Avoidance. Labels. Isolation. Less invites. Growing resentment. Blossoming bitterness. False praise just to shut me up.

This one kinda stung.

Your house is…nice. You musta worked hard on this. Hey Judy, remember Myrtle's house? This somewhat reminds me of her house except they had a great contractor who did a marvelous job. But this is nice.

Something's Hokey

What's the point, then? Should I believe in perfect timing or not? There's gotta be a reason why God has asked me this question. *Maybe it's a sick joke meant to amuse the reader.* It's plaguing me like mosquitoes at a picnic. A young man in his prime all but strapped to his bed, covered in everything healthcare, and day after grueling day is being forced to ponder the myriads of disturbing scenarios repeatedly playing in his mind like The Christmas Story on TBS, Christmas day. *Rude! How can this disability even remotely resemble perfect timing?*

And then God answers me with a text? Right in the middle of all this complaining?!

I can't give proper credit, who knows who penned it, but it says, "God has intention for your pain, a reason for your struggle, and a reward for your faithfulness. Don't give up!" *Jab my air mattress with a pin and shoot me to the moon, Alice! Maybe this perfect timing thing is real?!*

This is what it really says to me: *Yer unfaithful when ya ruminate on past struggles. Yer bitterness pillow is ugly and lumpy. Nice resentment blanket, Jason. Oh, and by the way, yer thoughts. Are they producing anything good? Offering ya a reward for yer faithlessness?*

The only reward I've received thus far is a participation ribbon. That's it. I've only endured whatever has come and that's it. My thoughts have been largely hindering my recovery. And deep down I've felt they've been damaging my body for a while now because my pain response has tripled with every negative response I've coughed up. It acts like a taser. The moment I lose composure, my left big toe starts to tap like a lunatic on a trash can lid, and then every inch of my left leg feels like you're jabbing me with 783 hat pins. And if I don't shut up and color a picture like a good little boy, I go into full-body convulsions. *Self-correction? No longer a suggestion but mandatory. Loud and clear, Sarge.* I have no plan, and it's leaving me vulnerable. Trusting myself for relief has been like eating horse poop and expecting fresh breath. I've never admitted the need for patience, mental clarity, rescuing from myself. But after this text, now's the time to change. To learn to wait on the LORD. To trust. But I can't seem to shut my mind up. *What's trusting gonna do? No one's worthy of my trust. God having a plan for my life? Yeah, right. Not a chance! If He removes the black cloud, then maybe I'll reconsider. Besides, I create my destiny. It's up to me to pull myself up by my bootstraps.*

CLICK!

But something mentally had changed that morning. A faint glimmer of hope flickered, reminding me of the revelations at the nursing home. It was dull but noticeable, nonetheless. That morsel of wisdom permeated my mind like a glow stick illuminates a portion of a dark room when slipped under the door. And instead of chewing the bitter road apple of the past and labeling myself a failure, I began to reminisce two cherished stories from my recent history. Ones that would become something of legend to my recovery.

Who's The Chick In The Blue Convertible?

When I took the job at Keystone Automotive in Escanaba, I immediately gained a huge perk the first day on the job: Tracy. For years I had been talking to her; she was my go-to while at the dealership. Her bubbly brand of customer service made her a crowd favorite and a hot commodity.

Need it right the first time? *Call Tracy.* Have an oddity other suppliers have given up on finding? *Call Tracy.* Need a perfect automotive color match for a vehicle yer struggling to mix the right color paint? You guessed it. *Call Tracy and she'll conjure up precision.* She'd been working at Keystone and in the paint business for years before I took the job, and she had proved herself as one of the best in the area. And still is. But knowing her skill level, it didn't take long to feel disadvantaged overshadowed by her competence. *Perk or not, I'm gonna hafta ramp up efforts or she'll make me look inexperienced.*

Tracy set the bar in the office and for our district. To reach her standards I'd hafta pole vault instead of high jump. Nonstop laughter filled the office most days, and I truly loved working with her, but, man, could she sweat the insecurities right out my pores. *Quit making me look bad.* Consistently, month after month, she put miles between my sales numbers and hers. *Let off the gas, Lady! Yer driving a wedge.* Her expertise was a sliver in my hiney, and it was starting to fester. Initially, her competence served as inspiration, but when our manager compared my numbers against Tracy's sales performance, my suppressed resentment surfaced like an ugly zit. When comparing employees—*why can't you be more like her?* —dark traits emerge in even the healthiest of individuals. And *I wasn't healthy.* In the back-storage room, right in plain sight, I indignantly shredded his foolish appraisal. Seconds into the rant, he erupted with a few *how dare yous* and quick-witted sarcastic rebuttals. Our chances of reconciling vanished as he flailed his arms, and I pointed my finger in his face. I viciously warned him I wasn't about to lose my friendship with Tracy to make his precious company a buck. *Perfect opportunity to blame the resentment chasm I'm digging on him.*

I don't understand the logic behind his tactics. I know he stirred the pot after that, putting me in a position to be at odds with both her and him, but what about integrity and respect? Sometimes his actions were cold, uncalculated, and ruthless; other times he was fun and unassuming. But Tracy's personality was simplistic and fun-loving. Her drive for excellence compelled her. She promoted healthy competition with a pin tip of dirty. But I had joined the wrong team. The chronically-waste-valuable-time-on-cyclic-anger team. I spent many days, weeks, months after the altercation, angrily staring at my computer screen and avoiding conversation with Tracy. A chainsaw would have struggled to cut through the tension that had surfaced in that office.

No matter how much I tried to ignore Tracy, she never gave up on our friendship. She's like the Energizer bunny. Drain her batteries, and she'll replace them while charging the other set. Somehow that woman knows how to take a pile of hot garbage and turn it into a tasty cinnamon roll. She's that good. Instead of biting back, she'd throw out hilarious remarks, *hey, did you ever notice this Santa statue looks like one of our delivery drivers?* Or misuse words. *I went to this shing-ding last week.* How can one stay mad at a lovable Kewpie Doll? Customers, coworkers, management loved Tracy. She had a wicked strong charm magnet; not even I could resist it. Deep down I loved her *like a fat kid loves cake.* (Her words, not mine!)

Charge Up The Paddles

Hang on. Before you get bored with the jerk I determined to be, I have a positive recollection to share. There's plenty of imperfections left to uncover in this book. But all of this happened in perfect timing, I promise. The story I'm about to share is one depicting right place, right time. Something I believed could never happen for me.

The Beginning of More Foolishness

One day I lowered my guard because I feared my resentment was causing me to miss out on all the fun. The previous afternoon, Tracy's cubicle resembled a Kenyan watering hole. All the animals were there except me.

"What ya looking at Jaybird? You've been staring at that screen and drooling for quite some time. Would Bernadette approve?"

I wanted to ignore her, but I couldn't. I missed her craziness and had to share my internet find.

"I'm just digging around looking at cars. Been wanting to get rid of the Uplander for a while now. I hate that stupid van. Gotta get Heather onboard."

"I know you do. Didn't Marisa's door open on you while driving down the road? I bet she screamed bloody murder. Poor little angel."

I grabbed for the phone to call Heather, but it rang as I picked the receiver up.

"Thanks a' calling Keystone. This is Jason." And then some other scripted nonsense we were instructed to annoy the customer with.

How Tracy had gotten Bernadette out of Heather, I'll never know. But I was about to discover whether my secret plan Tracy had uncovered would be approved by Bernadette. Anxiously awaiting the end of my sales call, Tracy sat in the ticket line drooling with anticipation for the upcoming circus ride.

"You're welcome. I'll send it right out. Yup. Ok. Goodbye." I held down the receiver and then put it back to my ear. "I'm looking at visual perfection, Trace" I said as I began dialing Heather's number.

"Oh, wow! Ok. And what is that?" she said with a chuckle.

"I'll email you a picture. I'm calling Heather cuz I want this thing."

"That's prrretttty! Jay. You gonna buy it?"

The conversation with Heather resembled a kid begging his parent for the third chocolate cupcake in a row.

"Did you get my email, Babe? Will you open it right away?"

A quick snicker from Tracy briefly interrupted our conversation. I looked at her and then refocused.

"I've loved these cars ever since high school. Remember that picture I drew? The Aurora. I sketched that in pencil from complete memory during English class."

Totally true. I spent the entire hour sketching and shading my favorite "grandpa" car. But I knew it would take more work than reminding her of a silly sketch to sell Heather on the idea. She could care less about cars. *I better step it up!*

"What are you talking about? Yeah, I'll open my email. I'm so confused. What email?"

She sounded skeptical. I was failing. *Quick! Recover lost ground.*

"I could put the hideous Uplander by the road for sale, and we could get this beauty! Isn't she beautiful? Wait. Did you get it yet?"

I looked up at the computer screen and noticed I hadn't yet sent the email titled, "I WANT THIS!"

"Check it now. I forgot to send it." Tracy had turned in her chair to gain full access to the freak show. She let out a belly laugh.

"Where is it? What's going on there? Is that Frieda? Tell her Bernadette says hi. I just got the email...Oh, that *is* pretty."

"Ohio. Isn't she beautiful?"

I tried to hide the fact that the car sat worlds away. Tracy let out another giggle, surprise dumped all over her expression.

"Ohio?! You want to go to Ohio to pick up a car you've never driven?"

"I'm gonna let you go and call the credit union. If they say yes, then what ya think? Road trip, Baby?"

An explosion of belly laughter from Tracy cracked the air again. I'm unsure if she spit her water or choked, but I remember how entertained by this whole mess she was. It must have registered that I had cut Heather off to get what I wanted.

"What'd she say, Jay? You roadtrippin' it?"

Her curiosity continued to drip out of her like the faucet in the lady's room to the right of my cubicle.

"Is she worried, Jay?"

"It's the Ohio thing. She's worried about never driving it."

"Those are good cars, hey?"

"The best. I'm not worried."

"I say who gives a crap. Ya only live once" spouted Donna, one of our feisty co-worker friends who stood drinking in the scene from the instant coffee machine we had conned our boss into rewarding us with.

"You should do it! It'll be so much fun"Tracy agreed in haste as I dialed the credit union's number.

"Shhh. I'm on the phone with the credit union. Hello, I'm looking for new loans…Jason Brunette…No. I haven't spoken to anyone yet...Ok, thank you."

Like two kids eagerly waiting to tear into the gift wrapping on Christmas Day, Tracy and Donna hovered over my desk, anticipating the news. *How'd they put aside their frustrations with me so easily?* I had never mastered sluffing off grievances, so it felt weird. Besides, I was buying an insignificant used car. Not a Lamborghini. What could be so exciting?

"She'll call me back this afternoon."

My office chair went lunging backward as I popped up, and I dashed toward the office.

"Tom, you got a minute?"

I spilled my plan to take the following Friday off to carve out a massive roadtrip weekend. I hadn't gotten the loan yet, but it would happen; oh, I'd see to it. No matter the cost.

"Yeah, that's fine. Check with the girls; see if they'll cover you. The calendar looks good, but next time, I need more notice, Jay."

Tom seemed uninterested in my foolish scheme and more enamored with his fresh-brewed hot chocolate. He took a sip too soon and burnt his lips, causing him to excitedly wipe away the pain with the sleeve of his shirt all the while hen pecking his keyboard. That guy could do a hundred things at once. Scattered but impressive at the same time.

"Perfect. Thanks, Tom. I'll check with them."

A voice came from the other room.

"Jay, line 1. I think it's the credit union."

It couldn't be this easy. But it was. I got the loan, the permitted time off, the unanimous, cheerful yes to cover my shift. *What's going on? What happened to always having to declare war with the universe to barely accomplish a simple task?* Apparently not this time. A stroke of luck.

My luck hadn't turned. The stars weren't aligning. God's perfect timing was about to take place. Only I couldn't see it coming. Lives were scheduled to change exponentially that following weekend. But even if I could see into the future, I would have missed it completely. Blinded by my new obsession I continued to crash full throttle through every barrier without giving any of it a single thought. I'd move heaven and earth for that lead sled slicked in chrome.

You Should Be Ashamed Of Yourself, Young Man

I found myself standing at the National Car Rental pickup counter the following Friday morning. Don't plan on being in a huge hurry, the place is largely vacant for hours on end. For those who haven't been to the airport in Escanaba—it's a ghost town. But this time steam built behind my ears after about fifteen minutes into waiting. No bell to ring, no human in sight. *Should I call or pound on the counter or stand on my head?* I chose to loudly clear my throat, but that didn't help. Finally, exasperation forced an exaggerated *hello* out of my mouth which produced results.

"Can I help you?"

"I'm here to pick up a rental." The unexpected calmness in my voice shocked me.

"Do you have a reservation?"

"No." Her valid question irritated me.

"When do you need the car?"

"Today." My face must have warned of a temperature change because her initial politeness vanished.

"I'm sorry sir. I don't have any availability for today."

"You don't have any vehicles? You've got to be kidding me! There's a parking lot out there full of them. I planned this ahead and you said you had some then."

The counter between us failed to protect her from the instantaneous surge of hot air. Her eyes squinted as the fully vented rage furnace blew her kind-hearted customer service right through the closed window behind her.

"What now?! You mean to tell me you're gonna wreck my plans because you won't find me a car?"

"When you called last week, I asked you if you wanted to reserve a car right then and there. And when you said no, I mentioned we should have a couple, but there were no guarantees. You said ok."

Firm and unrelenting I knew she had me. And the recollection flooded in. I did say I'd take my chances because I didn't want to run to the truck to get my credit card outta my wallet. I was in a pickle, and she knew it. Toning down the rigidity, she sheepishly stated, "It looks like there is a van at Sawyer International Airport in Gwinn if you want that one."

Full disclosure—my mama taught me better and my grandpa woulda slapped me sideways for what I blurted out.

"That'll be two hours out of my way! But I guess since you screwed me, I have no choice. Thanks for nothing. Goodbye!" And then stormed off.

As I huffed and ranted the whole way to the car, I rejected the urge to go back inside and make amends for going ape. I couldn't stomach rude people in customer service jobs because unruly patrons seldom have a single excuse for the way they behave. Even provocation doesn't afford the right. It's always been first come, first serve without a reservation in every sector. And tough guys know of chivalry.

Ignorance Is Not Bliss

Thinking back this reminds me of a time at the dealer when I was getting my head ripped off and then shoved up my backside by this guy who behaved the same way as I had. For a few minutes I allowed him to cuss and verbally tongue lash me. He thought I was splitting his lip with the price of the part he needed because I worked for the dealership. *This young punk is ripping me off! Typical of a dealership.* But then a lady walked down the hall, and I had enough of his dirty antics. I asked him to clean it up for the lady's sake, he ignored my warning, and I lost my cool.

"Listen, Sir. I've put up with yer crap for long enough. You have no respect for a lady if ya don't watch that sloppy mouth of yers. Find yer parts elsewhere. You can leave." Then I turned around and walked away. Sure, dealer parts are much higher than they need to be, but he had no right to subject an innocent lady to his poisonous spewing. Even the owner who had witnessed the whole thing commended me for my discernment. But I'm completely ashamed I had been such a hypocrite. Cleaner language or not, I was a real blockhead to the rental lady.

Soccer Moms, Unite!

No shade if you drive a minivan but give me a cool car to drive. I would've settled for a Nissan, even an Impala, but I was left with one option: a snot hauler. The equivalent to driving a Pinto or a Yugo through a classic car parade. *I'm gonna look like a schmuck! I already own one of those. I don't wanna travel in one.*

"Now what?" I sulked as I got into the truck and pouted at Heather.

"No cars? There's a pile of them parked out front."

"Nothing. And she said the nearest is Sawyer. A stupid van."

As usual I rage-vented to Heather. Boo-hooing and poor-me-ing the subject to death. But when she asked me the next question, I felt the furnace nearly explode.

"You still wanna go?"

"Well, yeah!" You know the tone.

"Well, then it looks like we're going to Gwinn. If you wanna go, yer gonna hafta make a choice. Van or stay home."

The blunt force of her comment stuffed one of Dylan's dirty socks in my lint trap. And it stunk. And tasted nasty. But I silently agreed from the backseat of my mother-in-law's Beetle and stared out the window the forty miles to Gwinn.

It took nearly every mile from Escanaba to Sawyer International Airport for the steam to escape. Just like a pressure canner, I'd build up steam, rattle a minute, and then settle back down for a bit. I had finally accepted our fate by the time the Beetle rolled to a stop in the airport parking lot.

Just like Escanaba, Sawyer is empty. If you aren't familiar with my neck of the woods, it might seem eerie, but for us Yoopers, it's nothin' new. However, quiet isn't what a person's looking for when he's in a hurry. There needs to be life. People available. Workers present. After wandering around the parking lot and terminal for what seemed like hours, I finally found a janitor who informed me of what I had already observed.

She ain't in yet. She might be…

I refused to let him finish. I stomped back to the parking lot, yanked the door open, and blurted, *she ain't in yet* somewhat mocking the janitor.

"Well, that's dumb" supported Heather as I climbed back into the car.

Back and forth my eyes raced, breath heavy with temper flares, as I hunched forward toward the seatback trying to calm myself down. Heather worked to lighten the mood with questions about the trip, but I responded to each with a *hmpf*. Eventually she disengaged and stared out the window. Disgusted.

About half an hour had passed before we spotted the rental lady nonchalantly wandering around every rental car in the lot. She lazily circled each one separately while jotting down notes on a clipboard. *Where had she come from? She's not gonna make it to the building before I tackle her!* I shoved off the seatback and charged at her like a bull after a muleta. But unlike a matador, she proudly wore the red flag as I stampeded. And then hardly moved at all when I approached her. The only way I could get her to go anywhere was to ask her a question and then walk away from her, almost luring her into the building. *Keep swallowing back the anger, Jason. Don't be a repeat offender.* What a challenge that was since the entire world revolved around her schedule, her sweet time.

"So, you said you needed a vehicle?"

"Yes. I'd like to get going. Got a long trip ahead. The lady in Esky said you have a van."

"Oh, where you headed?"

Keep smiling. Keep smiling.

"Downstate. You got that van?"

"Well, that's nice. Where downstate?"

"She mentioned it was a 12 Town & Country."

"You seem in a hurry. Let me check for you." She clacked out an extended tune on the keyboard and then said, "Yes, it's the black one that just came back this morning. I haven't had a chance to clean it. Oh, yeah, and do an inspection. Oh, boy! Let's go take a look see."

I walked ahead of her to the van hoping it would ignite a fire, but she rambled on and on about how nice it was outside and how quiet it had been. I avoided the small talk by looking away from her, hoping to rush the process along. But she continually sidestepped in complete distraction. She finally left Toto skipping on the yellow brick road and yanked on the sliding door handle of the van; I about dropped to my knees. In front of me sat my just reward for being a dink. A guy could've hosted a mud wrestling contest and a food fight inside that thing without needing supplies. When my head popped off, my ears quit working because the worker's apologies sounded like Miss Othmar's "Wah, wah, wah" from the Peanuts gang. I narrowly escaped rage washing the interior with word vomit, but somehow I pulled it together. Mid-stream explaining why the van appeared "untidy" I cut her off and blurted, "I'll take it as is. No worries."

What I wanted to say...*You know, lady, if you didn't waste your time doddlin' and flittin' about like a lunatic, you might find more time to satisfy your customers*...but my filter held. Knowing the netting to catch the chunks wouldn't hold much longer, I yanked the keys and clipboard from her hand, scribbled a signature, and shoved it back at her. "I'm gonna pull it over there to load up. We good?" I denied her the option to answer, and instead, jumped in, pulled the door shut while she was babbling, and backed out.

"What was that all about?" Heather had watched the whole scene unfold as she walked up and quickly got in the van.

"Don't ask. What did she mean she didn't have time to clean this thing? There's nobody here. If she wasn't so lazy and came to work on time, she might get something done." The filter broke. Completely. "If I tried that, I woulda been fired a long time ago. What are these companies coming to that they have such poor..."

I crabbed the entire time we transferred our luggage. *Great example for your daughter who's witnessing the bizarre ravings of a nutjob dad, Big Guy.*

"I'm gonna make sure National knows about this stupid mess! I'll tell them I'll cancel my loyalty subscription if this is the treatment I'm gonna consistently get!"

We had exited the parking lot long before I quit shouting my absurdities. I stopped long enough to say goodbye, but then continued for many miles later. Cancel my loyalty subscription? Who was I kidding? National is the only rental company in my neck of the woods. The loyalty rewards program? Through my employer.

Unfortunately for Heather, the childish fit gave way to a half hour of silence. Maybe it was a good thing? My mouth had quit flappin'. The hush was intermittently interrupted by heavy breathing and snorts, which cemented her silence. All she could really do was ride out the mess until the smoke cleared.

When the rant seemed to be over, Heather seized the moment. She cranked up the tunes, put her feet up on the dash, and waved the freedom flag. *Jay has finally shut up. Start the fun cause we're roadtrippin', man! Making memories!* But as she leaned forward to dig in the snack bag, a hard downshift violently shook the van, snuffing out the erratic happy flame.

"What was that?" she asked while pointing a stick of jerky at me. I read her snack question and responded by shaking my head.

"This thing's brand new, and still can't be trusted?!" I angrily shouted more obscenities, looking to Heather for the perfect solution instead of a beef stick. But instead of responding, she turned, looked out the window, and drank in the passing scenery. *Here we go again.* Is it a guy thing that when a woman ignores a foolish rant it causes him to pick a fight? Outburst or not, this really irritates me. Sometimes nothing is worse than something. For an argumentative person, that is.

Whatever the case, I acted like the motor had locked and the transmission had spilled its guts all over the highway when it only offered a hiccup. The transmission simply missed a calculated shift point. It's quite common in today's six, eight, and ten-speed transmissions regardless of the make or model.

And the Oscar goes to...the bald schmuck refusing a snack in the Brilliant Black Crystal Pearl coat Town & Country.

Without actually experiencing a mechanical issue that day, we came in smokin' hot into Ann Arbor. With celebratory hoots and hollers. We decided to stay the night in Ann Arbor because I had ridden the 3.6 like a stallion, and she needed a rest. Not to mention the thought of revisiting the Hilton

Garden Inn yanked us off the interstate. Posh and swanky, new, and upper class. We belonged. Or were scared into believing so after my fifteen-year class reunion. Any hotel would've outranked the janky no-tell we had endured in Warsaw. Stupid me procrastinated making reservations before the reunion, so we ended up having quite the memorable experience. But in my defense, second floor balcony side in the only place left available sounds good, right? Yeah, until the balcony proved to be a spongy walk-of-death held up by empty beer cans and crusty drug coolers. And was littered with passed out locals and cig butts paving the way to the murdery, musty room. Heather sat wide-eyed with panic nearly hyperventilating until dawn, wondering who would smash through the nicotine-filmed window a bloody mess smelling of skunk. Here's a great piece of advice: trust your gut. If there's a hole in the lobby ceiling the size of yer living room, yer guaranteed to be robbed of sleep. At best.

Anyway, if you're in love with deep dish pizza, the Pizza House in Ann Arbor is your ticket. This pizza joint is worth checking into. Just go before bar close. Ann Arbor's a college town. After midnight you're on your own. We decided on pizza and had satisfied our craving early that night, so I begged Heather for a premature turn in. Instead of lights out, she hit me with sarcasm.

"You can. I'm not goin' to bed this early. Jay-Jay can't run with the big dogs?"

"Hey! It's been a long day. Besides, the appointment's for 9 a.m. tomorrow. Otherwise, I'd stay up."

"Well, that was dumb."

"This train is leaving at 7 a.m."

"You shut yer mouth."

I had arranged to claim my prize early in the morning so we could enjoy the remainder of the day. Wherever the winds of excitement decided to blow us, we'd be ready to embrace the frenzy. But since I love structure and organization as much as freedom, I had set an appointment to ensure the best use of our time.

The Inside Scoop

If you know anything about the sales game, speaking the magical words *you've got the sale* always garners attention. No matter how stoic of a role a car salesman tries to play, you gotta understand one thing: a sale at the beginning of the month lights a salesman's fire. It breeds motivation to stalk the customer. Provides fuel to hound the looky-loos and tire kickers with postcards, phone calls, anything to keep the lines of communication open. And setting an appointment with a guarantee will hype the guy or gal up like nothing else. It has always paid off for me.

Besides, driving hundreds of miles to buy a car sight unseen without setting an appointment? Who does that? (Guilty as charged.)

Guarantee your spot of relevance if you're gonna buy the car. However, cars under five thousand usually get a person overlooked either way. Best of luck to ya. Maybe your adaptation of this narrative may help?

So, you do know I'm driving from Upper Michigan to buy this car. That's a long ride. I really don't need this thing, but it looks decent enough to drive. Yeah, I know it's not much money… Ok… Yup… I'll take the earliest appointment, that way I can get back on the road and you won't miss the big sale of the day when it walks in. I got yer best interest in mind, Sir, cause I'm throwing ya a sale—in and out—and freeing ya up for the lucky strike. Yup... Ha-ha… Yer the guy selling the cream puff that sat on the lot for almost a year. See, yer the hero! Yer boss will probably give you a raise! See? That alone'll bring you the lucky sale! Yup…I'll be safe…Ok…Yup. See you next Saturday.

What a schmoozer! Seldom had I shopped at the local dealerships because that's where I learned how to play the game. A person can't roll over on the teacher. It's game over at that point. Salespeople are a shrewd breed, and if one's looking to pull the proverbial wool, I've learned one's gotta leave town to do it.

You'll Be Fine

Slathering the butter on the staff who clutched my prize: easy. Convincing Heather she'd survive the forty-some mile hike back from the dealer to the Toledo airport: brutal. *Once the ring of keys tickles my palm, ditch the van in the scrap heap for all I care.* But that meant while I hot-rodded the freeway back north in my new car, Heather would have to drive the van back to Toledo. She wouldn't care about the ride if she remained a passenger. *Do what ya gotta do.* What had planted her backside in the bony, leg-numbing Town & Country in the first place? Getting out of town. Provided I drove. I had avoided the driving-in-a-big-city topic the whole way down, knowing my plans would implode the moment I failed to convince her of her competence the first go at it. Unfortunately, I knew persuading her would take finesse, something I lacked, so instead I skirted the subject for as long as I could. Then I dropped the bomb. Gently, of course. You know, tact with great renown…

Too late. Get over it, cuz you'll be fine. You didn't come along only as a passenger. Dork.

Then I reminded her of a trip we had taken to Chicago. The one where she punched me for drag racing the entire world in a worn-out grandma car. I owned my parent's early nineties Olds 98 with over 200,000 miles on the clock. Without a single concern for its age or mileage, I led the pack, swerving in and out of lanes at 80 plus miles an hour, using every available opening for advancement. Heather had rarely left her hometown, so picture the shade of white she sported as I tore down the interstate wheels a-blazin'. I had learned to drive near St. Louis, guys, so Carl Edwards took cues from me. As I squeezed between two semis while Heather nearly soiled her linens, the gas pedal just about pressed against the carpet, I educated my terrified student on how to draft and slingshot.

You gotta know the length of your car. Squeeze in, hold onto the gas, and then pull out like this.

Deep red pigment replaced the chalk white that had covered her face as she jabbed her tight fist into my right shoulder. Love convinced her to stop at one.

Who in her right mind clubs a race car driver at top speeds? Kinda life threatening, don't ya think? Now when the doctors ask, "Do you feel safe at home?" I gotta think twice and speak truthfully.

Love you, Babe.

Let's Go Get Her!

I sluggishly rolled outta bed the next morning like a teen on the weekend. Crawl. Whine. Yawn. Even the excitement of my waiting prize failed to motivate. Forty-five minutes into the hour-and-a-half drive, I had finally awakened the self-proclaimed race-car champion, and started compelling the 283 ponies under the hood of the kid hauler into a sprint like Seabiscuit. The throttle response was kinda impressive until the 62TE (transmission) bucked under the load. I remember thinking the guys at Dodge could reflash the TCM for better shift points, but then, why bother? I'd be taking out the trash in a few minutes. Furthermore, Heather's gentler approach would gracefully lull the kid hauler back to peace, so, it could rest then.

Moments later we arrived at the dealership, and I forced the shifter prematurely into park. Poor transmission grouched at me again. But there it was! Perfection glistening in the sunlight! The haunter of my dreams with blinding chrome rims! I must have looked like an idiot, drooling through the window of a bucking minivan halted by the parking pawl. But I didn't care.

The dark toreador red metallic. The glistening clearcoat accentuating alluring body lines. *An instant connection.*

"You going in?" snapped me back to reality. You guessed the tone.

Inside, handshake after annoying handshake commenced, and then several awkward minutes later, the anticipated question emerged.

"You wanna take her for a spin?"

"Yeah, I guess I could do that."

"I'll grab my jacket."

It's never good when the salesperson grabs a jacket. This means he or she is going with. And who wants that? When the salesman goes with, it's nonstop blabbing. Usually, a whole lot of nonsensical jargon working to sway the buyer.

How can I influence the decision? Lemme impress with fictitious facts…Maybe they won't catch me in a lie.

Truth be told, not all salespeople are like this, but how many have experienced such a display of unprofessionalism? *Know your facts.* Ask questions. Don't assume all salespeople have your best interest in mind. My advice to a salesperson: *Be honest and give a few details, but for crying out loud, don't flood a potential buyer with so much info, made up or not!*

Unsure of which one he'd be, annoying or helpful, I assumed the worst and bolted for the car. *Maybe he'd get the hint?* I admired as much of it alone as I could, ignoring his small talk as he walked until I heard the thud of the magnetic dealer plate adhering to the trunk. A wave of disgust mixed with nausea gut punched me. Hard. *Are you serious, dude? A magnetic plate on the clearcoat?! Yup, the annoying type.*

Every inch of that car he spewed baloney. I admit to several eye rolls and loud sighs while impatiently awaiting the test drive. *Please make it stop. Jason…Engage in conversation and it'll never stop; argue and it'll become a urinary distance contest.* So, I won another Oscar playing the role of a dense and inexperienced car buyer just to shift the focus off my disgust for his tactics. *Wow, you sure know your stuff. Thanks for sharing that with me.* He quit sharing his version of the truth after a bit of flattery which initiated the test drive. A classic move. The time had come for me to seem interested enough to keep him from walking back inside but nitpicky and largely dissatisfied in attempts to drive the price down. As he slid onto the tan leather behind me, I began to complain.

"Looks like there's quite the gouge on the bumper near the trunk."

"Yeah. The little old lady that traded this beauty confessed to dragging a suitcase over it."

"Gonna take quite a bit to fix that. I work for a paint company. This red is spendy."

"The car is solid otherwise. Not many flaws."

We rounded a corner and hit a sudden dip in the road.

"Feels like the rear shocks are soft. Probably air ride. Those are big money, you know." I knew what suspension carried us down the road. I continued to pretend. "Not sure it's worth putting a bunch of money into it."

"What ya think of her? She's a solid car. No trouble with these models. You'll get a lot of life outta her."

Not true. Long life with constant maintenance, maybe. The car was known for head gasket issues. Electrical problems. Radiator leaks. Crank sensor failure. To name a few. I knew what to anticipate.

"Kinda not what I expected. Lots of work. A few interior flaws to deal with. I don't know."

Heather shot me a puzzled glance. I winked. Reminds me of the verse in Proverbs that goes "'It's no good, it's no good!' says the buyer—then goes off and boasts about the purchase."

The back seat went silent as I whipped the car around and headed back to the dealership. What more could he say? He quickly got out when we arrived, and then asked if I wanted a moment to think about it while he attended to another customer. His pace toward the building spoke loudly, and I recognized his code. I had danced on a thin line. He'd move on if I pushed too hard.

"I'll be in in a minute. Thanks for going with."

I allowed him barely enough time to finish the handshake with his next client before I walked up and interrupted.

"We'll take it, but out the door, $4,500."

Not Again!

He motioned for us to follow him down a hall leading to the finance manager's office where he dumped us off and walked back to the showroom. Clearly, I had jabbed him too hard because his friendliness had turned strictly to business. But not the chatty finance manager. After a few minutes of his whirlwind gabbing, his-feet-up-on-the-desk demeanor complemented by his overstuffed-lounger-on-wheels office chair, I noticed he was in no hurry. Ever. I let him talk because I had already offended his colleague. *Please! Anywhere but in this guy's office! Oh, the perfect burn-out I could do on that steaming pavement!* But I knew if I wanted the lower out-the-door price, being rude would lessen the chances.

Didn't work. Minute by wasted minute we painstakingly digested every detail of the car-buying process. Something I had already done far too many times. I forced kindness out like juicing a lemon and dealt with his incessant gabbing. A few endearing smiles, a couple *Ha! I know what ya mean*s, hearty laughs; I was as fake as the hideous silk flowers sold at the dollar store.

An hour had passed before we left that office. But when the numbers aligned, I busted out before the ink had time to dry. With one hand full of documents and a pile of keys in the other, I strutted proudly down the hallway toward the exit. Before I made it to the door the weirdest celebration commenced. One right after another, dealership employees offered me a congratulatory handshake as if I had closed a long-awaited merger of two tech conglomerates. I awkwardly shuffled paperwork and keys back and forth before finally setting them down. *What in the world is going on? What's next? A camera crew and red carpet? How exhausting*. And then the weird scene abruptly ended. Old news. *Get out, peasant! We're done with you and your foolishness.* My palm connected with the glass door like a teenager escaping on the last day of school. Shoulders high and whiffing freedom. Get outta my way! Fresh air smelled sweet but would soon be heavy with CO2 emissions.

Remember, I knew nothing about that car other than the color and mileage and the little bits I had gained on the test drive. None of that mattered. The internet picture was the information I needed to form a ridiculous bond. Starter engaged, gear selected, rubber gripping pavement, exhaust thundering out the duals, Heather was left in the parking lot eating the byproduct of combustion. In the rearview sat an enormous gray and black cloud tinged with a hint of blue.

But all eight cylinders were just a singin', as I rocketed from the onramp onto I-75 North.

Oh, the adrenaline that coursed like nitrous through my veins as I pushed the pedal closer and closer to the floor. Teenage dreams had come true. The world had disappeared. And so did Heather. My heart sank as I scanned the mirrors to catch a glimpse of the familiar front end. *I'm never gonna hear the end of this!* Then she appeared. Rapidly closing the gap, I might add. Hotroddin' the kid hauler like a pro! And I gotta admit, my love for her, gearhead style, flourished that day. Heather had spanked her fears, enslaved the throttle, and owned the freeway. What a day!

As suspected, she wasn't impressed that I had dusted her, but later laughed it off with her usual *you suck* while we transferred everything to my Merry Oldsmobile. Glowing with pride with my wife riding shotgun again, I left the van in the past and began reliving the Chicago trip as we headed north. But this time she seemed pleased. *Was it my purchase? Would this be the car that would light her fire?* Not a chance. Ensuing conversation spoke of the truth. Being a passenger again is what afforded the smile.

The King Has Arrived

I was a changed man that day when we rolled into the hotel parking lot. I had become royalty, and everyone was breathlessly awaiting our majestic entrance.

Full disclosure—no one noticed. Except the fella exiting his fresh-off-the-lot Audi A8. Was it the car's beauty that garnered his attention? Maybe a fellow enthusiast thinking *man, where'd you pick up that beauty*? Dream on. He observed the horrendous scraping noises coming from the front end. That's what turned his head. So much for a grand and impressive arrival.

"Must be lot rot." I rallied to convince myself and Heather as I pumped the brake pedal like a lunatic. *Dude! Be quiet! You're killing my image.*

"What was that?!"

A shocking crunch filled the cabin that overrode the grinding by a mile. For those who are unaware, the ride height of the Aurora is rather low. This self-proclaimed aficionado announced his true amateur status by blasting the sidewalk as I parked. And as if resting the front end atop the concrete wasn't enough, I did what everyone seems to do in that situation... replayed the sound by immediately reversing it off the sidewalk.

Oh, my poor car!

I whimpered as I whipped the door open and poked my head toward the pavement. The Audi guy still watching the comedic freak show. Subconsciously, I knew that one can't see the nose of a car from the driver's seat, but I continued to bob my head up and down attempting to assess the damage. I'm convinced amused onlookers would've paid a premium for a chance to take cheap shots at my intelligence while watching the circus act. And what came next. Heather, ignoring her husband's usual tirade, searched for a trunk button. And for anything that'd rescue her from the raving crackpot who had crawled out of the car and had commenced bouncing around like a crouched monkey looking for a fight. The road rash was minimal, the fog light bezel had signature concrete bite marks, but I lamented the injury like I'd torn off the entire front cover. *You idiot! Only two seconds into ownership and you've already rammed your dream car into a cement wall.*

"Come on, Babe. It's fine."

"No, it's not!"

I kept turning around and looking at my diamond-now-rough masterpiece as I walked toward the lobby. Half swelling with pride and the other half in sackcloth and ashes mourning its recent step down from perfection.

It's Not a Delorean, But It'll Do

Punch 1995 into the keypad. There's my sixteen-year-old self, wandering the streets of Rolla, Missouri in a sun-faded and scraped-up gray lacquer 87 Cutlass Supreme two door! I look bored out of my mind. Where am I going? Oh, yeah! That's the day I spot the all-new-in-95 Aurora. Take a left! The Olds dealer is up and around the bend. Slow down, slow down! Well, if you would have slowed down you wouldn't have had to mash on the brakes. There's your new weekly habit/obsession. It's gonna cost you only a few gallons of gas a week, so keep going. Your buddy with the vintage Camaro will understand but the other guys are gonna ride you for not hanging and playing video games anymore. Quick! Drop to the ground before the salesman sees you, the lanky dork with humongous feet crawling *around on the ground around a $45,000 luxury car. Too late. Don't worry, he won't come out.*

Attention employees of the dealership, ignore the dork in the gray beater.

While I could only dream, each week some suit would parade his new copy defiantly past me, poking at my poverty with his glossy flagship. But instead of losing hope, I continued to search the dealer lot for models with new interior colors, admired once again the aluminum wheels compared to the chrome, and dreamed of the copy I'd buy when my time was right. What a pastime for a poor boy!

Earth to Jason

"It's just a car, Babe!" Heather suggested.

How long had I stood there?

"You're right, I just like it."

Almost defeated that she seemingly snubbed my treasure, I defended my new love as we entered the same ultra-modern lobby of the Hilton. New memories were scheduled for production, so I parked the obsession out of my head and back where it belonged: outside.

Are you sick of that dumb Olds yet? I don't think I'll ever be. Maybe you're confused on how perfect timing intersects with this car story. I promise, a used car purchase, the hip hotel—the story's been building. Besides, as I'm editing this story for the tenth time, I'm trimming the rambling. Thanks, Myra and my editor, for teaching me the KISS method. Keep. It. Short. Stupid.

Remember When?

Remember when checking in on Facebook bought you a label? *Ooh, trendy! Now you've graduated to the IN crowd.*

Hey, I'm getting my car washed. Gotta check in at Great North Auto Wash.

Yup, grabbing my prescriptions. Checking in at Walgreens, ya'll.

Kickin' it at Pizza Hut. Bet you wish you were eating bread-sticks, too...

You get the picture. We craved status back then like Black Friday shoppers clawing for the last coveted Chia Pet. *Don't worry about shutting the hotel door. It'll slam itself. Get checked in on Facebook before you lose your chance at relevance.* Although we subscribed, the craze implied bondage to society to me.

Was it to build jealousy? *Hey, focus on me. I'm living a life you wish you had.* Maybe for some.

Or was it fear? *You know guys, I might be kidnapped at any moment, so I need you to always know my exact whereabouts.* (I may have gone a bit too far on that one...or did I?)

Maybe it asserted socioeconomic status. *Aha! You thought I was too poor to have a bangin' life like this. Bet you feel dumb, eh?*

I'm genuinely unsure of why I checked in. I had never broadcasted my every move, even before it became the fad, but follow the in crowd, right? Gotta fit in somehow.

Regardless of our intent, we hung out and relaxed our cares away, surfing through the news feeds on Facebook ad nauseum and blaring some 80's movie on the tv. Well, shortly before the trip I had found a high school friend on Facebook whom I had lost contact with. She had posted some vague news about her life, but the post caught my eye because I had spent many nights after my high school reunion reconnecting with former classmates. I wanted to learn more about them. Who had they become? What had their life turn out to be like? Friending them became a sport, and Facebook made it easy. I decided to continue media stalking my friend, Mindy.

"Hey Babe. Remember Mindy?"

"From the credit union?"

"No. My friend from high school. The one I just friended."

"Oh, yeah. Why?"

"Where's Romulus?"

"I think it's near here. Look it up. Why do you ask?"

"She checked in at Romulus, Michigan. I know she lives downstate. Somewhere near Detroit."

"We're near Detroit, Jay. Send her a message."

Why didn't I think of that? Mindy had left Bourbon the year before my family had moved from Indiana to Missouri, so I had lost all contact. *Should I, or shouldn't I?* My heart pounded as I typed a quick message and smashed send. *No going back now!*

Mindy was the kind of friend everyone wanted in school. Loyal. Kind. Sassy. So sassy. Genuine. Truthful…very truthful. After a few minutes had passed, she responded. *Add responsive to the list.* As I read her reply my eyes widened.

"She's only a half hour away from here. And she said she wants to drive over!"

Excitement shot the words out my face like buckshot. Shocked that the stars had aligned, I rambled nervously all the anxieties surrounding seeing her again. It had been twenty years. *Would she still like me? Wait a sec. Did she even like me at all? I was a dope in school.* Many only tolerated my oddness. *Did we have a childhood feud to settle? Why couldn't I remember? She seemed nice enough on social media. How much had we changed? I'll impatiently await her arrival. Then accept the version that walks through the door.*

To prepare for the unexpected, Heather and I found a seat in the spacious lobby and ordered a drink. One would suffice. Just to calm the nerves and appear chill, I thought. And when Mindy arrived alongside her son and fiancé, I relaxed even more. *Oh, good. More is better. Just Mindy, Heather, and me would've been awkward. The fact that she came on a whim at 8 pm, fearless. Exactly what I remember!*

Hugs and enthusiastic greetings rang out for several minutes, and then conversations got awkward for a bit. But mysteriously the jitters cleared like midmorning fog, displacing uneasiness with laughter, crazy stories, and life. We hadn't changed a whole lot, only aged. Laughter had etched our faces. Stress had popped the familiar crow's feet next to our eyes. And gray. *Let's not talk about the gray.* Evidence of a hard yet fulfilling life had painted both our expressions. And as time fleeted, robbing us of our intent to spill every detail of our vastly different existences, the laughter ceased, tears dried up, the kidding ended. *What a night!* And before the goodbyes left our lips, we made each other promise that another twenty years wouldn't pass without at least dropping each other a line.

Let's Get Physical

"You got a great gal. Hang onto her" I softly spoke while shaking Noble's hand. Somehow, she meant more to me than I had realized, but it took that night to prove it. Long after the lobby door slid shut and the dark night swallowed the taillights of her Buick, I pondered her personality, her friendship, the joy of that night. And then the recollection flew in of the time she had horribly embarrassed me in front of the whole gym class. Warmup stretches, 7th grade, I was alongside Mindy in the lineup. Every time she said something, I mocked her word for word. And honestly, I mean no disrespect, but she was quite vocally animated back then, and I wanted a piece of the action ripping on her for it. She asked me to stop several times. *Not a chance, Lady!* After a couple more unheeded warnings, she turned to threatening. "I will pants you in front of everyone if you don't shut it!" Nope, didn't work. I kept taunting her with little noises and comments until she abruptly yanked my drawers straight to the floor. Red faced and put solidly in my place, I never challenged Miss Mindy again!

A Mind Is A Battlefield

The more I dwelt on that evening, our newly kindled friendship, the more mixed up my feelings got. I doubted the way I felt, her sincerity, my judgements, and I allowed trust and happiness to battle sorrow and apprehension for the spotlight.

"What's the matter, Jay?"

Concealing emotions has never been my strong suit because Heather has always been able to read the worry spelled all over my face. But I only spilled to her a half-truth that night.

"I don't know when we'll get to see them next. I had such a good time. And Mindy has it together and look at me, I'm a mess. Hard to let her go, I guess."

"That's not true. We'll find a way. Yeah, you're a mess."

I immediately noticed her words *we'll find a way* but kept quiet. *Mindy was our friend!* Before I mentioned her to Heather, I feared a marital storm, fierce winds of resentment, jealousy, and misunderstanding, if I pursued her friendship. Any woman showing an ounce of interest—a smile, simple dialog beyond hi and goodbye, a random act of kindness—sounded the intruder alarms. *Suit up. Full tactical. Machete in hand. War paint.* Heather safeguarded her man, her happiness, her world against all threats, perceived or true. And I'd explode. T*here's NO ROOM for jealousy in our relationship! NO ROOM!* Followed by a prolonged silence meant to drive my point into her subconscious. I blamed her for her distrust of me. But it wasn't until the women on her radar widened my eyes that I began to understand her reaction. The woman at Holiday who squeezed the pompon on my winter hat, and then brushed my face with the back of her hand. She was the one who rested her revealing top half through the open passenger window of my car while leaning in to say, *Hi, Hon. How you doin' today?* And then the ex-coworker who extended an awkward hug far too long, ending it with her hands on the small of my back. I had been naïve thinking they were innocent, and the woman I loved had the trusting issue. I doled out trust like the neighbor handing Halloween candy to the cutest kid. And to everyone. Each of those historical figures sported marriages dashed upon the rocks. Their boats were sinking, and they were grabbing at every life preserver from many different angles.

But the alarms in our marriage remained untriggered with Mindy. Heather latched onto her the same way I had. And why? Because Mindy encouraged love. Promoted a solid relationship. She wasn't out for a rebound like the freeloading water treaders of my past. They'd struck up a friendship because they cherished the same values. No wonder I had admired Mindy back in my school years. I'd later marry a woman of her caliber. What a true blessing! And peace for my troubled mind.

We'll Be Back

The following morning as we crammed our luggage into the trunk, I envisioned walking back into the hotel. We'd be back. Fellowship with Mindy, Noble, and Garrett would resurface. And that vision warmed my heart. However, if I could offer the troubled guy loading his car a heads up about the vision that day, I'd say this…*you're gonna return many times. Mostly in a wheelchair and riddled in pain, but the friendship knot will strengthen to unbreakable. Quit worrying. Just trust.*

Hand Me The Junk Food Bag

Undoubtedly, road trips are rowdy and memorable. Music blaring. Molars crunching chips. Pop bottles hissing and caps rethreading. Laughter, singing, and heart-to-hearts. And corn nuts. Don't forget the corn nuts. But sometimes there's silence. Only the hum of the tread patterns methodically singing against the porous asphalt. That's when I do my best thinking.

Why had we been so lucky to cross paths? It had been ages. What had caused our connection? There had to be a reason. What would come of our friendship?

I had already learned the hard way that always asking why is a-thief-in-the-night mistake, but I couldn't escape it. *There's gotta be a reason. Good things don't just happen for a guy like me.* And for hours I scratched that itch like a mosquito bite.

Please listen to me when I say this—*precious memories fade when you chase the why question. Joy dissipates on the endless search for explanations.* As Solomon repeatedly informs the reader throughout Ecclesiastes, "Meaningless. A chasing after the wind." Mile after mile, over 800 tire rotations per minute, the exhausted Michelins hauled my worry-laden mind homeward.

"Babe, you still wanna stay in Petoskey for the night? I gotta take this exit if you do."

Heather had been dozing off for a while, and I hated to wake her, but she had devised a plan earlier in the day to break up the trip and give the grandpa car a rest.

"If you want to. I'm good either way."

By the end of the exit ramp, the brake rotors went silent for the first time since buying the car. What a relief for the both of us! I'm fearless for the most part, but we had climbed into a car built in the previous decade, bet a full hand, and let the wheel spin. No warranty to fall back on. Roadside assistance unpromised. Trusting those noisy brakes was completely out of character for me, especially learning my lesson after hitting a pasty shop when the brake pedal went to the floor. I was nervous wreck up until that point.

Built In Bounce House

But when the punishing commenced on the horrendously rough US-131 N, we both did nothing but laugh. The rear shock absorbers had dampened for the last time, causing the tail end to bounce like a kid in a bounce house. However, instead of getting angry about it, I slowly applied the brakes, hoping it would slow the bounce, and continued to laugh until I cried. The brake maneuver and slowing the car down didn't help. The back end continued to hop all over the road like a frog on hot pavement. We musta looked like giggling goons on a trampoline, traversing 131 at 40mph. No matter what speed I chose, the suspension misbehaved so badly that we crawled our way north and back onto smoother highways. Forget the cars passing us and honking until they passed. And just embrace the discomfort from being jostled around. We had bought and paid for the ride of our life! I do admit the pounding headache from being repeatedly launched brain first into the loosening headliner for thirty plus miles became quite intense. And replacing the rear shocks the moment we got home became dire.

Sit There And Relax

A year passed, four flat tires and a dead battery later, the Aurora sat in the yard untouched while the detested Uplander still disgraced our driveway. All the vehicles we owned needed repairs at that point. Three car payments were draining the reserve. So were monthly insurance premiums. One had to go. *It won't be the Aurora. I'll see to that. 122 miles on the odometer in a year's time? No way!* The only fun I had driving the car had been the Ann Arbor trip. *Why did I buy that car? Had I jumped the gun figuring the van would sell?* But how could we sell it? Every opportunity it had it kicked an engine light and stalled. Or mysteriously opened one of the rear sliding doors and horrified the toddler sitting on that side. Who wanted a van that acted possessed?

Number 6,239,543. Your mission in life should you choose to accept it: torment the Brunette family. Stop at nothing, every idea is permissible. And if they try to dump you, resist.

Regardless of what rang true about any of the vehicles, one had to go. They were all on the chopping block. Each had their merits, but the only saving grace for the Aurora was reconnecting with Mindy. The van fit the family better, but we all hated it.

Bed Full Of Empty Attempts

"Hey, Babe. Let's refocus our plan on selling a vehicle. I'm gonna put the truck up for sale. We gotta lose one."

"But I like the truck."

"I do too. But I don't want all these payments, and I can't drive the Olds until we slim down. We got a trip to save for and the bank's getting our excess."

"Do it."

With her blessing, a desperate attempt commenced. I ran a newspaper ad. Created an attractive Craigs List posting. Found one of the busiest sections of highway M35 and parked it there for higher visibility. I figured two days, tops, and I'd have a buyer. A 2002 F150 four door, black, running boards and the FX4 off road package, Lariat leathered up with a sunroof should sell fast. And with low miles for the model year and little rust. An easy sell. But my two-day guess turned into weeks and then into months. Not even a bite. Obviously not salesman of the year! When I brought it home totally deflated, I saw red reflecting in the clear coat every time I walked by it.

One evening I stood outside with Heather staring at the headaches parked in the drive and wished for a break in the struggle. We bounced ideas off each other, but it quickly turned into a vomit session of hate. Heather, disgruntled and defeated, endured the rant quietly until I shocked her with the truth.

"The ONLY thing I haven't done is given this whole mess to God. I haven't asked Him for help."

Our eyes met; both our eyebrows lifted in shock.

"Where'd THAT come from?" Heather questioned completely puzzled.

Wasn't that the ticket dangling in front of my face all along? "Commit to the LORD whatever you do, and He will establish your plans." Proverbs 16:3.

"Maybe we should have prayed about this."

The bombshell still plastered her face with shock after I said it, but we both bowed our heads, and I began to pray out loud.

"LORD, I have put the truck in the paper, had it by the road with a huge for sale sign, put it on the internet, and still no buyer. I cannot keep making payments on all three. I'm sorry I was so hasty to buy another vehicle, but I felt like the trip was a lot of fun. But I quit. I can't do anything else to sell this truck. If You want the truck gone, You've gotta sell it. I've tried everything except ask for Your timing. Will You forgive me and help me?"

Desperation soaked the prayer as tears stained Heather's shirt. I had finally recognized my part in God's plan to solve our financial woes. And it wasn't the madman approach I'd taken. It was to trust and rely on God's timing after I committed my plans to Him. I knew we weren't in danger of losing any of the vehicles. Money wasn't tight back then, but we were financially bleeding. But developing patience in the LORD was on the roster, and I had finally registered for the class. I would wait on the LORD come what may.

Constant Winds Of Change

Despite all the time that had passed since the Ohio trip and the craziness life had thrown at me, I continued to sporadically reminisce the evening with Mindy. In a time where I had waged war with drama and emotionally draining relationships, God had orchestrated relief in His perfect timing. Through a night of blessing filled with laughter, relationships, and friendships, everything I had given up on became worth saving that night. Surprisingly, we all had grown from that impromptu visit, and the evidence would soon surface.

Day by day my life continued to change. I quit my job at Keystone and accepted a new position at Carquest. I sought advancement and ongoing training with compensation back then. Truthfully, as much money as I could make and the avenue to make it. And all of it seemed to fall in line. Weeks into my new job, my manager announced further management training in Wausau, so I fired up the Aurora and headed to Wisconsin.

Here's The Plan And How To Do It

Despite feeling lonely the entire trip, the training was incredible. I immersed myself to the point of exhaustion and sponged as much detail as I possibly could. I had witnessed the disorganization and chaos wreaking havoc on my home store, so when I could eat off the floors in the Wausau store, inspiration soaked my bones. *I'm gonna become the best manager in Michigan, starting with a thorough cleaning. And then I gotta tackle that filing system.* The list populated quickly. Build morale. Reorganize the sales floor. Add more shelves in the warehouse. Training kept me busy; however, when I clocked out the first day, boredom set in before I left the parking lot. In a town of roughly 30,000 people, none of which I knew, the week of weeknights cast a daunting anxiety. As I sat at the counter of a Denny's next to my hotel, I choked down a burnt breakfast skillet with my head resting like The Thinker statue guy. The bustling waitress kindly engaged me in the usual *hi, where are ya from* stuff, but it wasn't the conversation I wanted. I tried texting random family and friends but got no response. And then Mindy entered my thoughts. It had been a while, but I welcomed any kinda chat. *Score!* I remembered I had tucked her number away in my wallet for over a year. I had forgotten to program it, so I dug it outta the zippered pouch just ecstatic to have possible company. It would've been easier to chat online through Messenger, but back then data plans were stingy, and I was out of minutes. I'd hafta text. And text we did. We spent hours discussing our lives and the lessons we had learned from the cherished night in Ann Arbor. Long enough that the waitress quit asking if I wanted refills on coffee. I thought I had been the sole pupil learning valuable lessons, but I was wrong. I'll honor anonymity and sum up her replies: she had gained a renewal of faith. Multiple blessings for both of us had been waiting in the wings of God's mercy that could only be released that night. And sometimes when we're asked to wait on those blessings, we complain and curse them with our disbelief. *As if we know best.* We agreed that He makes no mistakes.

Millions repeat this but very few believe it wholeheartedly. But I'm one who is certain of it now.

I can't thank God enough for including me in His plan for Mindy and Noble. The precious memories that cultivated our friendship has helped carry me through this illness. And without His perfect timing, bringing me to the right place at the right time, self-discovery might have been delayed for much longer by foolish doubt. And like Mindy, I had received a renewal of my faith. Faith in God. Faith in people. A renewal strong enough to glue back together the shattered trust pieces I had scattered throughout my past. A renewal solid enough to prevent further willful loss. And the best gift? Being allowed to witness God's miraculous perfect timing in loved ones' lives. Seeing provisions appear that were otherwise considered unavailable.

Get a load of this: He sometimes uses a less-than-qualified person in His perfect plan. ME! *To answer Your question, God, do I believe in Your perfect timing? Yes, Sir! Thanks for patiently showing me why I should!*

The time has come for me to divorce myself of human impatience and wait on God's plan without complaint. That way I can accept His timing as a blessing and not a curse.

"Trust in the LORD with all thine heart; and lean not unto thine own understanding. In all thy ways acknowledge Him and He shall direct thy paths." Proverbs 3:5-6 KJV

How About You?

Is trusting God without reservation valuable to you, or do you have doubts surrounding God's perfect timing in your life? Maybe you have a perfect timing story that baffles, but you have shelved it because it caused you to see doubles. *Get that puppy out and share it!* If you don't have a story, maybe this will inspire you to trust God more freely…

Three days after asking God to help us sell the truck, it sold. A guy showed up while I was outside and asked if I had a truck for sale. When I asked him if he had seen it in the paper or alongside the road, he said neither. He was driving by and saw it in the yard and wondered if it was for sale.

How's that for perfect timing?

Chapter 11

←

DOUBLES?

You know what's a fun word to say? Doppelganger. It's almost as fun as saying Hasselhoff or Liechtenstein. Do you know what it means? It's a fancy German word for doubles. I've heard this word said numerous times over the years, and it somewhat intrigued me because it refers to the idea that everybody has a double somewhere on the planet. But…*Nah, that's just a silly delusion cooked up to wow the tabloids.*

Or so I thought.

To my bewilderment, everywhere in the mystical land called Marshfield lived doppelgangers to friends and family of mine. Ok, there wasn't a single thing mystical about it. I'll straighten up. Homesickness or just a simple resemblance might be a good explanation, but whatever the case, each of them left me scratching my head in amazement. I'm gonna need more evidence; I'm not a firm believer in the "mystery twins" concept yet. But, weirdly enough, after each time meeting a perceived double, I wondered whose twin would be next.

Remember Nurse Donna? The first time she came into my room, she walked right over to the dry erase board and started doodling. Then her phone rang, and quickly out the door she went without finishing her edits to the board. A few moments later, she popped back in, but then the phone rang again, and out she went for a second time. *Who is this lady?! She keeps runnin' off.* On a Dime Donna is what I began to refer to her as. Roughly forty minutes passed before she finally had the chance to introduce herself. The first person she reminded me of was my neighbor, Jackie, who also has brown hair about shoulder length, glasses, same height and build.

You already know Donna's kind and tenderhearted, well, so is Jackie, but neither of them is a pushover, though. Try telling these ladies they're wrong when it's clear they're right, you better expect the claws to come out. Nah, no claws, but get ready to adjust your thought patterns a bit. And don't worry. You won't have to guess what they're thinking because they're both straightforward. Neither of them is selfish in their attempts, but only determined to share the truth. What a breath of fresh air. Donna had transported me, the moment we finally connected, back to the white wooden fence separating our houses where I was gabbing with Miss Jackie. Donna spent every extra spare moment she could with me. Every morning she'd start her shift by organizing my things and tidying up the room. When encouragement cards came, she read them aloud to me, gave the balloons a tussle, and then scurried off. And returned with an extra snack, daily. She kept a watchful eye on her friend, just like Miss Jackie.

"And if you need any tools, just grab them outta the garage. Tom don't mind. Put them back, though."

The day she texted me at the home to tell me she was gonna take care of my yardwork while I was away, I accepted her kindness without hesitation because I knew how it'd go if I didn't.

"Hey, Jay. It's Jack. I'm gonna mow your grass while you're in the hospital."

"Oh, Miss Jackie. Thank you, but you don't have to do that. Dylan can try with Heather's help."

"No, he's not gonna do that. Why stress Heather out?"

"He's gotta learn some time, and you have lots to do yourself."

"Well, you're not here, and I've got the mower out. Don't be stubborn. What are you gonna do? Push mow it yourself in your wheelchair? I'll talk to you later. It'll be done. Click."

And just as promised, later in the summer when I arrived back home, my yard resembled hers. Beautiful, healthy, and well-groomed. *Disregard the brown patches and missing chunks since I refuse to water and fertilize, thatch, and spray for weeds.* When half the siding has fallen off, and several of the basement windows are busted because you've dropped your hammer from the scaffolding one too many times, forget the yard. Just climb back into bed at that point.

And, neighbor Cortney, you're included in this story, too! Thanks for teaming with Jack to maintain my yard, and so many other things. You've ALWAYS had our back through thick and thin!

The Home

The amount of people in a nursing home setting is mind boggling. I gave up trying to remember everyone's name who either walked through my door or walked by it. I should've had an old polaroid and a sharpie. But there were those choice few who left a lasting impression, and I'll never forget their names. One such impression came the day Aide C flung the door wide and strolled in. We'll call her Cora. (Ever watch the movie *Quigley Down Under*? The one where Laura San Giacomo plays Crazy Cora? Spirited doesn't even begin to describe San Giacomo's character.)

My heart raced with excitement when I looked up to see who caused all the commotion. At first glance, I thought I saw my niece, Katy. She would've been the last person I would have expected to visit, but I swore it was her. Until she announced her intentions before I could slip on my glasses.

"I'm Cora. I need your weight."

That gal's energy and charisma flowed into every room, nook, and cranny of the facility. It seemed the whole building warmed up when she clocked in. No one was exempt from her charm. She'd joke with everyone, offer a warm embrace, an extra heated blanket; she raised the mood from dreary to cheery. That girl wielded the magic touch. *Hey! There's the mystical part I alluded to in the beginning!* Even the crabby old cuss down the way on the left sported a wide grin whenever she bounded down the halls. How could he resist her bubbly nature? The same could be said about my niece, Katy, when she was a little shaver. The day I met her for the first time, she demonstrated her full-of-life—that's what I'll call it—nature. The family lovingly called her—Hurricane Kate. Barely two years old, the mischievous fire in her eyes roared ferociously. Although she was glued tight to Auntie Heather's hip, she'd bust away every chance she could get to seize the moment and prove she was in the house. Completely unpredictable, sometimes good, other times really bad, she always caused a smile. Well, mostly after she left. You know, the kid who makes you laugh until you cry and cry until you laugh? Katy. Over the years I've had the privilege to watch her strong-willed personality blossom, still fun-loving, *can't tell her much*, but just as fiery as the day I met her. I guess it's true that blondes have more fun. *Or was it redheads have more fun?* Either way, those girls' rosy cheeks and chubby little faces, infectious smiles and personalities were adorable and full of surprises. One thing's for sure: you'll have a memorable day should you be blessed to have either of them in it.

The Love Of Family

Speaking of family, my sister-in-law's twin worked as an aide at the Home. One night Aide M walked into my room; I did a double take that caught her attention. We'll call her Marsha.

"Didya miss something? What ya need?" She questioned me like my sister-in-law, Char, would. Full of sass, sarcastic, yet lovable. You know the type of person who almost offends you with his or her blunt nature but somehow, you're drawn in and want more? You can't fire back with even half the skill because he or she is too quick witted, yet you somehow enjoy the banter. Well, it all depends on the day and mood because sometimes sarcasm and sass can toss an edgy person off the cliff. *I would know because Ticking Time Bomb is another one of my middle names some days.*

Both these ladies have no interest in offending people for sport; their natures are loving and playful. But for a person who teeters on the edge of accepting a joke and emotionally sensitive, both these ladies are small dose until one becomes less crybaby. Just speaking from experience. One chooses to be offended. *Sis, if you are reading this...I just gave you a compliment!*

Well, Marsha and I became best buds. She refused to enter my room without harassing me, and I loved it. Felt like walking into Char's house back home.

Do you know the kind of pestering I'm talking about? Or am I rambling again? Picture it like this if you don't understand. Allow your feisty friend to pour into your cup love and provocation from the same pitcher. Raise the glass to your mouth. As you do, your friend smacks the bottom of the glass as you tip it back, causing you to frantically gulp the contents and spill the majority of it all down your face and shirt. And while you choke and spit everywhere, your friend laughs hysterically while handing you a towel. *First day drinking water?* Yup. To the letter. Char and Marsha.

But because of Marsha's familiar way of comforting, processing my loneliness in a healthy way became easier. *Remember the good times in the middle of the bad. Don't dwell on the heartache, focus on the belly laugh.* I looked forward to the evenings when she'd work. I needed the harassment to keep going, and she sensed it. But just like Sissy, I learned to avoid Marsha's hot buttons. Kind as she was, in an argument she was relentless. And truth be told I'd hate to see either of them in a dark alley after kicking sand at the helpless kids in the sandbox!

One evening while engaged in a showdown against cramps and muscle spasms throughout my whole body, Marsha sided with the nurse, and sarcastically suggested I quit the stubborn act and accept a pain pill. I barked out some ridiculous rebuttal; she whipped around and shot me a fierce look and said, "Have it your way, son. When you smarten up, hit the call button." Then she left the room. There were no gray areas with Marsha. Cut and dry. Black and white.

Marsha never argued to just argue or prove an absurd point. She spoke up about her beliefs. Many remain quiet and stew inside, allowing others to mow them over. And then become resentful because *nobody understands me and my opinions.* Well, share them! Society often classifies people like her as an irrelevant pot stirrer. *She won't hold her opinions, and they don't align with societal norm. Rubbish.* Does this mean an opinionated person should be considered a menace if he or she won't keep the trap shut? It takes all kinds to make the world go around. Or so they say. So, I say, drop the judgement and recognize that most would do nearly anything for someone in need. And then pester him or her for it. *Lighten up and have a little fun. Or walk away. And without labels.*

I Won't Let You Barf

To prove my point, listen to what she did for me one night. I was extremely nauseous from the pain I was in, and nothing seemed to help. Most days when nausea had set in, my pain level would be at a six or seven, but that night I blew past that, nearly reaching nine. I had no clue what was going on, and I was becoming desperate. Marsha popped in before her shift, inquiring how she could help.

"What can I do? Want a Sprite? Did they give you the anti-nausea pill, yet?"

I've never been a pop drinker, so I gently turned it down.

"Well, then. What do YOU do when this happens? How can I help you? Tell me how, and I'll do it."

"Yeah. That hasn't even touched it. Will you hand me the bucket?

What a sweetie she is. She wouldn't give up.

"You gonna tell me? They said you can't eat, you can't drink. We gotta do something."

I had to give an answer, or she'd drag it outta me. If that isn't my Sissy!

"I usually drink cilantro and lime mixed in water. I know it sounds strange, but the compounds in cilantro tell your stomach to behave, and..."

"Well, that's a new one" she interjected before I could finish.

You at home, try it. It's not that bad. I grind the cilantro and lime wedges together, mix in the water, and freeze the potion in ice cube trays. And *poof,* a safe and natural antacid.

To my surprise she left the room! *Did I freak her out with my enchanted brew?!* I wasn't quite sure what to make of her exit, but I figured she had spent enough time dawdling in my room. A few minutes later something in the parking lot grabbed my attention, and then I noticed Marsha driving away in her car! I'll be a monkey's uncle if she didn't run to Pick 'n Save, grab the fresh ingredients, and whittle me up a potion. I'll forever remember that night for the rest of my life. When people genuinely love and care about the welfare of others, they'll do whatever it takes to see them through a tough situation, even if they don't understand it. I'll also never forget her hugs, the love in her eyes, and the affectionate words she spoke over me the day I left the home. *How could you have so easily loved a stranger like your own son, Miss Marsha?* God bless my devoted friend. And my Sissy, too!!

STAND BACK! I'LL DO IT!

Making mention of running to Pick 'n Save brings me to Therapist P. Let's call her Peggy. During one of my mom's visits, this lady barges into my room and busts up our conversation with an unexpected announcement. "Hi, I'm Peggy. I'm an Occupational Therapist and you're on my schedule. You ready?" Hesitant and still processing her boldness, I sat somewhat speechless on my bed, wondering what would become of me that day. "I'll give ya a moment to collect your thoughts. I'll be right back" she said as she left the room. Mom and I looked at each other, and I kid you not, we both said *Mary* at the same time. In a flash, she was back and pounding the woodgrain off the door. As she rounded the corner, her mouth was firing off questions. I attempted to answer the drillings but made a grave error: I replied in a doubtful tone. She pounced on me like a lion on a bounding gazelle.

"What do you mean you don't know. Why haven't you demanded answers yet?"

The shredding relentlessly continued with only a moment in between each sentence for me to answer, or for her to catch her breath. Blood and guts were flying.

"You aren't settling, are you? Cause you can't do that. You're too young to sound this defeated. You need to stand up for yourself and get the answers."

Just like the others…same height, same age bracket, glasses, exact hair style, demeanor. The pouncing lioness resembled Miss Mary to the letter.

Say you've been looking for a fix for a problem you've been complaining about, but you keep comin' up short, so you've called it quits. You spill the issue to Mary in passing, and that you're unaware of any resolve, so you've given up the pursuit. Big mistake! Mary's the type that'll keep nudging you until you take care of it. Even if a month of Sundays goes by and she hasn't seen you, the moment her eyes spot you in a crowd, it's on! *Hey,*

Jay. How you been? Did you call a plumber yet? He'll be able to find a leak like that. It's gotta be in the drain because it swelled the cabinet bottom, but it's gonna ruin the linoleum and subfloor. And then you'll be complaining about that, too. Want me to call him for you? I'll tell him what I think it is.

How does one avoid a friend like her? Say no and never hear the end of it? Further reinforced by why nots and disdainful looks. Literally *don't come crying to me if you're unwilling to take the necessary steps.* Or simply fib and avoid the subject? She won't allow any of it. People like Mary are goal and task oriented and programmed to find a resolve. Mary has gone to major lengths in some cases in my life through hours of research, phone calls, reaching out to doctors on my behalf…anything to ease my mind and lighten the load. And Peggy, being cut of the same passionate cloth, did the same. The moment I revealed I had no idea of the date and time of my upcoming appointments at the Clinic, she stormed off to the nurse's station in search of the answers. Forget the exercises she had instructed; she was bent on keeping me in the know. With instructions written on ripped-up scratch paper in hand, she rushed into my room, pressed the wad into my palm, and bid me good luck. And then back out the door she went, and I never saw her again. After the dust had settled, and I reviewed the info several times, Mom and I repeated with a hearty chuckle, *Mary*. What a whirlwind!

Speaking Of Whirlwind

Every double I met was incredibly uplifting in a time when I thought all was lost. What a blessing and joyful reminder that I was never alone. But this story would be incomplete without my one-of-a-kind friend, Jody. There's none her equal. Maybe you've met or have a friend somewhat like her. Maybe you haven't. But she's someone quite unique. She's that friend who listens with love and support. Cries when you cry. Rips on ya and then hoots and fist pumps the air to lighten the mood. A tornado of epic proportions.

When I first met Jody, her large personality intimidated me. I didn't know what to do with all her energy. After hiding behind protective walls for years, a person like her obviously shocked my system. *You can't hide from her enthusiasm in life.* But she drew me out and welcomed me in. And it only took a few times hanging out and absorbing her vibes before the cows flew and the roof peeled off. Fear of being hurt got sucked up into the funnel cloud and was blasted hundreds of miles away. Love for my crazy new friend kindled a warmth in my heart that only Heather had the power to previously ignite. Loud noises and boisterous conversations had driven a guy like me outta the room and into seclusion, but now I was banging pots and pans with the best of them and willingly climbing aboard the crazy train.

But don't be fooled by her fun-loving side; it has a parallel. Mess with her friends and loved ones and you'd better run. Positive outlook on life or not, I've seen her walk right into the middle of a turd storm, grab her truth shovel, and smack down any and every projectile without fear. Don't expect her to back down until the truth is revealed. Period.

Same goes for Jody's twin at the home, Ruby. Funny thing is they could be literal twins. *No shade, Jody, but you're both short, rock the same expressive spikey hairdo, and have the identical in-your-face-love-for-life personality.*

Well, Ruby was the head nurse in charge at the home. Without her on the case, I wouldn't have gotten through any of the appointments at St. Joe's, Marshfield Clinic, or Mayo Clinic. Ruby knocked down insurance barriers, pushed to get appointments scheduled even when the facilities were booked, and coordinated my therapy. She kept bad news to herself and only shared it when she had run out of options. And if a whiff of defeat permeated the air, she'd bat it down with plan b and c. She'd headbutt any challenge like a sheep in the wild. And man did she face challenges. Many know injustice abounds in insurance companies. I suppose there's gotta be safety nets to mitigate loss, but sometimes their guidelines cause unnecessary stress in some cases and, sadly, casualties in others in the grueling process for authorization. In my situation, Marshfield Clinic and St. Joe's failed to diagnose me, so the insurance company deemed unnecessary nearly everything Ruby asked for. Yet she planted her feet without wavering and pushed for an auth. And when she couldn't get one, she would bring me all the pertinent information, and ask that I advocate for myself. "Sometimes if the patient calls and explains their position, the human element ties the necessity with the name" she'd say.

Ruby had a partner in crime, kinda like Batman and Robin. Remember my physical therapist, Sam? He reminded me of my grandpa, Lloyd. Serious, blunt but not rude, relatively quiet yet sociable, unassuming but inquisitive. Sam's dry humor was exactly grandpa, and that built the admiration. And just like Gramps, Sam would chuckle to himself, pause for a moment, and then spill his story that oftentimes didn't pertain one bit to his current surroundings. He'd just recall something comical and share it. Most folks need something relational, or they'll think yer a nutjob. But Gramps and Sam marched to the random beat because that's how life is. So, when I tied him to Grandpa's memory, trusting him became easy. He'd affirm my efforts, encourage me to employ the grit he knew I had within me, and then follow it all with a belly laugh and a story that had tickled his fancy. And that provided fertile soil for trust to flourish and determination to blossom. Sam had inherited a seemingly hopeless situation when Marshfield Clinic had decided to discharge me to the nursing home while crossing their fingers that I'd respond to therapy. And that meant a whole lotta pokin' and hopin' for Sam, blindly grasping at straws that something would stick and turn my situation around. And I was at my worst both mentally and physically. Like the time Grandpa allowed me to stay the whole summer at his house when I was at my most defiant, Sam kept adjusting and changing the techniques to pull me back to center. Relentless and determined, gentle yet firm, both men delivered their best. For the betterment of me.

You're Quite The Character—Please Change

Looking back on the doubles blessing, I can't help but think of it as a character-building lesson from God rather than Him comforting a tough guy. It was a time of adding in all the missing, unwanted ingredients that had made the cake bland and sleazeball-ish. I needed to add the salt, sugar, *and* baking soda in the recipe. Because, without the proper ingredients, the cake might bake, but it would still be a failure. I had to be willing to toss in the other ingredient without being forced, and then let them work together. You know what's the most annoying part about a tough guy in all that? The average macho man will take on the whole universe just to prove a point but won't flex a single muscle for self-repair. *Throw in the sugar, ya big doof!*

My grandfather forced me to add the extra ingredients, however. *Be respectful. Be punctual. Or go home.* Because he wasn't gonna put up with any of my nonsense. *When you say it, really mean it or you're full of hot air.* To him—and any respectable gent—a man's word is his bond. *Shake hands if someone puts it out there. Look a person in the eye if he or she is talking with you. Want respect? Then give it.*

And then Sam reinforced it. "Life goes on like it always has whether you're in pain or not. You can't change it, but you learn to adjust."

Dump The Pride Before It Dumps You

But what I've come to understand…adjusting is impossible if foolish pride hardens a once-soft heart. Again, refreshing tears need to flow sometimes. Ya gotta let wise counsel penetrate. It's medicine to the soul. Ever heard the phrase *I'm so mad I can't see straight*? Bottle it up until you pop; you'll be seeing doubles for sure. Run from your problems, and you'll crash right back into their evil arms again. Go ahead and expend valuable energy proving you're anything but weak. Maybe it'll work initially, but eventually you'll find yourself lost on some very lonely roads. And thankfully you won't meet me there anymore.

Luckily, Sam helped me realize that I could no longer take on the world, especially in the condition I was in. His gentle approach and stern wisdom showed me how to let some of it go. *Hey, Jay. Take a hard look at your stubbornness and pride and redirect your energy in a positive direction. Not all memories are worth focusing on. Try slowly letting go of what holds you back and purposefully readjust. But set the tools down once and a while and rest.* Solid advice. But I only dipped my toes in that pool here and there while in the home. *Was that the slow you spoke of? Oh, yeah. Purposefully. Got it.* Even after I had left the home I clung to *yeah, right,* until God allowed situations which demanded trust from me.

Please Breathe

Guys! Don't power through life trying to prove a point. Stubbornness can be a form of physical abuse to our bodies. Besides, coaches like Sam aren't trying to dominate, neither are your wives. (Pardon me. I don't really know your wife.) But, really, slow down and assess. Listen. Accept Godly advice.

And medical advice…

"Hey, Jason. Don't ignore me. I need you to breathe. Breathing is good. Look at the ceiling tile. Left side follow the tile, breathe in, one. Bottom side follow the tile, breathe out, two. Right side follow the tile, breathe in, three. Top side follow the tile, breathe out, four. Let's repeat…"

And my friend, Myra's advice.

"Smell the flowers. Blow out the candles. You're doin' good. The flowers smell good. Breathing is good..."

I feel so stupid sometimes remembering my obstinance toward their advice. But we all gotta learn some time, and it's never too late to learn the tools that help us avoid senseless pain. *And fainting.* Besides, stubbornness is a cheapskate. Won't even cough up the dough for participation ribbons. It'll just rob you of your inner peace, punch ya in the mouth, and run off like a bully when confronted.

20/20 Vision

Break out the compound microscope and take a hard look. A clearer look. Seek the Holy Spirit's guidance. Stubbornness, pride, all those worthless traits a tough guy thinks are macho are shoots from the bitterness root. Get out the axe and get to choppin' before it chokes the life outta ya. But if none of this resounds, at least take this with ya...breathe through yer pain, bust into tears, break down and fall apart when ya need to. Scatter your broken pieces before the LORD and ask Him to put ya back together. And then get yer butt back up and move away from it. We're meant to feel. Have emotions. Recognize that we need help and support. Meant to reach out to the only One who can solve our impossible situations. And sometimes through all this He reveals to us that tears are the insignificant tools that break the links in our chains. Forget about the key. Everybody's looking for the quick fix. Take out the trusty sledge and wedge and start swingin'. Smash that link repeatedly until you watch it separate. See double vision for a moment, and then wipe your eyes and straighten up. Cry out to God, raise your head high, and watch Him work in your life. Don't spend a fortune on tissues but have some around. Enjoy a good cry when the Spirit leads, or when your situation chips a fat chunk outta your backside. But recognize it's because of the grace of God you succeed. Because He sends a Sam. Some sort of coach. You just gotta have the will to press on.

Because of the love from the "doubles" I began to see life, my disability, my new path with clearer vision. I believe without this blessing from the good LORD, I might still be wallowing in the cesspool of stubbornness, pride, and bitterness. Had they not stood in the gap for me, I may have kept right on a'slippin' down the sludge-greased slide of depression and splattering wastewater on unsuspecting innocents along the way.

Let's Be Real

Maybe this chapter was a waste of time for you. Or maybe it set the fire of change burning in your heart. Whatever the case, I believe understanding that God has a lesson for every season we find ourselves in will produce a hunger for His refinements. We all desire a better version of ourselves, so I challenge you again to quit questioning *why* but rather ask God, *what would you have me learn?*

Seasons change rapidly, but there's beauty all around. No one's gonna force you to observe that beauty. Some will try to point it out to you, others will work to hide it, but if you're set only on negative beliefs and thought patterns, the beauty of life will quickly pass by on its own. And one thing's for certain! Hindsight loves to slap people with the truth, leaving behind either regret or amusement. So, don't be closeminded to the lessons coming your way. Be open and thankful. Don't overanalyze, and, again, listen to the still small voice of God in all situations.

"The fear of the LORD is the beginning of wisdom, and knowledge of the Holy One is understanding." Proverbs 9:10 NIV

People are brought into our lives for a specific purpose. Some to enrich, encourage, maybe guide. Others to refine and test. Some short term while others for a lifetime. And we may forever remain unaware of the reasons. So, take my advice or don't, patiently enjoy the ride no matter if it's smooth or bumpy. You don't wanna end up like the old me—noticing the gifts in my life a bit too late because I had trained myself to dwell on the potholes in the curvy road. Those potholes, bumps, and hilly roads chuck joy, people, blessings right outta our lives if we let them. Some leave for good. Others watch from a distance. Very few people will crawl their way back.

Is everyone strategically placed, then? Maybe. Does Romans 8:28 NIV pertain? Possibly. Won't know until I'm leprechaun-skippin' on the streets of gold. Decide for yourself. "And we know that in all things God works for the good of those who love Him, who have been called according to His purpose." I choose to believe He knew I desperately needed support, and He sent it in His timing.

Doppelgangers, Beware!

Before you find yourself lost in the afternoon of rebirth, I need you to know that not everyone wants *doubles* in their lives. Some twins…I cringe at the thought of it. Cloning people? *Vote it down!* One sun-filled afternoon while in a gutsy and sarcastic mood, I told my wife she needed to clone me so she could be genuinely happy. And without skipping a beat she fired back, "I'd shoot you both and live with the memory!" The video capture of that letdown would've gone viral. Overinflated ego—popped without notice. Hilarious!

Chapter 12

←

THE AFTERNOON OF REBIRTH

Dreading the incessant chatter and the daily bombardment of *why not, Dad?* one early June evening while driving home from work, I lazily followed the white line along the highway. *Two more minutes and I'll be home. I'd rather not be in that chaotic environment right now.* Over fourteen thousand steps on the pedometer, nonstop needy customers, and a phone that rang off the hook, I was thoroughly exhausted. Back to dad mode in less than a mile. *Should I be cringing over the thought of going home? What's causing this mental war? The little noise monsters? Could it be the current remodel job stealing all my free time? The water trickling down the freshly installed windows every time it rains? New job stress? My co-workers? Yup! That's it! It's gotta be them. They all hate me because I'm the outsider. If they'd support me, even a tad bit, I probably wouldn't be leaving a shift feeling so haggard.*

The fleeting moments of solitude continued to vanish as the wind fluttered my seat belt like the wings of a hummingbird. I had seconds left to shrug off the day, otherwise, I knew I'd project the gloom onto my family. *How am I gonna boost sales if they all hate me? How in the world am I supposed to promote unity in such a hostile environment? What am I gonna do with all that paperwork I gotta sort through and file? Good luck shrugging this off!* My mind raced back and forth as my car sailed into a beating. Daydreaming blocked out what lie ahead, and I had no time to avoid the crumbling intersection. I blasted through 14th Street and Michigan as water flooded over the car and in through the open windows. The previous day's torrential rains had filled in the usually exposed intersection, and the ever-widening crater lie hidden underneath gallons of water. My flagship sunk into the muddy mess, and my head bounced off the side pillar as expletives flew out the window.

If there's so much as a scratch on the undercarriage of this car, they're going to repaint the whole thing! Where the heck's my tax money going? Probably in their vacation funds! Filthy crooks! There's no reason I should hafta drop back to five miles per hour to cross this slop hole they call a road! (clean version)

The profanity continued while I gassed my way outta the abyss. An older gentleman walking his dog turned sharply and shot rebuke directly into my eyes as I inched toward the stop sign. His bewildered and offended expression said it all. *You kiss your mom with that mouth? Learn how to drive, Jackwagon!* I quickly looked away, finished rolling up the mud-soaked windows, and shot through the intersection near our house. At that moment the sky darkened, and the Arctic blew icy winds into my soul as my brain registered what my eyes beheld.

Bulldoze The House And Watch It Fall

Is that the flower BOX? NO FLIPPIN WAY! YOU'VE GOT TO BE KIDDING ME!! GRRRR! NOT ANOTHER PROBLEM WITH THIS DUMP! I CAN'T TAKE MUCH MORE.

You know that defeated whine/cry/growl a person lets out when the unexpected rips his/her heart out the seat of his/her pants? My voice cracked under the load as the pitch changed.

Smashed beneath the weight of stagnant dirt and splintered redwood siding spread what was once daffodils and tulips in full bloom. The splash of red, pink, and yellow that had drawn the attention of the passerby? History! Along with my dignity. Shredded tar paper intermixed with giant toothpicks lie strewn about the front yard like a tornado had whipped through. What used to be a weather beaten and desperate-to-be-painted front façade now screamed remodeler's nightmare. The entire under half of the window, studs and all, had rotted away and was forcefully removed when the window box slumped from the house. In plain sight. Exposed. For all the world to see.

Evidently, I knew nothing about the condition of my fixer upper because reinforcing the whole front half of the house and an emergency window replacement had just taken me by surprise. Who wouldn't be shocked? I never saw it coming. *So, no more replacing windows one by one, then? I see how you're gonna play this. You do remember just yesterday that half your power went dead when I unknowingly clipped the wires you had dangling between the living room windows, right? Now you're forcing me to pay for a facelift and a chin raise?! What's next? A tummy tuck?! (Yes, actually. That summer the crack in the basement walls started leaking…)*

The structural integrity of the fiercely pitched roof was now at stake. Fix it or lose the front wall *and* the roof. The wiring issues? A frolic in the park. Without my permission, years of rot had unleashed its fury. React or watch the house implode.

I whipped open the door of the Aurora as soon as the nose of the car met the driveway and leaped over the retaining wall. All before the car had halted. If you've ever thrown a car into park before it comes to a complete stop, you're probably aware of the horrendous noise that comes outta the transmission. I had heard it several times before; remember the Ohio trip? It makes me cringe every time, but I was more concerned that day about landing in the newly sprouting hostas rather than ripping the guts outta my transmission. The neighbors must have thought I was playing hopscotch as I bounced back and forth trying to avoid grinding the new shoots back into the ground. It wasn't first grade hopscotch filled with joy and exhilaration, and the sidewalk chalk wasn't providing the color, either.

"How the heck did this happen?? KIDS! GET YOUR BUTTS OUT HERE RIGHT NOW! HEATHER!!"

After a closer look, four eight-foot rows of siding lie torn off in the front flower bed, and the remains of an attached, six-foot-long wooden window box, collapsed like a folding chair, stretched into the mangled yard,. *Why am I yelling at the kids for this?*

I screamed out *this CANNOT be happening right now!* as frightened faces appeared from around the corner only to disappear again. Overtaken by despair from the dreadful scene, and knowing the extra work would be far too much for me to handle alone, the doom set in. I had lost the entire war in one unexpected ambush.

Snapshots Are Lovely, Doncha Think?

Let's examine the surroundings for a moment. Across the street there's an enormous brick beauty sportin' a red door and beautiful white windows, sitting on lush golf course greens accented by symmetrical shrubbery. Right next door at the Joneses, a cozy, old-fashioned blue and white charmer with stately pillars resting on a spacious, painted covered porch, positioned on a gorgeously landscaped corner lot. And here I am, standing in front of the Delta County Landfill. The only thing missing…a flock of seagulls swooping down to pick at the junk.

The Main Problem In Life

As far as the true answers to the questions at the beginning of this chapter, the ones pertaining to who rightfully deserved a finger jabbed in their face for the stressors in my life, I had identified the culprit. My kids' inquisitive and mischievous natures weren't to blame. And neither could I cuss my coworkers. Who likes authority, anyway? Singling myself out as the only one hated for being partly in charge at work or at home is stupidity on my part. *The slop hole with the flashing marquee, that's the problem.* It had been repeatedly punching me in the face for quite some time and was seeking the TKO. I held the deed to the only dandelion-infested yard on the block lacking an ounce of professional landscaping. I owned the rights to the sun-scorched siding flaking paint chips like a bird pecking at a feeder. I palmed the certificate to the drafty shack with single-paned wood windows inviting the drifting snow to mound on the laps of anyone daring to sit on the couch. *Zip up your parka, kids. Tonight's episode will be worth your frozen eyeballs. I promise. Quickly eat your snacks or you'll have to chisel them outta the bowl.*

I deserved to be scorned! Meanwhile, next door and across the street…balmy Jamaican bliss.

What's The Meaning Of This?

"HEATHER!!!" I yelled as I entered the house.

"I'm in the living room."

"What happened out front? Did the kids climb on the flower box? And why didn't you come out when I called?"

"What are you talking about? I didn't hear you."

"So, you haven't looked out front? The flower box's annihilated and whipped all over the yard, and a crapload of siding is ripped off! You mean to tell me you didn't know about it?! I sure don't need any more work added to the list!!"

"What are you yelling at me for? I didn't do it, and I'm sure the kids wouldn't do something like that! You need to calm down!"

Not what I wanted to hear. It soaked my anger in lighter fluid.

"DYLAN!! WHERE ARE YOU??!!"

Around the corner came a nervous 10-year-old, fearful of taking another step toward me.

"Yeah Dad?"

"Don't yeah me. Get your shoes on. We've got a mess to clean up."

"Yes, sir."

"And don't take forever, either. I wanna sit down sometime today, too, ya know."

I believe the house responded to my intense ranting as I pounded down the side entrance steps. Seconds before I whipped the screen door past the plunger limits, the walls in the entrance shifted and settled, producing a gigantic cracking noise. Followed by a *shriek* and *snap!* Awkwardly flexing beyond its capabilities, the plunger snapped, the door banged against the siding, and then slammed shut as the spring and chain yanked it backward. I barely made it out the door before it smashed me in the face. *What was I thinking shoving on the screen door that hard? Because of the shifting noises the house had made? Was I becoming a raving lunatic?* The creaking and moaning noises I had heard were merely the sounds a hundred-year-old two story makes while soaking up the warmth of the morning sun. Besides, nearly all the plaster walls inside the house had cracked. Clearly it had been settling and shifting over the years. *Was the house plotting my demise while signaling the impending doom lurking on the horizon? Dun Dun Dunn!*

Hey tough guy. Yeah, you. Ya better settle down. Ya keep abusing me and yerself and yer family, and it's gonna cost ya.

Could this be likened to God's conversation with Cain in Genesis 4:7 NIV? Or am I taking this out of context?

"If you do what is right, will you not be accepted? But if you do not do what is right, sin is crouching at your door; it desires to have you, but you must rule over it."

Heed The Warning Or Else

Warning or warming, an uneasiness hovered over me like a thunderhead from that day on. Justification boomed but condemnation did also. And to further torture was the recollection of the time I worked on a decorative cabinet I was refinishing. I was scraping off the forty-nine layers of paint, and with every layer I uncovered, the job got harder and harder. The more I angrily scraped, the more I cussed and carried on. What I figured would take only one tiresome afternoon stretched into several days of intense work. Me and tedious never got along, but on this one, stubborn took over and perfectionism overwhelmed, and I persevered to the end. While carefully sanding but cursing the job, mysteriously a corner section of glass in the upper half of the door cracked without warning. A new reverence for the cabinet terrified me into silence, and I took the glass breakage as a warning to keep my floppin' trap shut. And it's quite alarming how one's mind can become irrational during the unexplained. The glass breakage had to be a sign… or a punishment.

Had I been careless and angered the ghosts in my house? Should I plead my case?! On second thought, no way! Just shut up!

Somebody's To Blame

No one was punishing me. The mess out front. The broken screen door. The cracked glass. All proof that time erodes. *A destructive lack of self-control doesn't help, though.* Nonetheless, I employed a victim mindset to the extreme, allowing all rationale to fly out the window.

"GUYS! The stupid screen door broke. Hang onto the piece of junk when you open it, or it'll fly away. I'll fix this worthless thing later. DYLAN! LET'S GO!!"

For a moment my temp evened out after I word cursed the screen door to death, but I think the sheer terror of *what next?* cooled me off rather than common sense.

Silence threatened mine and my son's relationship as we cleaned up the front yard. I think what kept him quiet was the pent-up rage that flew outta his dad during stressful moments. Hours passed without saying a word as we hauled the wreckage to the back yard and outta the sightlines of prestigious Michigan Ave. Poor kid worked his tail off and was exhausted halfway through. I finally set him free, but I continued wandering around the house begging for a solution from my overtaxed mind.

What am I gonna do? The neighbors must hate me by now. Our house is bringing down the value of the block. I'm doomed, and this is gonna cost me more than I got.

Mr. Jones appeared from around his side of the fence. Observing the damage, he looked around for a bit, and then offered some kindness.

"How's it going, neighbor? Looks like the flower box fell off, eh? Need any help?"

"Hey. Nah. I'll get it."

"I'm heading off to camp. Want me to take the wood scraps? I'll burn them for you."

"You'd do that for me? That'd be great. Thanks!"

"Yeah. I'll stick around if you want help out front."

"Nah. Thanks for the offer. Taking that pile away would be great, though."

Nothing about marring the image of the block? He's being too nice. What's his angle? Give it some time and the truth will come out. He thought the Brunettes were sinking deeper and deeper into the slums, and I knew it. *He sees the plywood blocking in the windows, the I'm-too-poor-to-maintain-my-house look, right?*

Have you ever worked on an older home? Drywall mud by the gallons and so many buckets of nails and screws. And don't forget to buy stock in the lumber yard while you're at it. Remodeling is no picnic. And if it were a picnic, it'd be a torrential rain with lightening, baseball-sized hail, swarms of mosquitoes, and soggy pb&j. I knew repairing the inside alone spelled endless days of frustration for an inexperienced diy-er like me. Every plaster wall inside the house was about to sport a sledgehammer hole if I decided to replace the twenty-one wood windows with new ones. And that number didn't include the basement. But first I'd be switching gears to focus on the outside since the front looked like Jaws took a bite outta my charming cottage. *There's no way I can do all this!* And under the neighbors' watchful eye? The noose was tightening, and I nearly lost my grip. *What am I gonna do? I gotta reduce the workload somehow.* After several more trips around the house, the solution slapped me upside the head.

"HEATHER, C'MERE! Please, I mean."

One of the wooden windows in the dining room lifted, and she poked her head where a screen should have been.

"What are you doing? You've been wandering around like a weirdo for the last twenty minutes."

"I'm trying to make sense of this disaster. I don't know why this crap always happens to me. I'm so sick of all this piling up. Now I gotta start siding the house, and I'm not even finished with the windows. But I've got no choice. I can't leave it like this. Did you even look? Never mind. You don't care."

"Yes, I looked."

"Well, you seem so calm about it all."

"What do you want me to do? Yell and scream like you are? What good will that do?"

"You don't understand."

"Yes, I do! Getting mad and flying off the handle won't help. What do you want? You called me for a reason, what is it?"

"Never mind."

"Don't do that. What ya need?"

"I think I have a solution for all this mess. Will you please come out here so I can explain it to you?"

The Brilliant Plan

We hadn't spent our tax return yet, and as I expressed my hopes of piecing the house back together before fall, I painted an elaborate view of how we'd stretch out our return to the extreme limit. We'd have beautiful vinyl siding, crisp white windows with the crosshatches just like the mansion across the street, and a beautifully landscaped yard complete with a white picket fence. *And a dog.* But carefully I brushed in the details of eliminating several windows as a cost saving measure. I knew words like eliminating and reduction would make some waves, so, I blended them in.

"If we strategically repurpose six windows into wall space, we'll save a ton, and it'll be easier on me to run the siding."

"What windows though?" Plan failed, so I plainly spelled it out.

"I figure if we replace the two sets in the living room with one big one in each, take out both windows alongside the fireplace, and replace the two in the dining room with one, that'll save a ton. What ya think?"

"I'm worried about enough light. That's eliminating a lot. Plus, that's only five. Where's the sixth?"

"The sixth is in our bedroom. We haven't opened that window since we bought the place."

"As long as there's enough light, do what ya gotta do."

"I promise it'll look nice when I'm done."

Day after day, closer and closer to a carpenter, an electrician, and plumber I inched as repairs on our desperate house drilled experience into me. Have you ever worked forty hours a week and then on a project until sundown for weeks? It takes a toll. All throughout June, I dragged myself inside at dusk like a cartoon character flattened by a steamroller. Every morning the dreaded *beep-beep-beep* woke me to my reality: it's gonna be physically impossible to complete this remodel before the first snow fall if I don't ask for help. But instead of doing what I knew I had to do, I complained to whomever dared to ask about my summer project.

"Did ya get yer windows in yet?" asked a fellow co-worker.

And then I continued to hear, "How's that project coming along?" from regulars at Carquest.

"You look exhausted. That's a big job you got going on," observed the UPS driver.

Each question became more disturbing than the previous one. *It'll look good when I'm done. What? Ya think I can't handle it? It's just gonna take a bit of work, and I've never been afraid of exertion, so this is no different than the average project. But I inherited a mess. If the previous owner had kept up on the house, I wouldn't be in such a mess! Obviously the inspector screwed me on this one."* I spoke of defeat everywhere I went, and everybody noticed. Burnin' the 'ol candle at both ends as they say, and the heat was reachin' my backside.

"Why don't you call my brothers to see if they'll help you set the scaffolding today? You can barely walk. How you gonna move it?" Heather asked one late June morning after I slugged only coffee for breakfast. "You won't even sit long enough for me to make you something to eat? Jay?! Come on, you're killing yourself."

"I don't need yer brothers. I'll scoot it across the yard myself."

You want them to think I can't hack it? I've already replaced the west side windows, reconstructed the interior walls, nearly sided the south and west sections myself. Why ask now? Even though I could barely walk, let alone stand up straight, visible progress propelled me forward. I figured if they hadn't offered to help, it was an admission of unwillingness. *Don't bother yourself now.*

What a terrible mindset for a Christian to cultivate. The Bible labels such beliefs as a mental stronghold, which will eventually destroy us if we celebrate lies instead of truths.

The Heat of July

"Babe, you worked away the entire 4th of July. You stay out until after dark every night. You never take a break. The summer's gonna be over, and I wanted to do some camping, or go somewhere with the kids. Anywhere but here watching you kill yourself on this stupid house!"

Wrong choice of words, Babe. They produced dreaded word vomit.

"Hey! Who's gonna do it, then? Who's gonna complete it? I don't see your family, my family, our friends knocking down the door to help me. They know I'm bustin' my hump on this house, and then act like they're too busy to drive by. I'm not gonna ask people for help. If they don't offer, then they don't wanna. Plain and simple. People don't give a crap when you're struggling, they're selfish and refuse to lift a finger unless pressured. I WILL NOT BEG! DYLAN!! COME HELP ME AND YOUR MOM MOVE THIS STUPID SCAFFOLDING."

That horrible scaffolding was just as stubborn as the guy reefing on it. It wouldn't budge. The wheels had rusted solid, and with every ounce of strength we could muster, we yanked and pushed but only tore up small chunks of sod. Soaked in perspiration and frustration, I slumped to the ground.

"CAN'T I GET A BREAK!! Dylan, stop pushing! Can't you see I quit?!"

"Now what, Babe?! Call someone. Please! Maybe Caleb can help us."

"Caleb said he'd be over later, but he's not home right now. I need it moved right now. I'll just take it apart."

"That's way too much work for you. Lemme call Joel and see if he can help."

"NO! I said I'll just take it apart."

"Whatever, do what you want."

And with a wonderful attitude, so supportive and accommodating, I ran off the only help I had. Heather went back inside the house and refused to talk to me for the rest of the night. Dylan ran off with his tail tucked between his legs.

The Tower Of Doom

On the east side of the house, the scaffolding towered a near thirty feet in the air. My neighbor, Tom, had helped me set up the lower half the week before, but he too had problems to solve that day. I reluctantly accepted my self-induced fate and began disassembling the tower. The burn! Oh, the burn as I raised my arms above my head and lifted my legs, shaking like a frightened teenager on a talent show stage. I rebelled against sound judgement as I climbed the looming menace; my body warned of being too exhausted to accomplish what I had set out to do.

That day I birthed my anthem. ***I will not give up. I will not give in.***

Piece by burdensome piece, I despairingly dismantled the structure barefoot and alone. Like a gibbon in the jungle, I'd wrap my toes around the metal bars for extra support, bend over the top bar and press my sixpack against it, and then hang my upper half over the side to lower each section to the ground. It was obviously dangerous what I was doing, but how else does one get the job done? *I'll do what it takes. Admit defeat? Not today. Not ever.* However, I'd be lying if I said I wasn't tempted to give in. Every individual section of scaffolding weighed nearly forty pounds, and at the end of dismantling the second section, razor blades pumped through my veins. *But dream on, peasant, there's no breather for the obstinate. The end is a long ways off.* Even after disassembling it I knew I couldn't rest. The skads of cursed iron crowding the lawn would then have to be hauled to the opposite side of the house and then be reassembled.

Halfway done, Manly man. Snow's a-comin' so get busy. You see that crusty tar paper? You think it flaps in the wind now. Wait until the brutal winds of an Upper Peninsula winter get after it! Oh, by the way, the partially attached corner pieces of your sage vinyl siding look amazing sailing through the air and onto your neighbor's shoveled porch. Yeah, that's gonna happen. Well played, Big Fella. The disdainful looks irritate you now... Wait until this winter when your neighbors stand in their windows and articulate their indignant conclusions! It's not the snowfall they abhor... it's you.

Luckily, a welcomed realization flooded me with peace and washed away that horrendous visual. *You've a whole day's work before you need to climb that miserable jungle gym again. Do the ground stuff first and wait for Caleb. You deserve a break.* With absolute exhilaration, I slumped to the ground in relief and spent the next twenty minutes staring at the clear blue sky. *Thank God!*

Scram, Timewasters!

One of the most annoying traits I've perfected over the years still haunts me to this day, even though my body can't perform like before. I never sit still for long. My father-in-law used to lovingly joke, *he never lets grass grow under his tires*. I knew what he meant. *Park that car and take a five, Young Man.* This curse has been a real buzz kill for many. *We stop over to visit because you're whining about being lonely, but you won't sit down long enough to say more than hello.* It not only bothers others, but it has caused me an enormous amount of grief as well. It's a real stinger for me for two big reasons. Inescapable fatigue is the number one. I can't quit sprinting on the endeavor treadmill. *It's ok, Jason, just keep running yourself into the ground at full bore daily until you either achieve your goal or collapse into a hateful pile of goo. Joy's gonna go AWOL, you'll miscalculate every step you take, and the wick on your rage furnace will get clipped shorter and shorter. No worries, right? All in the name of progress. Brilliant.* And the second reason is like the first. If I catch a single soul watching me or resting while I'm snapping necks and cashing checks, it'll throw me over the edge and light the ol' furnace. *If I'm working you better be, too, Buster! There's no time for laziness, EVER! Burn some calories or I'll give ya fifty lashes with a wet noodle. Ya got time to lean ya got time to clean* (unsure of origin, but I loved saying this). *Sleep when yer dead.*

Has anyone been given fifty lashes with a wet noodle before? Do you use spaghetti or linguine? I'm so confused.

Time's Up!

Twenty minutes of staring at the sky and allowing fatigue to subside was far too generous from a guy like me. *You're burning daylight.* Remorse pushed me off the ground and to my feet while regret replayed the winter scene over and over in my head. That's all it took to rebuke the smile right off my face and whip me back into submission. *The sections can't stay where they are. Some are resting in the neighbor's yard, and some are propped against the fence. That's gonna go over like a fart in church.* (I wanna ask, but I'll refrain.) But having to nearly drag each of the five foot by five-foot sections down the slight grassy hill and around the concrete retaining wall to the driveway made me wanna cry. I couldn't imagine taking one more step without landing face-first on the pavement, passed out in a bloody mess.

Get busy or yer gonna fall behind. Yer already teetering on the tightrope. Suck it up or yer gonna fall off and look like an idiot.

I slumped down again next to the daunting stack of iron. *What am I gonna do?* The grueling pace was destroying me. I had taken on the largest project of my life without experience, and the mounting weight of depression was flattening me. I sprawled back out on the warm ground and fought back the tears. *Who's gonna rescue me from this dreadful situation?* I gave up for the night.

Not By A Long Shot

What I had proposed to be a *day's work* before I would need the scaffolding turned into two weeks of struggle and continuous shortcutting. I hadn't factored in all the job variables, so my thoughts were quite misled with allowing myself a single day to get it all done. For instance, I wanted to remove and brick in the side door. The garage roof pitches steeply toward the side entrance, so when it rains, you either get soaked from the flash runoff, or you've gotta whip the door open and dart inside. Sounds easy enough, right? Wrong. As soon as you pass the threshold, there's a dinky six-foot landing with steps directly in front of the door and then to the right of the door. Try shoving five people into that crowded space during a downpour, and then add tile flooring to the mix. We've had far too many people bounce and shriek from the vicious spanking that floor loves to provide. So, I planned out a reroute into the garage door opening and through the doorway into the house from inside the garage. Brick in the old doorway, throw in a window, and voila! Problem solved. *What a wonderful solution to soggy groceries and water splashing down the crack of you know what.* But in all the hasty planning I had completely forgotten to factor in the fire-hazard outdoor light perched above the old side door. And instead of eliminating the light while I had the walls open, I foolishly decided to avoid the mess so I could get started on the siding. A word of advice when working construction…never ignore gut feelings. Because when you've already drywalled and mudded the inside, covering up the exposed wires you needed to eliminate, the job's now gonna require a hack job on the outside to expose the dangerous wiring. Picture this: a circular saw, a Sawzall, and a jigsaw all chewing at the ancient tongue and groove-like outer boarding of our house. Wiring is seldom run in a straight line. The results: a wonky puzzle requiring loads of glue, nails, caulking, and screws. *Never mind the fact that you could've fixed this mess from the inside when it was open. By all means just mud the whole mess in and then mangle the outside like an amateur. Great call, Sparky.* Any logical and common-sense driven carpenter would've taken the time to do the job right the first time. Not me. *Ignore logic because you're already overwhelmed.*

A Postcard From The Author

Dear Reader,

Should you decide to promote this book and its sequel, you will be party to a well-done remodel job by a professional and not a novice!

Sincerely,

J.P. Brunette

The Mess Continues

While chasing the wiring from the old light into the garage, guesswork created a hole the size of my head in the plaster on the staircase wall leading to the second floor. Timely advice #2—Swing a hammer in haste without double checking your whereabouts and you're bound to leave a mark. A big one. Write that down.

Before I knew it July and August had passed, and September had crept in unannounced. Kiss summer goodbye, bring on the new school year, and find a place for the thousands of feet of siding still waiting to be nailed up. Winter would now be able to seize the prize for winning the competition—ravage the Brunette home.

"It's gonna be ok, Jay. You got a lot done this summer" consoled my neighbor one fall evening.

"I know you see it that way, Cort, but I'm far from finished."

Seeing me struggle day in day out, she understood the challenge I faced but refused to be anything but positive. As she hopped up her steps to go inside, she reassured my efforts.

"It looks great! I'll continue to help as much as I can, but I don't know how much good I'll actually be."

Even though she was forever willing, I felt horrible for asking her for help. She had already worked hard enough, popping in and helping with small jobs all summer long. She picked up scraps, hauled and handed me siding, scoured the ground for nails and screws whenever she stepped outside. From the ground she'd hoist supplies up to me so I wouldn't have to keep climbing up and down. But being the only weekend I'd have off for the whole month of September, I blurted, *are ya busy?* I nearly missed her as she grabbed for her screen door, so I shouted louder as she stepped out of sight.

"Hey, Cort! Is Caleb home?"

She poked her head around the side of the house and then leaned over her porch railing. "Yeah. Why? What ya need?"

"You think he'd help, again? I need to set up the last section of scaffolding so I can get to the peak tomorrow. There's rain in the forecast. I gotta get this side done before that happens."

"Yeah, sure. No problem. We'll be right over."

Cort To The Rescue...Again.

We erected the familiar skyscraper rather quickly that night. Everyone huffing and puffing by the time our feet touched the ground. *Oh, man, why hadn't I grabbed Caleb and Cort more often? Wow can that kid work! Great job, Mom!* I couldn't thank them enough that night; they had rescued me yet again. I think by the ninetieth time, it had finally annoyed them because they eventually went in the house and shut the door while I was still talking. The chill of the damp grass soothed while I panted like a dog in the sun. *What a successful night!* Things had finally taken a turn in the right direction, and it felt good. *Tomorrow's gonna be even better! Take that, Snowstorm. In your face, Defeat.* But then an eerie feeling wiped the smile off my face as I reminisced the previous work. *What if I had hurt myself because I wouldn't ask for help? Maybe I should listen to Heather and Cort. I'm spinning out of control.* But then pride fired back. *Shut up! They don't care. They pity you. That's why they help.* As I pondered the racing thoughts, I grew sullen and despondent. *Which ones are true?* One day Cort climbed the scaffolding—something she said she'd never do—and helped me nail up one of the longest sheets of siding without complaint. She saw me struggling and put aside her own fears to help a friend. Not because she felt sorry for me but because she's a supportive and helpful person who adheres to her core values. And she's always been that way since the day I met her. Without a moment's notice I've witnessed her stepping in and saving someone's day. I felt so ashamed for questioning her intentions. *You know better than that.* But numerous boxes of siding and trim pieces blocked the drive. Half empty boxes of nails and screws sat spilled out on the concrete. Every tool imaginable littered the garage floor. Chunks of foam insulation lie strewn about in the yard. Heaps of cut off house wrap, 2X4 scraps, and the mountains of sawdust blocked the house entrance. I couldn't escape the mess, and it consumed me. *I need sleep. I'll think more clearly if I get some sleep.* And then the side support panels buckled on the garage door, causing the center to cave in as I tried to shut the door...I jumped right off the ledge and into utter insanity. Up and down I violently reefed on the door, cussing and stomping until it finally decided to sit flush on the cement. My thoughts, my life, my yard, my house had exploded! There was no turning back from the rage-a-thon. I stormed into the house and both my girls plopped on my feet, wrapping their arms and legs around mine in anticipation of a "bigfoot ride". I nearly snapped again but, luckily, Heather interjected when she sensed my foul mood.

"Girls, get ready for dinner. Let Dad take his shoes off."

The girls slowly climbed off my feet but continued to look up with longing faces.

"I'm fine. Just gonna need a whole lot more help than the neighbors to get this dump fixed. The garage door busted. The yard's a mess. There's junk everywhere. And there's no end in sight. I shoulda listened to your dad when he said not to buy this house. I'm going to bed."

"Eat something first. The kids and I'll go out and clean up."

The Day It All Changed

Sunshine flooded our room the following morning, 7 a.m. *No time to waste.* The warming rays welcomed me to a bright new day, and while I listened to the melodious songbirds singing out their praises to the Creator, I slid off the bed and quickly got dressed. (I describe it this way now, but, given the time that day, I'm convinced I would've target practiced the day away.) Eyes open, covers off, clothes on. The hardwood floors spoke volumes of the chill of the morning. *Wow! I need to wear shoes today. Can't believe it's this cold!* And as I transferred full weight to the heels and pads of my feet, the alarms in my body went off. Stabbing pains throughout the lower back. Tearing sensations in the abdomen. A threatening imbalance from buckling knees and burning calves. The pain shooting from one end to the other forced me to sit down and wonder if my plans for the day had been overruled. Achieving perfect posture would be a prerequisite for the workload. *Body, we've got work to do. Muscles, I'm in charge now. Brain, I'll take it from here, thanks.* I pinballed down the hall to the kitchen to grab some chow, slugged down the leftover, day-old coffee in my mug, and headed for the door. *I'll make it to the peak today no matter what.*

I'm unsure if you believe breakfast to be supremely important or not, but I had ignored my own convictions all summer long. Toast and jelly would suffice, again, and the few sips of cold coffee would supply adequate energy to fire the cylinders until lunch. However, when you exert yourself as much as I was, filling the tank is vital.

Outside the dewy ground stung the bottoms of my feet every step I took. Clearly, it was too cold of a morning to be barefoot, but shoes and socks reduced traction, so I reasoned them hazardous. On the way outta the garage, I grabbed the old metal Stanley tape measure and crammed it into my pocket. I leaped for the scaffolding and started upward. The frigid metal bars felt like icy swords stabbing at my feet. *I might need a coat, too* exited my mouth in a frozen vapor as I fearfully squeezed for a tighter grip.

Advice #47 of ten billion—climbing barefoot on a metal structure in chilly conditions is not smart. And especially when it's covered in dew.

In the few seconds it took to reach the second level, I could barely handle the stinging pain from the frozen bars; I decided to take a second to dangle my tender feet from the rickety platform stretched between the two sections. I swung myself around the bars to the inside and stepped onto the make-shift platform. It wasn't safe—two ridiculously long and bouncy 2X8 rough-sawn boards overhanging each side of the scaffolding by all of four feet—but it worked great for piling up extra supplies to keep them outta the way. Just as I stepped onto the boards, they sagged heavily, I lost balance, and went into a squatting position. And then the old Stanley popped out of my pocket and smashed onto the cement below. I foolishly grabbed at the plummeting tape measure, misjudged the width of the boards, and fell forward into the empty space. Luckily, the platform stretched out above me between the second and third section held position as I reached for it, and I caught myself before I fell. But then the boards slid, rammed against the back poles of the scaffolding, and I nearly lost grip of the platform. With tip toes on the 2X8's and white fingertips on the pick above me, I lengthened myself to the limit to keep from falling. Fortunately, I was able to shove off from my fingers hard enough to balance on the boards and stand up straight. *That was awfully close!!* But instead of sitting down to allow my heart a moment to normalize, I cursed the boards and continued to climb. *The first piece should've been cut by now. Stupid boards. I never wanted these useless things in the first place. By all means, add to my scrap heap to diminish yours! All I've got to work with is junk that's trying to kill me!"*

What's A Pick?

If you don't know what a scaffolding pick is, it's a platform that has two support beams with hooks on each side that wrap around the bars of the scaffolding. On top of the support beams can be a wood or a fully formed aluminum floor used for walking between or atop the scaffolding structure. My dad had lent me an aluminum and a wooden pick, and I used one for walking and one for tools and supplies. The wooden one worked great for a work bench, but going up to the peak, I chose to rely on the solid aluminum for a sturdy walkway.

What's Missing?

Once I got to the top, I noticed the sudden shift while trying to prevent falling had knocked the siding and insulation nails off the top, and they had spilled all over the cement. Completely enraged because my supplies had fallen, I leaped off the ladder-like bars of the scaffolding, plopped down on the aluminum pick, and slammed my fist against the house. I only needed the first measurement to get started, but the fallen nails were just plain rude. Right next to me sat the hammer and my nail pouch emptied of all its contents, as well. Luckily, the hammer hadn't fallen with the nails. Because if it had, I'm sure it would've clocked me right on the bald spot. But while whimpering over spilled nails, I discovered gold amid all the disaster—the neon green tape measure I had seemingly lost the day before sat close to the edge. Another major stroke of luck! I carefully squirmed my way to the other side of the pick to grab the tape. It was extremely wobbly that high up, so I had to delicately inch closer to the tape measure so it wouldn't fall off. A worthwhile investment of my time.

With measurements in hand several minutes later, I started the descent to cut the first piece. Excitement turned into fear, however, because about halfway down my legs began to bounce. I knew I had pushed them past exhaustion for months, but it was a new day. *Can't I get a mulligan? There's no quitting now!* Nailing in the first piece drew like a magnet. *I thought cutting the angles would hold me back, not weakness…but I'll be taking a huge risk if I keep ignoring the warning signs. I could get seriously hurt.* History generally repeats itself if one decides against applying the wisdom behind the necessity to change, but I chose to take the risk and hit the ground running. Out I yanked the first chunk of siding, rushed to slice off the angle, and then raced up the tower with the golden piece in hand like a ravenous spider after a trapped insect. Almost to the top, however, I realized I had forgotten to grab the nails. But instead of burning valuable energy, I laid the first piece on the wooden pick, measured another section, and slithered back down to the ground. This time with a new energy-saving plan. *Determine the next piece by anticipating its dimensions from the previous piece. Measure up and over. Mark it. Determine the length from the guesstimate. Chop off the length according to the staggering end laps and cut both the angles.* I knew it would work for only a moment because the pieces would get shorter as I moved skyward, thus moving my stagger joints, but I figured the plan would save numerous painful up and down trips. And it did. But what I hadn't allotted for—how far out-of-square my roof line was, and what a mess that would create for me as I moved upward.

Please Take A Break

By the time I had sided above the third section of the towering metal structure, my body screamed with pain. It had taken hours to reach the attic vent hole, and nausea, dizziness, notable weakness threatened to halt progress. But I could see the end in sight, so I pressed on. Dylan handed me the new vent, and with it secured in place, I measured off the chunks to go around it, jotted down the dimensions on scrap paper, and then slowly climbed down. My pace had dwindled from spider monkey to sloth. Shortly before placing the vent, Heather had stepped outside to announce lunch, making me promise to eat after nailing in a few more pieces. Lunch sounded amazing. And so did laughing and chatting, relaxation before Monday's unpredictable workload. Anything but hard labor. But when her phone rang and she became preoccupied with the conversation, I determined the few more pieces she spoke of would be the ones that finished the job. Only a small section remained. Another hour and it'd be done. *Hold on, Sparky. Ya just gonna leave the mess on the ground? There goes your chance at happiness. Let me poke another hole in yer sails just for fun. And bust off the rudder while I'm at it. Why not?* Everywhere I looked there was ten more minutes of work strewn about. Frustration regarding the crushing workload yet to perform spilled out my mouth as I hobbled with pieces in hand over to the scaffolding, gripped the bars, and commenced yet another climb. As I had done all day long, I clutched the cut pieces in one hand and worked the bars with the other hand. Pockets loaded with everything imaginable, and the marker tucked behind my ear. Still barefoot and loaded down like a bread bike in the Dominican, I must've been quite the spectacle to the traffic on Michigan Avenue. Google a picture of a bread bike in the Dominican Republic. It's quite impressive!

Can't Fix Jason

As prepped and ready as I tried to be all day, nothing could have prepared me for what happened next. Most intelligent and experienced carpenters would've never climbed scaffolding loaded down with as much as I carried, but I had become accustomed to the climb without struggling, so I kept doing it. Once I learned to balance and juggle things while shifting my weight, it became commonplace. However, as experienced as I felt, this specific climb proved to be different. It was that one slip up that most people work to avoid by refusing to participate in the first place. But not me, because half-way to the peak my foot slipped, and I smashed my face and ribs off the bars.

I've combed that day numerous times since the accident, and I cannot recall any reason for my foot to have slipped. I had wrapped my toes securely around the ladder bar and used the opposite foot to grip the next before moving my hands. So, when I did slip, without a single thought, reflex caused my climbing arm to embrace the side bar, and I swung toward the center opening of the second section of scaffolding. Unknowingly, I wrapped both legs around the side bar and managed to secure the piece of cut siding before it fell. Split seconds. All reflexive. The stinging pain throughout my face and chest verbalized into angry ranting as I readjusted and continued upward with heart racing. With climbing hand clenching the next bar above me, I shifted all weight to the right and raised the left leg while pulling with the climbing arm. Steadied myself as I pressed against both legs to stand while still pulling with the right hand. Stood up, let go with the right, and then reached for the next bar. Only this time I couldn't grip the bar. Almost as if my fingers wouldn't bend and could only palm it. And then time froze, and I panicked in slow motion as I watched my hand refuse to respond. It felt like I was suspended in that moment long enough to fight for safety. I flailed my arms, worked to wrap my free arm around the ladder bar in front of me, anything, but I wasn't positioned high enough to successfully hook onto it or hang from it. Scrambling to secure my grip, I violently grabbed at the bars, the side rails, the wood planks, however, everything seemed just out of reach. And then gravity took over, and I fell backward off the bars. Trust me, you don't wanna experience the sheer terror that comes over a person as you fall off something high off the ground. It's a mixture of confusing and shocking blended with dreamlike meets I'm gonna die. Time seems to cease long enough for the mind to ponder the situation before registering impending catastrophe. And then subconsciously our brains react. Without my intellectual input, I whipped my arms out to the side, released the piece of siding, and pulled my legs into a crouch position to prepare for impact. Kinda like a posing superhero or a gymnast sticking the landing. But don't picture graceful or gold medal worthy. Excruciating pain unlike I've ever felt coursed like lightening throughout my body. There's no adequate way to describe it. I remember how popular it was for schoolboys to kick each other in the groin, and those kicks insanely hurt. I'm ashamed to say I participated in that, but those foolish assaults on the playground paled in comparison to the pressure and horrible pain I felt the moment of impact. The day I rolled my truck numerous times down a hill tickled a bit; the jarring and smashing rattled my teeth as each side connected with the ground. Even that pain seemed like a gentle love touch. But this occasion, the second my bare feet hit the concrete, it felt as if every organ in my body had attempted to dislodge simultaneously, and then competed for first place exit out my backside. My lungs deflated. My blood pressure tanked while my pulse skyrocketed. I dropped to my knees in agony and then fell on my back. Writhing and gasping for breath, I felt the world around me fading in and out from color to gray tones to blinding flashes of light. My vision blurred, my ears shrieked with every heartbeat and then muffled, and my body convulsed. I had fallen right onto concrete from twenty feet up, and my spine had absorbed the shock waves of gravitational compression. I remember praying for enough strength to crawl into the house to notify Heather so she wouldn't find me dead in the driveway. I tried to yell, but nothing but a hoarse groaning sound came out. In all that, you know the life-flashing-before-your-eyes bit that everyone speaks of? It didn't happen to me. I knew I was in bad shape, but I didn't see the bright light. *Maybe my screen is defective?*

I'm unaware of how long I twitched in the driveway; it seemed like an eternity. I'm positive at least forty-five minutes passed because the sun had clearly moved from its previous position by the time I was strong enough to get up. And oddly enough I remember the accident and the events leading up to it, but the recovery period is a blur. I do remember, however, finding myself cutting more pieces and climbing right back up to the top to finish the job I had started. After the last pieces were nailed in place, I left the entire mess, tools and all, and crawled my way into the house.

That's Not Funny, Jason

The most comical part of the whole mess was Heather's response after learning of my accident. *That was you?! I saw something outta the corner of my eye fly past the window, but I thought it was a piece of siding. You've been throwing things down all day long. I never thought it was you!* No one laughs with me when I speak of that part of the story.

For weeks after the accident, overwhelming symptoms racked my body. Muscles worked and then quit working. Severe headaches and fatigue brought me to my knees. Numerous oddities occurred, and the symptom list is still a mile long to this day. But like a true tough guy, I went back to work like nothing had happened. I struggled daily to perform my duties until finally I couldn't function properly at all. Even though I began staggering and falling without explanation, I continued to refuse to seek medical attention. Heather begged me to go in. My boss and coworkers kept pressuring me but to no avail. I'd sleep for twelve to fourteen hours a day and would have to call in to work because I couldn't get out of bed. Many days I sat in my chair holding my legs straight up in the air because they hurt so bad, and I didn't know what else to do with them. My heart began erratically beating, and my breathing became shallow and labored. Slowly and painfully, my body fought to recover but my brain and nerves refused to relay the signals. *Should I shut down or just violently convulse?* Nothing health wise remained the same. I was in dangerous and unchartered waters, and I was scared, but I continued to dismiss all pleadings to improve my condition. It wasn't until my legs quit working altogether, became locked in a bent position, before I caved.

Two things I was unaware of at the time: I should have been in the ICU for weeks to monitor my organs (according to a nurse in the trauma unit at Mayo Clinic) and my life would never be the same from that day on.

Who Are You?

A new me had emerged the day of the accident and little did I know that it would take years to grow accustomed to the new version of me. Many good things were gonna take place, but not without first exhibiting a surrendered heart, a firm grip on *am I complaining* or not, a new Christ-centered outlook, and the desire to cultivate gratitude in every situation. Otherwise, the character lessons and trials would be too overwhelming to endure, and it'd be defeat for sure.

And when the proverbial dump trucks showed up only a couple weeks after the accident to haul off the wreckage of my shattered life, I didn't know what to do at first. But then it clicked the moment the construction crew began to unload their rebuilding equipment onto the site. The time for a major overhaul had arrived.

But wait a second. WAIT! S*hould I fight them? Or support them?*

Chapter 13

AM I COMPLAINING?

Because of the life I've led, oftentimes after a conversation with family or friends, I've sat back and wondered: *am I a chronic complainer?* I chew on the words used in the conversation, and then analyze it to death until it becomes a hang up for me. *Did you see so and so's face? Wow, Sally's body language seemed off. Should I have used different verbiage to describe that situation. When I saw Sally the other day, she seemed uninterested, maybe put off by my presence. I wonder if she's offended because of it.* Oftentimes, I've had to mentally record the conversation, the reactions, the responses for later review because it was too much to deal with in the moment. The fear of being labeled a complainer hampered attempts to self-correct, and I became what I had feared I'd become: a real bummer. Someone who has nothing better to talk about than the misfortunes that have befallen him his entire pitiful life. The ticket master to Jason's pity party. Remember the invite? And then I would worry I had said too much. *Should I have said that? Can Tammy be trusted with that information? Will Bill use that against me?* It bred like jackrabbits the irrational fear of people's judgements against me. Mainly the people I desired to get closer to. But since I've felt disregarded and replaceable, irrelevant, unworthy, I've cultivated this fear into an overwhelming reality that's nearly inescapable. Even when dedicating my thoughts over to Christ, and then arresting the ones that destroy the budding peace He gives, I struggled to believe the truth.

So let me ask you this. Have you ever asked yourself, *do I work from a complaining spirit?* I ask this because I've found that a complaining and critical spirit are key ingredients to conjuring up a miserable life.

I find it healthy to analyze whether I'm perceived as a complainer, but only if I do it correctly. You know the *nothing in excess* suggestion? Yeah, that. Do that. If a complaining spirit is left unchecked, it becomes a serious downfall. But so is overanalyzing it because it can become an obsession; however, analysis consistently performed for self-regulation is a good practice. In today's world it's easy to be classified a real bummer because many refuse to allow others to freely speak of the negative in life without placing a value statement on it. *Oh, well, it sucks to be you. Maybe you should tell him to tuck and roll. You should have said this…* Many only want the flowery, yippee-ki-yay false reality from others. As soon as there's signs of withering and fading, *move along, please. We only have room for the fresh-cut bouquets.* Or a person has wronged you in some fashion and view your distaste for their shortcomings as whining. *That Judy. All she does is complain. I wouldn't support her in her ministry when I promised I would and now she's sniveling.*

May I Help You?

However, long ago in a distant land called America, all across the plains, complaints were heard by many as a cry for help. The folks inclined to do good, *the do-gooders*, would come to the complaining person's aid. Families would pull together to help one another. Friends would form bonds that misfortune couldn't easily break. Life was hard but richly rewarding. Selfishness was shunned and togetherness was celebrated as vital.

Maybe these sentiments are antiquated? *Get with the times, Jason. You're overthinking it again. You expect too much out of people. Lower your standards, Complainer.* Is it out of text to read Jeremiah 6:16 NIV and apply it to this sentiment? "This is what the LORD says: 'Stand at the crossroads and look; ask for the ancient paths, ask were the good way is, and walk in it, and you will find rest for your souls. But you said, 'We will not walk in it.'"' Take a moment and read Jeremiah 6 for yourself and maybe you'll agree? Don't agree with me, though. Agree with God.

Is the love-one-another sentiment in today's world only for the Season of Giving? *I give at Christmastime, Silly.* When there's a natural disaster? *Those people are unworthy until a hurricane hits.* Am I missing something? Because, if we speed up the Memorex, fast forward to today's reality, we generally hear recordings drenched in *what about me? What do I get out of it if I help out a "complainer"?*

Before you get bent outta shape and start naming off different organizations and non-profits doing good in this world, recognize why I speak of this. Selfish intent finds its roots in a complaining spirit. Out of it breeds competition and envy. *I deserve…*

Get Ready For A Steep Incline

And if a person rebels against this prevalent spirit in society, he or she is gonna commence a gigantic uphill climb to accomplish anything worthy in others' eyes. I've noticed even the smallest gestures of kindness are expectations now. Hold the door for someone in public, once, and gauge his or her initial response. Are they grateful, or do they simply walk in without a peep? And then six hundred more people seize the opportunity to rush in while you stand there like a doorman at a posh British hotel. What about the *selfie queen* who's holding up the line while snapping multiple shots of her pursed lips? Can you avoid her with complaining about it? Obviously I'm guilty. What about offering a simple good morning or waving at a passerby on the street without getting the *creeper* label? What do you observe? Is it kindness and love the first response, or do ya gotta really work at it to get a positive immediate reaction? The Bible teaches do it anyway. Or do you still live in Small Town, USA, where peaches and Cool whip and please and thank you abundantly abounds? Maybe you see this societal decline and feel the weight of its crushing force grinding your soul to powder. *Life as I knew it is gone. LORD, get me outta here!* Let me assure you, all of this was not in God's original plan, but we gotta keep doing what is righteous and just in His eyes. Remember, we're strangers on this earth headed for a better life. Hang in there and do what pleases God and not men. (Galatians 1:10)

Yer Complainin' Again, Sir

Maybe in today's world, many would see this as an example of me complaining instead of speaking the truth. They might be right depending on how they classify the word. After all, the world's truth is ever changing from one philosophy to the next. *Wishing for a better world that hasn't been lost to inevitable moral decay is old-fashioned and therefore archaic.* But I don't see this as complaining. What I'm longing for is a reality that shows compassion for others without a single thought of how it'll affect him or her personally. A society filled with people who understand their actions have positive and negative consequences, so, before acting on choices, they weigh out their decisions for the good of all involved. And should they irrationally choose, and their choices pay them and others adverse dividends, they refrain from complaining or finger-pointing and gain wisdom from the circumstances. And then work to self-correct for the betterment of themselves and society. *Your actions affect others whether you accept it or not.*

Double The Trouble

I believe there are two types of complainers in the world: The Rowdy and The Mute.

The Rowdy we all know. Whether good or bad comes his way, he whines, points out every flaw, cries victim, works every angle to ensure at least an ounce of sympathy is his for the taking. Granted, his situation might deserve a bit of commiseration, but he demands a ton. However, when presented with the opportunity to grow from the trial and show appreciation for those who've supported him through it all, he shrinks back and wallows in his own self-pity. And then intensifies the complaints when others grow weary of his incessant bellyaching. Nothing's ever good enough. Every situation is dire and requires all-out catastrophizing to feed the addiction to chronically complain.

Then there's The Mute. He's the one who refuses to speak up yet grumbles when no one's around and is convinced that nobody cares. He's the only one left in the world with compassion. He's been abandoned and there's no hope for rescue. He could shout his complaints from the mountaintops, but he believes it'd only fall on deaf ears. This causes him to withdraw and reject any opportunity to be heard because he's doing the world a favor. He's the hero of the story because he's successfully convinced everyone that he's the happy-go-lucky type who's forever satisfied. Yet, at the core, he's bitter, resentful, and proud.

The world wants to avoid both these guys. He's the essence of a complaining spirit. Not a single positive complaint comes out, *please help me with my need.* That'd necessitate a change, and he doesn't want that. How would I know? Because I've been a combination of both for some time. But the LORD has been requesting the removal of this behavior from my character because it's not what He requires. Psalm 100:4 speaks volumes to this, "Enter his gates with thanksgiving and his courts with praise; give thanks to him and praise his name." Listen to Philippians 2:14 NIV, "Do everything without grumbling or arguing…" **Why does the squeaky wheel deserve the grease only when it's noisy? What ever happened to maintenance? Keeping a close eye on problem areas and moving toward a resolve?**

I've ferociously struggled to defeat this giant in my life. One minute it's smooth sailing and the next I'm falling prey to the sympathy vote. But what has nursed a healthy mindset is knowing the line between stating a fact and spewing a complaint. There's nothing wrong with sharing facts if that's all a person desires to do. But don't take my word for it; you decide after what dictionary.com defines as a complaint.

Yay! A Definition!

"An expression of discontent, regret, pain, censure, resentment, or grief, lament, fault finding."

And another way the site defines the same word: "A cause of bodily pain or ailment, malady" (*complaint*)

Well, how's that for a definition? Did it fit into how you view a complaint? I don't see anything in the definition about stating a fact but only uttering an expression. My point is: a complaint can become a word curse if used improperly. Maybe this will help. *I don't feel well today. Thanks for asking.* That's the expression in complaining. You don't feel well, but you will feel better, so you kindly accept a person's inquiry for what it is: genuine concern. But the other side. *I am sick, and the doctor said I possibly have strep. Guess it's just my luck to get strep when I've got so much going on.* That's the word curse, the "fact" that drives the sympathy campaign whose main candidate is false information.

Possibly is not certainty, so don't accept the news. Yes, you don't feel well, but, no, you shouldn't make it into a fact by repeating it. I'm learning to reject that kind of complaint.

I don't wanna split hairs here. I'm merely suggesting a repetitive nature turns expressing discontent or, if you'd rather, sharing a fact, into a complaint. At this point, the repetition, is where most turn down the hearing aid.

What's Your Take?

How do you view complaining? Should society turn a deaf ear the moment a complaint is heard? Or weaponize it to obtain things? Allow it freely or avoid it like a plague? Help any and every person crying out or categorize it like everything else? I personally use complaining as an expression pointing to a fact, but I've learned to reject the word cursing end of it which leads to demanding the sympathy vote. But I gotta continually be careful on how I express a complaint because it's a razor thin tight rope. Am I stating it and then moving on, or did I beat it to death, again? Have I sought a specific audience who will feed into the negative side of things, or was I willing to air it to the party with whom it concerns? (Look up Numbers 12) Have I found a resolve or in some cases, have agreed to disagree if there's no plausible solution? Was the complaint dripping in poor me or was I seeking advice? The questions could be endless.

But let's be honest here, if I don't allow a trusted someone to hear my complaint and then speak life into my situation, then I'm campaigning for the sympathy vote.

It's Time To Pass The Test

The way I've moved from uneducated to undergoing wisdom installments has been dreadfully gradual. I'm a slow learner but largely by choice. But know this, when a person embraces a relationship with Christ, He promises to give us the necessary tools to become more like Him. It takes a willing heart and loads of discipline washed in repentance. This speaks volumes to us taking charge of our own attitudes, behavioral patterns, and praying for discernment to replace the complaining spirit. We have been given the power and the tools of self-discipline to refuse the chronic complainer's lifestyle. We just gotta choose it.

But let me ask you this? Does this mean we gotta take everything in stride, hold back the expressions, and force out *I'm all good* when we're not? No way! That's what the silent complainer does, and I'm unwilling to be an advocate for that anymore. Here's what I'm learning: I believe getting things off your chest in a healthy way to a trusted individual for the sole purpose of personal growth is one of the keys to recovering from a grumbling lifestyle. Plan to recover and deny fertile soil to a bitterness root. Cultivate a self-love that refuses to harbor toxic weight on your soul. Dump the whining and moaning before it hinders your God-given abilities. Become someone who's sensitive to your own needs and the needs of others but also promotes growth. Add a touch of sympathy, a personal element, because everyone wants to be valued and heard, but don't allow any self-seeking or catastrophizing.

Needy People? Eew!

What if society *has* deemed all complainers as annoying? It's no longer an acceptable form of crying out for help. *People, shut down if you hear a complaint. Run and hide cuz it's the end of the world.* Totally understandable, right? Chronic complainers are overwhelmingly annoying. A repeated woe tends to agitate even the kindest of folks. The worst is when you haven't seen that person in a long time, and then the first words outta his or her mouth is the peeve you worked to avoid. And his or her refusal to self-regulate, to at least say *hello first*, anything but go right at it, causes the strain to fester. *For crying out loud!!* Literally! Remember the adage? *Misery loves company.* But shouldn't we speak up instead of enduring or walling ourselves off? I say yes. But what a tough situation!

Reclassify?

If the word *complain* strikes fear in even the strongest of warriors, then perhaps the issue lies in my classification of the word. Could it be that the fix is in the analysis? If I skip the person's true intent because I've immediately affixed a label, and thereby, refuse to listen to understand, then I've already dove into a conclusion. And hasty conclusions are widely incorrect. Man, this is easily done. We generally hear to respond before we hear to listen and understand. How many arguments and divisions does this cause?!

What if we reclassified the word to alleviate the fear element, and then categorized the complaints we hear according to love? What if we listened and processed them accordingly, and then came to a proper conclusion without pre-judging even the chronic complainer? *Because not all expressions of distaste are meant to be disregarded.*

Break Out The Bunsen Burner and Beakers

Maybe doing a quick experiment might help. Ask these questions regarding your latest complaint. I know I've touched on this already, but let's dial it in.

1. How many times have I expressed this complaint? To this person? To others?
2. Was I looking for sympathy?

3. Was I seeking help? Am I desiring growth?
4. Did I speak up because I crave attention from a person who seems to misunderstand me? Because I want to kindle or rebuild a relationship?
5. Is complaining a way of life for me? Are my words intentional or am I generally flippant with my speech?
6. Do the vast majority of people ignore my complaints or has a trusted someone(s) walked alongside me to see me through my issue?

Now recall the person or persons reaction. His or her facial expressions and body language.

1. Did he or she blow me off? Walk away mid-sentence?
2. Appear irritated and disengaged?
3. Change the subject?
4. Give me what I was seeking? Was it healthy or caustic?
5. Express concern as a trusted friend?
6. Ask me kindly to stop complaining?

Word Choice Is Key

In my life I had become accustomed to incessant grumbling. The world observed, and, instead of assisting, sought shelter. *Did you notice the word change? From complaint to grumbling?* Initially I was *expressing* the discontentment and pain surrounding my life and sought to gain understanding through airing my difficulties. I wanted people to figure me out, help me, but when their effort level fell short of my expectations, an obsession over my woes quickly formed. Facial expressions, thoughts, my conversations, they all turned sour. I failed to realize while ramping up efforts to get a single soul on my side that a deep-rooted lamenting spirit had attached. That's the exact moment when people become immune to the cry for help.

My wife…for the last fifteen years has shut me down the second a conversation seems to be turning into a gripe session. Her lip quivers a bit, a dimple appears on her chin, and her face reddens. Remember the van ride to Ohio to pick up the Aurora? She refused to join my absurd rant about the rental van, and it angered me. I wanted her to agree with me, to understand what I meant, to get angry over the things that make me angry. *Please complain already! Speak up and agree with me! Do something!* But experience has taught her uttering a single word would give full vent to crazy. And all I actually wanted in that moment was a solution for the thirty plus years of rejection that surfaces every time I feel ignored. *I want to belong, to fit in, have others affirm me and my opinions.* But none of this will ever come to fruition by employing a complaining spirit.

I Do. But Not Like That

Much to my surprise, I've come to realize people do want to hear about my feelings, to listen to my complaints, to understand me as a person. But with emotions in check. Respecting boundaries. Exercising self-discipline.

Pondering my life from this bed, I've been reliving the many memories of the people who have tried to console me, offer comfort, show support. Not only when I became disabled but before and on an ongoing basis. But, because I haven't been in the proper headspace to embrace it, I've dismissed far too many attempts as inadequate. Or as doting and under false pretenses. *If I accept their kindness their gonna want some sort of reciprocation.* If you're reading this, and I've done this to you, please reach out to me. I wanna make it right. Because shouldn't a person who's complaining to fulfill a need be accepting of, without stipulations, any positive help from the party he or she's complaining to? *Accept his or her contribution, give thanks for the relationship, and affirm the attempts to comfort.* Selfishness and a grumbling nature chips away at friendships. Avoidance creeps in. And Proverbs 17:9 NIV comes true. "Whoever would foster love covers over an offense, but whoever repeats the matter separates close friends." Hopefully at that point, he or she is a great friend, and will offer a loving rebuke to facilitate correction.

And honestly, if all I do is complain, am I not writing out my own certificate of rejection? Am I not re-inserting the *what about me* statement that annoys so many? To be completely dramatic about it…am I not taking a million selfies and gluing them to my friends' foreheads? Honestly, what do I expect from a friend?

Have you ever heard it said that expectations kill relationships?

Please, Momma, No Salad

Whenever we went through McDonald's, my kids would ask for a chicken sandwich with no salad. Because I knew the lettuce was all wilty and nasty, I never forced them to eat it. *Don't try that at home, though. Yer gonna eat yer greens or else. I suffered as a kid, so will you!*

But why not analyze the child's viewpoint after the poor kid has heard *oh, quit yer complaining* for the hundredth time? Ever hear that as a child? I did and all too often. Green leafy veggies on my plate…yuck! Mom had us eating Brussel sprouts and kohlrabi from the moment we were conceived, but that would never change the fact I hated those upchucks waiting to happen. *Serve it a hundred times if ya want, and I'll still mud wrestle ya. And keep whining.* I whimpered and whined until someone responded, and even though I knew it wouldn't end well, I tried anyway. Wouldn't it be easier to process the complaint with a kind response? Can't we decipher the difference between a true dislike and senseless grumbling before it becomes a chronic behavior? Rather than forcing a person who longs to be heard into a repetitive rant?

I've learned through all God's leading that a chronic complainer is a person lacking self-control. Guess who needs to be taught self-control...children.

Back to me as a salad hater.

Shouldn't Mom and Dad have listened to me? Heard my valid complaints? Most children barf a little in their mouths when fed vegetables. And as a nutritionist at heart, don't come at me with the whole *it's-healthy routine*; I completely understand the merits of balanced diets. But hear me out. Isn't the child giving the parent valuable information? He or she doesn't like that vegetable. So, try another. Offer the kid a wide array of vegetables. Lay down the law, per say, only if the child attempts to rule out all health foods. Isn't the answer right in front of our faces? Quit forcing our children to eat things he or she despises. I'm a drill sergeant Dad, so typing that last sentence was torture.

Eat it or else! And the else is no ice cream until yer 38. Don't test me, kid.

I'm terrible when it comes to threats like this. I'll spout off in anger, but then have to follow through because I refuse to go back on my word. Stupid temper. Withholding ice cream from a child should be a capital offense.

But, honestly, give the kid some grace. Taste buds develop as children grow, so, don't die on every hill. Offer the kid a pardon before forcing dislikes becomes a foothold for chronic complaining. And if the child's complaints are always rejected, it'll become the start of a war never won. Why not win the war before the first battle? Take the time to truly listen to the complaint and put it to rest.

Ok, kiddo, I understand you dislike vegetables. But veggies are a part of the meal we're having. If you don't want the broccoli, you gotta have a different vegetable with the dinner. There are green beans or there's sliced cucumbers in the fridge. Which one do you want? We eat healthy foods so our bodies can handle unhealthy options like cookies and ice cream. The choice is yours, but if you choose no veggies tonight, you also choose no dessert tonight.

Or maybe learn how to properly prepare the vegetable?

For my kids, down the hatch goes the broccoli. And when they complain about the flavor or texture, I remind them of how delicious the bowl of triple chocolate brownie blast will be. Don't be fooled...getting them to eat balanced hasn't always come this easy, but kids are counting on parents who will stand their ground.

Children long for consistency even when they screech and whine and carry on during the battle. But the same goes in friendships, work relationships, in families, and any other facet of life. Maybe ignoring a simple complaint is snowballing an issue into an avalanche. What if the person is at a crossroads, the tipping point of evolution of his or her character? In a kid's case, how will the child ever learn to trust a parent if his or her opinions are always disregarded?

And I've come to understand that some big problems originate from always excusing the smaller ones. Causing a search for comfort from someone or something else. What a scary thought when children are involved! Could this be one of the reasons why the prisons are so full?

Blame It On The Rain

Being a person who never really understood the difference between complaining and grumbling and its costly outcome caused numerous trials and rough patches in my life. But the worst part came shortly after becoming disabled. I went from being the openly verbal chronic complainer to the silent type. I began to internalize everything and refused to speak of it. I refer to it as the worst part because it led to doctors misunderstanding my situation, misdiagnosing, and misreading my nonverbal cues. But it wasn't until my second trip to Mayo Clinic before I began to understand how dangerous to my health this behavior had become. Remember the second definition for complaint? "A cause of bodily pain..."

The neurologist at Mayo questioned my chipper demeanor after reviewing the charts. *Fuse lit.*

"I don't wanna constantly complain because who really gives a crap anyway? You doctors sit in judgement of me every time I arrive. You put me in neat little boxes but don't fully understand where I'm coming from. What's the point of actin' all sad and mopey? You don't get it either way."

"You gotta understand my position here. You come in complaining of chronic pain and reduced ambulation in your lower extremities. Your charts speak of severe trauma, yet your non-congruency is confusing. You wear a smile, and you seem like a really likable guy, but I'm unsure what to think."

"Well, everyone either dotes over me or ignores me. I gotta move on. And keep my mouth shut." Angry tears started to run down my cheek. "I'm tired of it all."

"I'm sure you are, but I want to hear you complain. I want to hear what's going on because how else will I figure this out? I can't read your mind, but I can see you're in rough shape, but all I've got to go on is your charts and your behaviors. I'm not your family or your friend; I'm your doctor. The best place to complain is at your doctor's office."

The very same evening back at the hotel I began writing this chapter. She had slapped me so hard with the truth that it jarred loose some examples I felt inclined to share.

Complaining Is Necessary

There's a place and time for complaining, but we gotta be careful. When done in the proper context, it can produce large dividends. Whether or not you've heard complaining to be a bad habit, or hard for others to wanna listen, or plain annoying, when done in the right spirit, it can save one's backside. In many ways.

The Bible says in 1 Peter 5:7 NIV to "Cast all your anxiety on Him because He cares for you." It doesn't say *grumble and whine at Jesus because He loves to hear it.* Rather, it says "cast all your anxiety on Him because He cares for you."

Let me ask you this. Do you cast a baited hook, worm and all, into the lake and then jump in after it? The entire time treading water and monitoring for activity? Well, of course not. That's utter foolishness. Then why do we refuse to cast our grief, our troubles, our concerns on the One who genuinely cares? Is it because we know we're sinning, so we don't dare cast our care? Is that why we continually moan and groan to human sources? Mutter our way out of relationships and friendships, hoping one magical time our complaints will produce the desired goal? Why do we carry our lament like bait, cast it to catch some sympathy, and swim violently after it until we can no longer tread water? *We know we're gonna sink and take others down with us.*

Remember the verse that I shared earlier in Philippians 2? Let me finish it. There's a comma instead of a period at the end of the verse, and Paul used a comma for a specific purpose. It's to show us that a life full of *gratitude* has no room for a complaining spirit. "Do everything without grumbling or arguing, so that you may become blameless and pure, children of God without fault in a warped and crooked generation. Then you will shine among them like stars in the sky." Philippians 2:14-15 NIV

Graciously express your malady if you must, but then move on and rise above. We were meant to fly. Live set apart from the rest of the grumblers. Be a shining light in utter darkness.

Chapter 14

GRATITUDE

As you have read, I've done an immense amount of self-reflecting and soul searching over the last several years. Mostly resultant of the accident. Maybe some out of boredom. I wish I could admit it happened out of a pure willingness and drive to self-improve, but that would be a fat lie. Stubborn tough guys don't willingly change. Most need a punch in the mouth to wake up, and even then, it's a fifty-fifty chance.

Much of my self-reflection has been gut wrenching and difficult to express, therefore easier to suppress than to deal with. What macho man wants to uncover his own baggage and spread it worldwide for people to observe? *Why not bury it? It's safer that way. Live fake, act fake, die fake.*

But behaving this way leaves behind huge foundationally human questions in its wake, and they're troublesome to folks who refuse to answer them honestly. *Who am I? Where do I belong? Do I fit in? Who holds the truth? And do I wanna conform to such societal tension?*

The stressful life I've lived up to this point has taken a toll mentally and physically. But now that this disability has destroyed the chance of seamlessly fitting in anywhere, the mental strain has intensified. The dream of being the cool kid, the popular guy, the well-liked socialite, the put-together role model for the world to follow flew out the window and shattered into a billion stupid pieces.

Reality has decided and not in favor of this guy.

The Judge Has Spoken

I've made my ruling…I know you've been bullied and for every possible reason. Your friends and family sometimes ditch you when a better option comes along. Your bosses have passed on rightfully promoting you regardless of the competence and loyalty you've shown. It's your fault you're bald, so quit whining about that. And since you've refused to correct the anger issues that have riddled your life with pain and turmoil, you're gonna really struggle with this disability until you choose to straighten up. Choose heightened pain and continual frustration leading to uncontrollable physical distress, depression, and possible death, or you can choose self-correction and manageable pain with joy abounding. Your choice. But you can't have both. I'll accept your plea now, Sir.

Surprisingly, despite the ruling against me, full-on depression from being a social outcast never came. It should have destroyed my life, my resolve, my personal worth, but it didn't. It certainly tried, and I nearly allowed it, but instead of falling into that black hole, the LORD showed me how to be thankful. But first He showed me some of the past…

Let's Revisit

Rather than developing mutual social bonds with people I knew were trustworthy, I had constructed multiple escape routes to remain unaccountable and free from responsibility for many years. I loved to give up on nearly everything I set out to do. Rejected tried-yet-true family members and friends for any and every mistake they made. Avoided agreeing to larger commitments to remain a free agent. Flew the reckless banner on all fronts. So, what better place and position to be in than a wheelchair, seeking support from others for normal everyday tasks? It's either full submission or fail. Thankfully, someone's always available to help me. Seems like proper justice for a guy like me!

Truth Be Told

In what ways have I ever fit in, anyway? Have I ever really been influential? Now that I'm less productive, do I even have a purpose anymore? I've heard it said that God has a reason for every part of His flawless plan, so what is it? Maybe He messed up and left me hangin' in the wind. How can I truly be content in life with all this weight on my shoulders?

Let me reassure, these feelings and questions are valid. But their answers are deep and require a person to recognize that he or she *is* blessed in life, regardless of the circumstances. However, all it takes is leaving out one important ingredient for the blessings to dry up and to cloud the memory of the previous ones.

There's a key to receiving blessings?! Are you sure?

Yup!

And it's not working to fit in. Let's dispel that rumor immediately. I've come to believe relentlessly working to fit in is a cry for help directed at the wrong audience. I don't need to conform to the in crowd to build my identity. I'll come up empty. Depressed. Stressed out. Romans 12:2 instructs a child of God to avoid conforming to the patterns of this world because it'll lead to chaos. And God is not into chaos.

The missing link isn't found in becoming influential, either. How can I influence others if I fail to influence myself to self-correct in troublesome areas? As an influencer, burying the truth instead of exposing the flaws will lead to the hypocrite label.

Thus, expanding the void already felt. I'm paraphrasing Pascal when he said *the God-shaped void I feel can only be filled by Him.*

What's the missing ingredient, then, since I've already accepted Christ into my heart?

Gratitude.

More Reminiscing

I spent the better half of this crazy life of mine boo-hooing, wishing for a more enjoyable outcome, coveting the neighbors' good fortunes, dealing-promoting-playing the victim card, being largely ungrateful for any and every blessing I had received; I hardly feel qualified in this area, either. Yet, because of the infinite grace the LORD has given me, I'm gonna share what He's taught me on the subject. And perhaps you'll accept into your life the lesson that corrected my ill-fated path before you spend one more second denying and deeming unfit His continuous blessings.

God Is Love? Yeah, Right!

Before I move on, however, I need to address the elephant in the room. How can a guy like me offer gratitude toward God when he's been afflicted with an unexplained illness that has robbed him of nearly everything he once enjoyed? Do you feel the same? Maybe for you it's a loss. A friend. A loved one. A child or a spouse. Or maybe it's cancer or another scary diagnosis. What if it's being stuck in a go nowhere job? Or owning a clunker that caused you to appear unreliable too many times, and it cost you your dream job. Or you live with an abusive spouse, child, or family member and you're living in hell. Or a co-worker tortures you to your breaking point. We've all got an example of the *oh, HER, yeah, THAT GUY* situation to gossip about around the water cooler. But let me restate the question. How can I unearth a single reason to be thankful while in the middle of a horrible situation when I know full well God has the wherewithal to poof the problem away? And then chooses not to. *Is everyone asking this?* I've heard it from even the strongest in the faith. And rightfully so because we all trip sometimes. But the command to love the LORD your God with all your heart, soul, mind, and strength and in everything give thanks remains unchanged. Because His plan requires a rock-solid faith without an ounce of doubt in His goodness. A belief beyond head knowledge and repetition. Over the past several years battling my disability, I've traversed some rough roads. Fought with every ounce of my being to build back the strength to keep a smile on my face. Endured so much heartache, separation, anxiety, loneliness, and pain that I've begged God to end my life. *Where's your love, God, in all this suffering and pain? How can I be grateful when you've abandoned me and forced me to go it alone?*

Hike The Skivvies

The answer's simple. I haven't been deserted. And neither have you. God's never left. And sure, maybe you're thinking cliché, but if He promises, He delivers. He promised never to leave us nor forsake us, but in the trials, He might just be checking to see what we're made of. What we're gonna do. Whine and complain? Or look to the One who's got it all together? To the One who's working for the good of those who've been called according to His purposes. And if we fully trust Him like we say we do, then we understand He hasn't left us. We move past the head knowledge, repetition, and walk out what we say we believe. Which means we gotta plant our feet, grit our teeth, and march outta the muck. Without complaining. Not even a whimper. Maybe a grunt, and soak our face and shirt with tears, but never once be moved in our faith. And that's what I have determined to do. Come what may. And why? Because I've left the faith more times than I can count over silly expectations that God had never promised. It's high time I pull up my big boy panties and be the man God designed me to be. With or without a disability or male pattern baldness. Even though none go with me.

Another Postcard

Dear Reader,

What do you believe the author is referring to when he said, *though none go with me?* Strands of hair or laborers in the harvest field serving Jesus? Hmmm…

Sincerely,

J.P. Brunette

Start Marching, Soldier

Without a single doubt of God's faithfulness placed in my head by the enemy or formed into a stronghold through less-than-ideal situations, I gotta keep marching. *Hey, Jason. If you can be bullheaded in other areas of your life, refusing to hear and apply truths, then you certainly can reverse all that and stand strong in God's love.* I fully understand a person's mental stronghold can only endure so much embattlement before his or her will is broken down and disbanded. But that's why we're lovingly instructed to refresh ourselves in the LORD and draw on His strength for endurance. Daily. Not go our own way because that'll lead to disaster. Maybe not immediately but all too soon. And then we'll receive discipline to correct our paths. *Shoulda done the right thing in the first place!* Listen to Hebrews 12:11

NIV and you decide. "No discipline seems pleasant at the time, but painful. Later on, however, it produces a harvest of righteousness and peace for those who have been trained by it." Notice the phrase *trained by it*? Trained is past tense meaning it has occurred already. *LORD, I know what this discipline is all about. You have taught me ever so patiently, and I accept it willingly because I know You only want what's best for me. Thank You for taking the time to correct me.* The Holy Spirit reminded me of Isaiah 30:21 NIV while typing this, "Whether you turn to the right or to the left, your ears will hear a voice behind you, saying, 'This is the way, walk in it.'" Go back and read that passage. Eye opening!

Topple It By Removing That One Brick

The miles I've travelled on this new journey have taught me gratitude is one of the few if not the only brick securing our faith walls. This brick requires continual sealing and reconditioning because it erodes quickly. Allow gratitude to crumble and watch the faith wall topple. Because good ol' envy easily finds a crack in the brick. Justification quickly widens the gap, and then the brick starts to crumble, thus replacing faith with despair and depression. *Why is this happening to me? Why can't I be happy? Mrs. Jones has it all!* Our thoughts and perceptions widen the visible gaps in our faith walls, and the desire to prove our point knocks the bricks out. *Wait a second! How did I get this far into misery?!* A rampant mind is wicked good at chiseling, that's how! And the cares-of-this-world's expertise cementing the vicious search for happiness in place is astounding! And worse yet, they both dump the rubble onto the beautiful memory of when Christ rescued us from the crushing weight of our sins when we first met Him. We come up empty, chained down again, choked by the pressure as the search for happiness silently robs us of the original joy we once felt in Christ. What a mess!

If that's not enough to make your head spin, get a load of this. While on the road of recovery, I've discovered that the word *gratitude* is often misused. Misconstrued and left one-sided as merely meaning *to be thankful*. Like many out there, that's how I internalized the definition. I showed a thankful side while hiding the truth, and it cost me dearly. *I'm thankful and all, but it's not quite what I'm looking for. Thanks, anyway.*

Bald Guys Have Mad Skills

Several years before becoming disabled I formed a group called *Uncle Shiny's Outreach*. We aimed to help anyone and everyone regardless of their background or request. From a minor boost up to a huge undertaking, we wanted to do it all. *Just apply, and we'll jump into action.* For instance. *Short on groceries?* A friend of a friend could refer you to us, and we'd help. *Elderly Ms. Hazel needs her yard mowed and raked?* Send in a referral. *Oh, you're a single mom moving out of your apartment to a cheaper facility? Perfect! I'm sure we can oblige. By the way, do you need extra diapers and butt wipes?*

But we didn't stop there. *You said the women's shelter needs supplies? Can you get me a list? I've got donors waiting for the call.*

You get the picture. We'd step in. And all this sounds fantastic, right? It sure was.

I began recruiting members and worked tirelessly to grow my idea. I visited local businesses, spoke at luncheons, compelled local churches into action, went door-to-door. As the group expanded, we helped numerous people. Provided meals to the sick, moved a woman's whole apartment from one town to another, put together food baskets for veteran families. The list was endless. I continued promoting my lofty program dreams at every venue available; I was offering salvation to so many. We built a clothing collection group called the *Family Closet*, a food collection group called the *Compassion Cupboard*, and a veteran-targeted task force called *Project Red, White, and Blue*. The groups flourished as donations poured in, and a board member panel developed to handle the decisions. A passionate desire to help others propelled us forward.

Detonation In 3...2...1...

But then it all fell apart. Horribly. Fundraising efforts ceased. Donations dried up. Members shied away. My dream of growing the non-profit into superstardom fizzled.

And here's why. I designed the whole program with impure motives. To onlookers I was a Rockstar philanthropist with a heart of gold. But to God, I was a broken man running myself ragged in search of love for my fellow man, and without an ounce of gratitude in my heart for where my paths had led me. I would not include Him in the process because *I know what I'm doing thank you very much* was my attitude. I was a glory grabber full of self-serving pride. As I poured hours upon back breaking hours of my heart and soul into my idea, not once did I seek God's heart on the matter or recognize my need to repent of the hatefulness behind the wheel of the whole thing. I was regaining a love for mankind because secretly I knew I despised most people and helping them was godly enough to absolve me of my sins. I considered myself arrogantly superior to most, and *Uncle Shiny's* was my golden ticket to a happy life. *Help others and God will finally smile at me. Maybe He'll even bless me with more.* Little did I know that the good LORD had a huge lesson in humility planned to correct my selfish schemes. He was about to show me He doesn't work that way.

Listen to 1 John 4:20 ESV as it relates what I had done. "If anyone says, 'I love God,' and hates his brother, he is a liar; for he who does not love his brother whom he has seen cannot love God whom he has not seen." I could be the nicest guy in the world but without love, "I am only a resounding gong or a clanging cymbal" 1 Corinthians 13:1b NIV. You catch that? I'm a noisy distraction and an annoyance without love.

BOOM!

My heart sank the day it all exploded and became just another piece of the past. Dreams of grandeur, the thought of changing the world flew out the window without a moment's notice. God had taken out the pruning shears and lopped my golden ticket right in half before my very eyes. And why? Because He gets all the glory for remarkable things He has done. And maybe you're confused with how this all ties in with gratitude? Let me bring it back around.

More Definitions!

Grab the dictionary again and look up the definition of gratitude; you'll understand where I'm going with this. I'm pulling from the part that implies you must be willing to show wholehearted thankfulness for everything you've received. ***Gratitude is a heart condition.*** A lifestyle. Not just reciprocation to look good, but a willingness to open your own arms to accept wholeheartedly any form of kindness from others without judgement. It's clear where I went wrong. I wanted every ounce of praise, feelings of accomplishment, and relevance all to myself without having any responsibility for mistakes. *You accept my help and that makes me good. Don't try to guide me onto the right path or convince me I have a terrible attitude. I'm gonna pave my own road. Sorry yours is bumpy. I'll work for my salvation. I'm a free agent.*

I'll forgive others and their failures, shortcomings, through random acts of kindness and that's God's path to freedom in Him.

So many people seem to give because it makes him or her feel good. They'll even tell ya that. But that's not true gratitude. Feeling good is a byproduct, not the reason to do it. That can lead to one-sided, self-gratification if one isn't careful. Leaving God robbed and man exalted.

Open Arms Lifted High

Can you accept every form of blessing with open arms and then give thanks to God for His goodness? That's the easy part. Well, if I'm truthful, I forget to honor God in all situations, so it's easier said than done. But can you give with your arms open wide to receive? Let others reciprocate and then thank the good LORD? Maybe you can, but that has always been difficult for a superhero like me. If you're able to give and receive without reservation, thank the LORD for blessing you with this character trait; but if you can't, then I dare say you need to pray for a lesson in gratitude before the seas get too rough. We clearly don't deserve His grace, yet He freely gives it. To whomever He wishes. Expecting us to meditate on His goodness and praise Him for it.

I've learned if we can't easily accept kindness and grace from God without doubting His intentions, then we can't give it unconditionally to others. We KNOW God is good because the evidence is everywhere. And if we aren't meant to earn His merit by doing whatever we think is good and kind, then we ought to submit to the One who knows best and do what He created us to do.

I Can't Show It If I Don't Understand It

I wouldn't show my team a drop of gratitude for their faithful work, brilliant ideas, creative abilities because I didn't see a need for it. Words of affirmation? As foreign to me as Dutch in a Spanish-speaking country. And what do people do when they feel used and underappreciated? They walk. Yet when everyone began to disperse, I angrily blamed the group for their lack of devotion. Even though they felt undervalued and discarded, reprimanded, and insulted, *don't blame me they can't take a little coaching*. And consequently, my gentleness halted long-standing relationships with friends on the team. *Pansies! What they gonna do in the real world?* I can't keep all the blame to myself for every slip-up because many mistakes were made, but I hold myself largely responsible being the supposed leader and all. Sure gave it my best, though. Sorry guys.

Costly Lessons

But let's look at a simple truth I've largely glossed over. Gratitude in its purest form is difficult to convey if a person refuses to learn what it truly is. And the fact that humans aren't happy-go-lucky every moment of the day makes it especially difficult, even with lots of effort and practice after a person has properly defined it. Which means we're gonna be offensive or offended at one time or another. We're gonna slip from time to time. We're gonna be ungrateful in relationships, when others attempt to help us and fall short of our expectations, when someone tries to speak life and truth into our hearts and it's not what we wanna hear.

Maybe you feel your significant other fails you in showing the kind of love you desire. Or completes a project the exact opposite of the way you would've done it. Maybe a friend attempts to speak life into a tricky situation you're facing, and in desperation you get bent outta shape. These moments require a ton of grace and gratitude for those people's efforts because at least they're trying. Being grateful for their support is necessary, whether it's up to our standards or not. Wow is this difficult! Especially when numerous times I've properly instructed someone on how to complete a chore, yet it ends in frustration and disaster. *And I still gotta be grateful? How?* Show grace anyway. Offer patient instruction, again. I'm at the beginning of this journey, let me tell you. But if you're wary of the pin poke from this message, then you're further along than you think. Most would broom it and spout off the names of others who need this advice. Trust me, if you're doing that, YOU need this message.

Dust Off The Bunsen Burner, Again

Let's do another experiment. You'll need a lab partner. Ask someone to hand you an object, preferably something unbreakable, and when they hand it off to you, keep your fists clenched shut as they release it. See you after. *This one's being graded.*

Did you successfully receive the object or have to catch it before it hit the ground? If you caught the item with closed fists, I want to shake your hand. If you're gonna truthfully admit you had to catch it, ask yourself: Can I effectively receive anything with my fists clenched? *Maybe a fist bump if you wanna be literal, but let's not go there right now.* The same goes for love, gratitude, emotions, and/or actions. You can only get away with partially accepting something for so long before whomever is doing the giving eventually senses the rejection and calls you on it. Or ultimately quits trying. And why is that? Humans hate rejection. They want to belong. Rejection on any level is still rejection. It can't be effectively hidden. Besides, negative emotions awaken the amygdala, causing a person to recall the most recent hardship, thus activating other areas of the brain in attempts to mitigate pain. I lack scientific data to back this up, but put me on trial for what I just said, and I'll build such a case around it that no one will be able to successfully refute me. I've observed it in action throughout all facets of life. And I've also observed that not even the kindest of intentions can protect benevolence when rejection enters the room. Rejection wrecks everything because we all want to belong.

The Joy Of Gift Giving

Have you ever given a gift to someone, and *you didn't have to do that* is the first thing outta his or her mouth? Was that the response you looked forward to while preparing the surprise? Probably not, but it's usually the go-to phrase. Every time I've heard that phrase or its equivalent, I've felt somewhat rejected. *Of course I didn't have to, but I wanted to.* To me the original phrase reads, it's *nice of you, but I don't deserve it.* Or *you're too broke to do something like this.* Well, how does that grab ya? It's dismissing and rude. The joy I had experienced from desiring to spread kindness is lost, and I begin to doubt the person's gratefulness. And maybe I need to work on this end of my perception because I warned about being one-sided, giving to feel good; but what happened to a simple *thank you* or *I love it* instead of the go-to? Be assertive and tell the truth. You're thankful someone thought of you, that's it. Instead of having to go through the awkward *I really do love it* mess when ya gotta nearly be shamed for others being kind to you. Yer putting people on the defensive for being benevolent. *Do we really feel guilty if others wanna bless us?* That might be a different issue in need of some checking into.

A Societal Solution

I dare say pure gratitude may be a solution for many societal issues. Of course, love remains number one, but gratitude and thankfulness score high in ranking as well. Might I suggest allowing people to do what they feel led to do will reduce awkward flailing? Promote more love. Breed harmony and peace. Don't worry, though. You have the right to refuse a kindness. It's your prerogative.

Reminds me of a time I offered to bake a pie for a fellow member at church.

"I'm sending you a message because I'm baking pies each week for the whole month of February. This week I randomly chose your name along with three other families. Do you have a favorite flavor you'd like me to make?"

"No thanks. I'd rather not."

I was completely shocked and taken aback. But after a few hours of bewilderment, I began to understand. *Maybe they have gluten sensitivities like me. Or they hate pie and prefer cheesecake instead. Had they tasted one of my flops? I bet they've had Mrs. Schoen's blueberry pie! That thing's a national treasure.*

Take Up Battle Stations

Troops. Listen up. The world's falling apart out there. Be on guard. There's gonna be some casualties. We've already suffered innumerable collateral damage. Lindahl! Haswell! Breault! Man your post. Whatever happens, do not let Mrs. Schoen's Blueberry Pie outta your sight. Guard it with your life, Boys! It's the last one left. Stay strong. And may God have mercy on your souls.

The Truth

They can't have sugar! That's it!

Diabetics beware! Baking is a passion of mine. I'm unable to eat most of the creations I concoct because sugar causes me immense amounts of pain, but that doesn't stop me from snacking here and there or from doling out the pastries. In my cabinet right now there's at least thirty pounds of sugar, the equivalent in flour, two cakes of yeast, and twelve bags of chocolate chips. I've got vegetable oil by the gallons, a farmer on call for fresh eggs, and enough baking soda to conduct a 6th grade science experiment. Don't forget the 2 Kitchen-aid mixers and enough countertop space for kneading dough.

But to be offended by a simple no means I'm in serious need of a reality check. I've come to understand that ya gotta respect people where they're at. Maybe a little more in the explanation would be nice, but I really don't need that either. If a person gives you a gift, ya need to accept or decline without foolishness. Be a day maker. And regardless of what it is or how it came outta the pan. Less insulted people equal more random acts of kindness. *Don't quote me on that one. Just sounds plausible.*

Christmas 2016

Let me share a doozy of a story that finished the lecture on gratitude. I could stop at wow!

Because of my accident, Heather and I had to pinch pennies to stay current on bills, keep food on the table, and gas in the car. I hadn't worked since May of the same year and the coffers were empty. Month after month we consistently fell short, and panic started to set in. Daily life is expensive! But the back-and-forth doctoring in multiple states is bankrupting. One day Heather thumbed through the bills we couldn't meet, and she searched for a way to pay them but came up short. Only one option remained. The one I had previously refused.

"You wanna go up to St. Vinny's today, Jay?"

"No. I'd rather puke in my mouth and swallow it than beg for assistance."

"Jay, the City posted a shut-off notice on the door a week ago. We gotta do something."

"They can't shut us off in the winter. We got time."

"No. No, we don't. Let's go. We've got kids to think about. It's no longer just you and me."

She had a valid point, and I knew it, so I reluctantly caved. The stress on the kids from my disability was already weighing heavy on my mind, and that certainly didn't help.

We parked close to the building and exited the car slowly. My guts churned with anxiety as the U.P. wintery winds reminded me of my condition. Nothing could touch my left foot without making me cry out in pain, so the vicious wind on my bare foot hurried me along. But I'm unsure of what felt worse. For the first time in my life paying the bills required groveling for assistance, and it mimicked food poisoning working its way up my throat. But to make matters worse, as Heather pushed me through the *help-me-I'm-poor*-door, the wheelie-bars on my wheelchair got stuck on the threshold. Blowing snow and flapping papers alerted a couple workers as the wintery winds rapidly cooled the warehouse down. *So much for discreetly sneaking in and out undetected.* The commotion and brisk air brought several more workers from multiple directions scurrying to offer their assistance. *Now instead of tripping over a threshold, I gotta get stuck on it? And lifted and yanked and shoved over it. Good grief!*

Wonder Woman & Cheetah

A few moments later, my rescuer, Wonder Woman, wheeled me into a small office and began rearranging the entire room to make adequate space for my golden throne. Meanwhile, a rigid-looking woman entered the room and promptly commenced the interrogation. Wonder Woman left after she finished arranging furniture and in bounded Cheetah. She silently took a seat next to her cohort, patiently waiting to pounce if I spoke out of turn. I paused briefly before nervously answering the straightforward and demanding questions, the whole time planning an escape route. Then the unthinkable happened. Instead of being dumped out of my wheelchair and beaten with it, Cheetah stopped the questioning and asked if she could give me a hug. Tears welled up in her eyes as she went off script and began to inquire. *Hun, how are ya doin' emotionally? Do you have adequate care, do you need anything other than what yer requestin'?* No shame. No embarrassing rhetoric. Only simple kindness. Heather began gushing all the difficulties we had been facing and then bawled like a baby. The whole scene was a hot mess for an unfeeling guy like me! But then moments later, I broke down. Tissues sailed through the air. Sniffling and the occasional snort rang out. I wanted to shrink into the fetal position in the corner and rock while sucking my thumb.

The women at St. Vincent's I had never met, but I knew my wife quite well. My stubbornness had pushed her to her breaking point. For months I had noticed the desperation building, however, she hid it well. To lose composure in public was out of character, but this time the overwhelming stress surrounding our situation gushed out her pores. Unfortunately, it took her sobbing in an office with complete strangers, openly expressing her fears, consumed by despair, to blast through the tough guy barriers I had built. *What had I done to the love of my life? To my family? And why were these women so overwhelmingly compassionate and accommodating for a guy like me?* For several minutes I curled up in my own little reality and bawled the sight right outta my eye sockets. But while I worked on destroying several tissues and eventually composed myself, I realized where the conversation had moved. They had been discussing every angle of benevolence they had to offer, and then had signed our family up for a Christmas gift basket and food delivery. A charity case I had become, and strangely it felt wonderful. Not because I was grabby, but because I felt loved. The kid's sizes and color preferences, hobbies and toy choices began floating gently across the airwaves, as if the brutal winds whipping through the side entrance had blown in a breath of fresh air. *Am I stuck in one of those sickening Hallmark Christmas movies? STOP SHAKING THE SNOW GLOBE!*

"Is there something you and Jason might enjoy that we can put on the list?"

"Um..." Heather looked puzzled.

Don't look at me! I just made a spectacle of myself over here, and now you want me to ask for another gift?!

"I think you've done enough. I'm so overwhelmed by your generosity that I can't think right now" I blurted.

"We'll add in something special then. God is blessing you and your family. Just accept it freely."

I hadn't given Christmas shopping a thought before that day; it was literally one day at a time back then. Sometimes hour by hour. I subconsciously knew, however, that if we couldn't pay the electric bill, Christmas shopping was outta the question. And how does one explain to the kids the unavoidable empty space underneath the Christmas tree?

I was only joking, kids, when I sang, "you're getting nothing for Christmas because you've been nuttin' but bad. Sorry about your bad luck, wish you weren't such a schmuck. It's your fault you're nuttin' but sad."

Regardless of the hardship they had already endured, I figured they'd understand, but who was I trying to kid? It was Christmas. They had gotten accustomed to barely enough, but could they remain exceptionally tolerant through the holidays? I couldn't handle the thought of them having to endure much more. Heather and I had never spoiled our kids because of their past, but we also never denied them of a want if they were obedient and earned it. We decided early on to shower them with love and affection more than stuff, and they learned to appreciate everything around them. But Christmas has always brought out the softer side of my hardened exterior. I began picturing sad little faces staring at the lights on the tree glimmering brightly. The empty red stockings hung over the white fireplace. The excitement savagely snatched away by the taunting empty space below the glowing tree.

Brutal.

I had no idea that when we crawled into St. Vinny's to beg for mercy that they'd oblige Christmas, too. With tears and humility pouring out of me, I passionately sought from the workers an opportunity to repay their kindness.

"All you can do to repay us is to pray, Honey. Pray that God will provide."

Bewildered and saddened, I wheeled out of the room after the meeting. *That's it?!* Moments later as we drove away, I felt my fists clenching shut again.

"Pray?! That's it? Prayers are powerful and all, but I can't just pray as a form of repayment."

"Jay, that's all we got right now."

"There's gotta be something I can do."

"Pray about it." *Real funny, Heather. Real funny.*

Here...Have More

The rest of the afternoon I searched my thoughts, begging for a way to give back for what I felt I didn't deserve. I was profoundly thankful, but I couldn't accept their kindness without reciprocation. Period. *There's gotta be something I can do to clear my name.* And then my phone rang out with another lesson in gratitude.

"Good afternoon. Is this Jason?"

"Yes, this is Jason."

"Hi, this is Bellin in Escanaba. Do you have a moment to chat?"

"Sure."

"Great. Our staff adopts a family in need each year and supplies a Christmas basket to that family. We picked yous."

Before I could say another word, I began to sob, and then handed the phone off to Heather. Not what I had expected to hear. An update from a previous doctor's visit. Instructions for the next visit. Med changes. Anything but what she spoke. *Why were we being remarkably blessed again?* After the conversation had ended, I grabbed Heather and held her tight. Our worries surrounding Christmas seemed to be over. We melted into another hot pile of goo until I could no longer handle the pain from standing up. So much had changed in my heart that day. Yet one thing remained. I couldn't dispose of my guilt. *It's my job to help others. If I take it, even though we need it, I'll be robbing someone who's far worse off than us. Besides, why do people suddenly care? Do they pity me because I'm now a charity case?* Apprehension broke past the thought barrier and began spilling out my mouth before I could stop it. Heather soaked in my concerns for a moment but then interjected when she had heard enough.

"Jay. I hear what you're saying, but we need this kindness right now. Accept it and be grateful."

"I *AM* grateful, Babe. But it's too much."

And then I think it was the good LORD who flashed before my eyes the ones Uncle Shiny's had helped. I saw a vision of numerous smiles racing across the big screen of my mind. It was then that I could feel myself miraculously giving in to the whole meaning of gratitude. Out of my mouth started spewing wholehearted pure appreciation without reservation, and I only felt blessed. But it wasn't until being humbled yet again with more unbelievable news that the wall fell for good.

Benjamins

A few days after the St. Vinny's and Bellin incident, a friend from down the block stopped by with a Christmas card full of holiday wishes. He chatted for a moment, but in his usual fashion, he abruptly ended the conversation and left. We hadn't opened the card yet; I've never been able to open a gift in front of someone unless pushed into it. It's like when a person asks me to taste something he or she has made and then eyeballs me as I cram the food into my mouth, anxiously awaiting my approval. Half of it usually falls out of my mouth, and I gotta scramble to save face. I just can't do it. But the moment our friend left, Heather popped the envelope open. Numerous hundred-dollar bills spilled out, and she gasped loud enough for me to hear it from the other room.

"Jay! C'mere!!"

"What, Babe? What's up?"

I was kinda freaked out by her gasp, so I kicked it up a notch. Grabbed the card from her outstretched hand, and then palmed the door frame as my jaw hit the floor. I gushed *we could finish cleaning up the bills, spread some holiday cheer, and still have a bit in savings!*

But the story doesn't end there. The blessings kept coming. Later that week, we had two more anonymous monetary gifts, and then a year's worth of coin savings left on our front porch from a generous friend. And then the following week our kids' teachers, church family, my boss all dropped by one by one with food donations, cards full of money, wrapped gifts. We had such an immense outpouring of love around the holidays that my heart burst with joy and a newfound gratitude. Finally, I had internalized the lab experiment and opened my arms to love. And without ruining anyone's joy or insulting them. *Score! Put a gold star next to my name on the board!*

Psalm 100:4 NIV comes to mind, again, "Enter His gates with thanksgiving and His courts with praise; give thanks to

Him and praise His name." And James 1:17 also in the NIV, "Every good and perfect gift is from above, coming down from the Father of the heavenly lights, who does not change like shifting shadows." All thanks to God!

The Heart Change

Looking back on these events I ask myself, *what changed your mind? You've been close-minded your entire life. Why now? Because it's Christmas? The gift-giving-and-receiving season?* No. Christmas hadn't been the only time in my life I had received crazy kindness from God. You've read the chapter on blessings filled with examples that barely scratch the surface of God's goodness. *Is it cuz yer a stingy gift giver?* Nah. If I had it, I'd give it. *Did others finally succeed in convincing you to be more accepting of offered gifts?* Nope. Many had tried. Very few had succeeded. *Then what did it?*

The LORD granted me a softened heart when I witnessed the expression of utter relief painted all over Heather's face. When I felt terribly sorry and desired to repent of my stubborn streak, then I was granted the emotional heart transplant. Stubbornness had wreaked havoc on my relationships and realizing that finished smashing down the walls.

"Godly sorrow brings repentance that leads to salvation and leaves no regret, but worldly sorrow brings death." 2 Corinthians 7:10 NIV

No longer had I the desire to dominate the playing field. I could ask for and receive help, but if I couldn't be the one saving the day, so be it. I had offended far too many benevolent people, and in the process alienated nearly everyone who had experienced my demeanor. But because of my heart change, I determined to correct my mistakes. I had to unlearn and no longer agree with the spirit of pride. Understand that some may consider me a failure, but the LORD calls me His child. Others may see me as another person living off the system, but God provides in many ways. And as far as contributing and helping others, I know my time to support will come.

I've been shown that gratitude should flow freely from the heart for every aspect in our lives. Dissatisfaction and a sense of entitlement springs from a deficiency in gratitude. For a Jesus follower in a world void of Godly gratitude, I can't exhibit the same behaviors as everyone else and expect to stand out in the crowd. God commands us to give thanks in every situation because it produces the best outcome. To shine our lights because others have no clue without a Godly example. To mirror the image of Jesus because He lived the very love of God. I understand difficult seasons come and go because I'm in the thick of it right now. But we've gotta remain appreciative, walking out that appreciation through both the smooth sailing and the rough patches. Doing this will teach us the endurance we need and build the love for God that continues to perfect our hearts in Him. Picture this, if you can't express thankfulness during the stress-free times, imagine trying to show it atop an angry bull trying to buck you off so he can gore you to death.

"As God's co-workers we urge you not to receive God's grace in vain. For He says, 'In the time of my favor I heard you, and in the day of salvation I helped you.' I tell you, now is the time of God's favor, now is the day of salvation." 2 Corinthians 6:1-2 NIV

Now's the time for change. Do you need a perspective change? Do you need to properly redefine gratitude? Don't wait like I did. Take a good, hard look around you right now. Anything in your life come to mind that may demonstrate ungratefulness? Do you need to seek forgiveness from family or friends? From God? Have you repeatedly refuted an act of kindness with a negative phrase? Reacted in such a way that was perceived as ungrateful? Or you flat out refused a kindness because you assumed you didn't need it? I don't ask you this to generate shame and guilt. I'm hoping to promote growth.

Butterscotch Discs Abound

On my own corrected path, I've had to think about how my actions have affected the people around me. Ruminated on a better way to handle the same scenario in the future. Practiced the new me and moved away from the past indiscretions. I've learned that correction in the present will streamline the future. Understood that no one can undo the past so I can't dwell on it. Gotta leave it be and keep walking. Grow from it but don't recycle it. Take the piece of hard candy when it's offered.

Did I throw you off with that last statement? Do you know any old men who carry a pocket full of hard candy? Not the creepy guys trying to attract little kids. The kind old man who randomly says, "Want a butterscotch disc? Or a mint?" There's one in every town, and I'll probably end up one of them. But I say take the candy for crying out loud. I'm sure you've got a niece or nephew, know of a kid who'd enjoy it. Make the old dude happy and take it. You obviously have the right to refuse anything you don't want. But why? A harmless piece of candy may be the only act of kindness the old man has to offer. Maybe that piece of candy is his ticket to relevance in a world bent on rejecting him. And what if the entire world denied his kindness and robbed him of his joy? The old man might be counting on you to accept his kindness to keep his spark of benevolence alive.

Who Doesn't Like Food?

Maybe you don't mesh with the old dude. Let's work another angle and revisit your favorite restaurant. You're stuck with that waitress again who messes up your order. After numerous attempts she still can't seem to get it right. Do you word curse her or offer compassion? *Wait a second. Is the place known for terrible service? If yes, then why do you go there? It's really none of my business, but I gotta ask. Is it your only option? I'll bet it's because you think the waitress is cute or the busboy's been flirting with you.* I know, I know, the narrative says she messes up repeatedly. But what if you're unaware of a difficult season she's walking through? Maybe she's a single mom barely making ends meet. Going through a divorce or experiencing a loss in the family or relationship. Or she seriously needs the practice to become a better waitress. Who knows? But imagine what a bit of grace and a tip filled with gratitude might do for this woman in a hard situation. Take a moment to realize we've all been there ourselves and have been found lacking in many areas as well. Society tends to talk only about the bad. Spread negative publicity, ruin businesses out of spite, trash talk the employees. And for what? *I'll show her not to bring me a medium well when I ordered medium rare!* Will this one incident be the very last time you'll ever enjoy a medium rare ribeye? Maybe. Only God knows. But I'll bet ya ten to one in that situation, too, He'd require kindness to be the first response. Because if we're modeling gratefulness like Jesus, then forgiving the mistake, and giving her another chance is on the menu.

And what comes to mind when I say this? I'm glad to have food choices in my neighborhood. I'm grateful so many have a job. Thankful for the money they earn because it filters throughout the local economy, thus promoting community growth. Grateful again because, frankly, I don't gotta cook it. Plus, somebody's serving me. Many have never had such a luxury we take for granted. Oh, yeah, happy that I've got enough money in my wallet to eat out, instead of holding up a sign and wondering if a passerby will consider me worthy of more than pocket lint and a disdainful look.

Only By The Grace Of God

Because of God's grace I've learned that gratefulness demands a closer look at our attitude in every aspect of our lives.

I've only started to recover from being the *tough guy*, and it's taken too many years to get where I'm at. You've discovered how I've offended far too many people to list, and then refused to make amends even when made aware of my shortcomings. Grateful I was not, and for that I am truly ashamed. However, God has a funny way of bringing His children full circle and humbling them when He has a plan for their lives. Think this doesn't apply to you? Ask yourself, *am I a Christian, born again and willing to serve God?* Then He has a plan for your life, and it involves gratitude. And if you don't have it, you'll wanna develop it before you go any further in your journey. Everywhere in the Bible we find instructions to praise the LORD. To thank Him for His goodness. To give Him all the glory and honor. But without gratefulness, this is impossible. But with gratitude, wholehearted thankfulness, acceptance of blessings with an attitude of praise, reciprocating without a selfish intent will be your first response and all glory will go to the LORD. Effortlessly.

So do what I've learned to do: drop the baggage, unclench yer fists, and give it a go.

One For The Road

There's one last part of gratitude I learned that is vital. Forgive freely. Especially yourself. It's a major part of God's perfect love. People we meet, friendships we cultivate, grace we've been given are gifts from God. Unforgiveness is being ungrateful toward God, and it's saying His gifts are no good because they come with flaws.

Today I'm sincerely grateful for the trials I'm enduring because they've brought about repentance, acceptance of God's forgiveness, and recovery from my hatefulness. I never wanna go back to that darkness. But I've forgiven myself for living there for so long. And when situations attempt to hijack my peace, Ephesians 4:32 ESV often swoops in to remind, "Be kind to one another, tenderhearted, forgiving one another, as God in Christ forgave you."

Life's gonna be hopeless and rough without gratitude. But appreciating all that God has blessed me with will smooth out those bumps because my mind will be fixed on His goodness alone. But I keep having to remind myself that forgiveness is intentional. Although hard to do, it's nearly impossible to be thankful for someone you won't forgive.

Forever Grateful

Thinking back over my life while authoring this book, I feel I should offer again one of the verses I shared previously. But this time I need to back it up a few verses because it pertains so well to my situation. "I am not saying this because I am in need for I have learned to be content whatever the circumstances. I know what it is to be in need, and I know what it is to have plenty. I have learned the secret of being content in any and every situation, whether well fed or hungry, whether living in plenty or in want. I can do everything through Him who gives me strength." Philippians 4:11-13 NIV.

We as a family have weathered so many storms because of God's love for us. We have trusted Him, and He has delivered. Every time. And even when I've consistently fallen short, His grace was always there to save. If God sent His Son to die on the cross for my sins, chooses to forgive me every time I repent, continues to bless me repeatedly, and provides for my every need, then I have no reason to be ungrateful. Regardless of the situation. Life's gonna throw a ridiculous number of challenges at me; I'm guaranteed nothing in this pilgrimage. But if I don't choose to act in His frame of mind, make choices based on His design, then the trials will rob me of my gratitude, kill my joy, and cause me to fail miserably. Every time.

Thank You, LORD, for continuing to teach me, forgive me, provide for me, lead me. There's overwhelming evidence of my unworthiness, but You continue to show me grace. I am truly grateful. If You should decide to stop blessing me altogether, right now, I still will have no cause to complain, but have every reason to continue to thank You for the rest of my life. I love You, Jesus. Amen.

Notes

Chapter 13 Am I Complaining?

"Complaint." *Dictionary.com*, Dictionary.com, www.dictionary.com/browse/complaint

CPSIA information can be obtained
at www.ICGtesting.com
Printed in the USA
BVHW071434291221
625052BV00020B/1081

9 781662 835124